The Properties Director's Toolkit

The Properties Director's Toolkit is a concise guide to managing a prop shop and show build. Sandra Strawn and Lisa Schlenker skillfully explain and provide templates for organizing and managing a prop shop, from pre-production organization to production processes, budgeting, and collaborations with other production areas. This thoroughly revised second edition includes interviews with prop directors and collaborators as well as two additional chapters: one exploring more deeply the role of the Properties Director as a creative collaborator and one on managing co-productions. Individual chapters were expanded to include prop management for opera, musical theatre, film, Broadway, community/academic theatre, union and commercial shops in the evolution of titles and job duties, online management processes for digital information sharing and collaboration, and detailing in more depth and with examples, photos, and forms the foundational processes of prop production and management. The *Toolkit* also explores how to plan, organize, and maintain a prop shop for safe and efficient production work.

Sandra J. Strawn has enjoyed over four decades of theatre prop and design experience highlighted by six seasons at Actor's Theatre of Louisville and five seasons at Milwaukee Repertory Theater. Leading the properties production/design curriculum and designing for the mainstage theatre at UW-Milwaukee for the past twenty-seven seasons, Sandra recently retired Professor Emeritus.

Lisa Schlenker has been the properties director for Skylight Music Theatre for the past twenty-seven years. Graduating with an MFA in Theatre Technology from UW-Madison (1988) her prolific scenic design and prop career is highlighted by work with Renaissance Theaterworks, Milwaukee Shakespeare, Milwaukee Chamber Theater, Northern Sky Theatre, the Florentine Opera, and Milwaukee Opera Theatre.

The Properties Director's Toolkit

Creativity, Collaboration, and Communication
for Prop Shop Management in the Theatre
and Performing Arts

Second Edition

Sandra J. Strawn and Lisa Schlenker

Routledge
Taylor & Francis Group

NEW YORK AND LONDON

Second edition published 2018
by Routledge
711 Third Avenue, New York, NY 10017

and by Routledge
2 Park Square, Milton Park, Abingdon, Oxon, OX14 4RN

Routledge is an imprint of the Taylor & Francis Group, an informa business

First edition published by Focal Press 2012

Library of Congress Cataloging-in-Publication Data
Names: Strawn, Sandra J., author. | Schlenker, Lisa, author.
Title: The properties director's toolkit : creativity, collaboration and communication for prop shop
    management in the theatre and performing arts / Sandra J. Strawn and Lisa Schlenker.
Description: Second edition. | Abingdon, Oxon ; New York, NY : Routledge, 2018. | Includes index.
Identifiers: LCCN 2017048632 | ISBN 9781138084148 (hardback) | ISBN 9781138084155 (pbk.)
Subjects: LCSH: Stage props—Design and construction. | Theaters—Stage-setting and scenery.
Classification: LCC PN2091.S8 S763 2018 | DDC 792.02/5—dc23
LC record available at https://lccn.loc.gov/2017048632

ISBN: 978-1-138-08414-8 (hbk)
ISBN: 978-1-138-08415-5 (pbk)
ISBN: 978-1-315-14620-1 (ebk)

Typeset in Times New Roman and Helvetica
by Apex CoVantage, LLC

Contents

Figures

Introduction

Welcome to *The Properties Director's Toolkit.* As co-authors, we have enjoyed writing about the process of being a properties director and the joy and struggle of managing a prop shop.

Theatre has been an important part of our lives for decades. Working in the prop shop, managing a show, and creating a world on stage to take the audience (and ourselves) on an adventure of story, character, and place is a career unlike many others. Collaborating with other artists and designers creates a community of creativity and possibility, rewarding in ways beyond the usual compensations of a job. We play with elements of time, place, and character; bound by the script, defined by the design, and open to every possibility within our imagination. Lisa and I have prospered in the world of props throughout our professional lives as properties artisans, properties directors, and as designers.

This book explores the process of being a properties director, managing a prop shop, and organizing the build on a show. Like all management, it's about the efficient use of resources— time, money, and people. In theatre, layered on top of being a manager of a shop and the people who work in it, the properties director fulfills the design teams' challenge through imagination, craft, and skill-based experience. This is the duality of the practical and the imaginative.

As collaborators in the theatre, writing this book as co-authors took the best of both of us and combined it into a singular informed voice of "how-to" for being a properties director. Lisa is the properties director at Skylight Opera/Music Theatre in Milwaukee, going on now almost three decades, and has worked as a freelance prop master and scenic designer for numerous theatres in the upper Midwest. My first properties director job was in 1977 at the Utah Shakespearean Festival, followed by stints at Actor's Theatre of Louisville and Milwaukee Repertory Theater before being wooed to lead the properties production/design curriculum at the University of Wisconsin-Milwaukee for the past twenty-seven years. We have been friends for over three decades, finding common passion in our prop work and the love of producing theatre.

Those years sparked many discussions on product, process, and management techniques/ skills as well as how to pass on and mentor others in learning about props. At UWM, I created an arc of training in properties production, teaching the skills of being a prop artisan (sewing, casting and molding, furniture construction, metalworking, plastic work, floral/craft work, etc.), and students were immersed in afternoon production work on shows. Lisa opened the doors at Skylight to welcome prop interns and apprentices to her shop, challenging them to meet the standards of production work in the profession, fine-tuning what they had learned in my classes and working on university productions. Passing on our knowledge and passion for theatre is part of who we are as artists and as teachers of the craft, but the far subtler talent of management remained elusive to many students as well as to colleagues working in community, educational, and professional companies.

What our discipline needed was a handbook guiding someone through the entire process of managing a prop shop and a show build. The original edition, *The Properties Director's Handbook* (Focal Press, 2012), evolved from my webpage (prophandbook.com), exploring those intangible skills of being a properties director for the student, prop professional, and prop enthusiast. Lisa offered encouragement and editing on the original edition, so when Focal Press requested a second edition expanding on the first foundational copy, it was time to bring her on as co-author. By adding Lisa's insightful voice, a wider examination of the management process was possible, exploring more contemporary prop shop management and adding her experience in the world of opera and music theatre. I had been using the book for my properties production classes at the university, making notes and planning revisions to the writing. In reviewing the book, Lisa and I wanted to update the information to include online management processes, the evolution of titles and job duties, working on co-productions, and detailing in more depth and with examples/photos/forms the foundational processes examined in the original edition.

May this book bring the duality of management and artistry to future projects, infusing the work with creativity, joyous collaboration, effective communication, and humanity.

Acknowledgments

We would like to acknowledge Stacey Walker, Senior Editor with Focal Press and Routledge, for her unflagging enthusiasm, supporting the writing of valuable theatre "how-to" books from the production side. Without her willingness to appreciate what we do behind the scenes, these books—and especially this one on props—would not have been written. Our appreciation also extends to Hollie Christian-Brookes and Hannah Rowe, who swept in halfway through the writing process to advise us on everything editorial and production. Thank you!

Numerous people have contributed in a variety of ways, from offering suggestions about content, allowing photos to be taken in their shops, contributing forms and documents, and lending a supportive voice. Our appreciation for their cheerful willingness to be interviewed and provide information/assistance goes to:

Jolene Obertin (Seattle Repertory Theatre—Properties Director)

Mark Walston (Actors Theatre of Louisville—Properties Director)

Karin Rabe Vance (The Alley Theatre—Properties Director)

Lori Harrison (San Francisco Opera—Properties Director)

Megan Freemantle (Houston Grand Opera—Properties Design Department)

Elizabeth (Fried) Friedrich (Seattle Children's Theatre—Properties Director)

Rich Gilles (Geffen Playhouse—Properties Director)

Jim Guy (Milwaukee Repertory Theater—Properties Director)

Deb Morgan (Freelance Properties Director, Kansas City)

Nikki Kulas (First Stage Children's Theatre—Properties Director)

Vicky Smith (Scenic Designer, Minneapolis)

Hugh Landwehr (Scenic Designer, New York)

Sarah Brandner (Scenic Designer, Minneapolis)

Takeshi Kata (Scenic Designer, Los Angeles)

Van Santvoord (Scenic Designer, New York)

Robert Perdziola (Scenic Designer, New York)

Kurt Sharp (Scenic Designer, Chicago)

Paul Owen (Scenic Designer, Louisville)

James Ortiz (Scenic and Puppet Designer, New York)

Shima Orans (Costume Designer, Milwaukee)

Melissa Woods (Freelance Assistant Art Director, Los Angeles)

Katie Kragiel Elder (Stage Manager, West Virginia)

Dan Hanson (Production Stage Manager, Chicago and Milwaukee)

and

Members of SPAM (Society of Properties Artisans/Managers)

Deep appreciation goes to our partners, George Abraham and Steve Gillingham, for their enduring patience and goodwill, as we have worked these many months on finalizing this project.

CHAPTER 1

Sense and Sensibility

If you were to google props, it might be surprising to discover props seems to have something to do with boating or airplanes instead of theatre. Actually, a propeller hung as décor on the wall of a stage set, carried in by an actor as part of their character, or attached to a modified bicycle to represent an airplane as it is peddled about the stage would indeed be a prop. Props, or **stage properties**, embrace the enormous possibility of being just about anything to help tell the story on stage and to support the understanding of character for the audience.

Unique talents and skills are necessary to build stage properties. Frankly, the skill set needed to be an artisan in a prop shop is endless, as one never knows what experience or knowledge will pop up as helpful in the process of creating props for the stage. The "hard" skill sets (upholstery, welding, woodworking, molding, design layout, crafting, to name just a few) might all be learned through education and diligent study. However, the "soft" skills seem more innate, and prized above all are curiosity, a thirst for knowledge/exploration, and the desire to nurture ideas, relationships, stories, and storytellers.

The head of the prop shop is often called the properties director or the prop master. A **director** is a person who is in charge of an activity, department, or organization; from *dirigere*, meaning 'to guide'. A **master** is a skilled practitioner of a particular art or activity—or having or showing very great skill or proficiency. Leading a prop shop requires a balance of both definitions, which may be why the titles are used so interchangeably. Managing a prop shop for an individual show build in a season of shows requires the alchemy of being an active artist and storyteller as well as strong leadership in managing and inspiring other creative artists, understanding and channeling the vision of the director/designer, and the constant challenge of organization, communication, collaboration, resource allocation, budgeting, and deadlines.

A properties director needs the willingness to embrace constant change and will thrive on the shifting sands of the creative process. As the creative team's ideas coalesce, concepts are embraced and abandoned, finally maturing into clarity within the developmental journey to show creation.

This arc presents multiple opportunities for the "3Cs of leadership and management":

Collaboration   Communication   Creativity

As you navigate through the rest of your life, be open to collaboration. Other people and other people's ideas are often better than your own. Find a group of people who challenge and inspire you, spend a lot of time with them, and it will change your life.

—Amy Poehler

Collaboration is the heartbeat of working in props. *Everything* from start to finish involves the input and ideas of others.

A good collaborator:

* Builds trust and promotes buy-in and inclusion
* Understands prioritization and time management
* Is a good listener
* Can communicate ideas with clarity
* Exhibits a calm, supportive, caring, and committed demeanor
* Is willing to explore, dream, challenge, and offer "what if" ideas
* Plays well with others.

Being a collaborator in the design process allows the team charged with creating the world seen on stage to develop solutions or alternatives by contributing toward the whole vision. Building on ideas developed in the initial director and designer concept discussions, the properties director joins the process to give input into the design and definition of the stage props, from the things the actors handle to the furniture on the stage to the décor on the wall. This might be done individually in a meeting just with the prop shop or in a larger group including all area heads. Often times things overlap into multiple production departments, and having input from all areas allows the information and problem-solving process to embrace everyone's talents and ideas. The area heads in scenery, paint, lighting, sound, special effects (FX), and costumes can contribute their ideas and experience as they help to define unknowns, present solutions, bring alternatives for consideration, and share the load.

As the designer delivers the initial prop list, drawings, and research, the properties director often invites the prop shop artisans to contribute ideas on construction methods, product usage, or supplemental research information. This adds to the collective foundation of discovery and creation. Like an interesting layout of dominoes, each decision or choice can alter other choices. Each idea presented might trigger another thought and develop a new or better solution. Dreams can become reality as alternatives are presented and priorities are determined. Budgets and deadlines can be "massaged" to support crucial aesthetic and story-telling elements when viewing the greater whole.

> *The single biggest problem in communication is the illusion that it has taken place.*
> —George Bernard Shaw

Communication is vital to good collaboration. Regardless of where any one person sits within the structure of the organization, having the ability to communicate well with colleagues is the key to success.

A good communicator:

- Speaks with diplomacy to reach understanding
- Is truthful in representing issues and presenting challenges
- Is proactive in taking responsibility and ownership of their part of the process
- Demonstrates integrity in the information flow
- Maintains accurate, organized files/documents and shares them openly
- Utilizes appropriate levels of notification and inclusion
- Advocates for appropriate expectations—for the shop, for the designer, for administration, and for other areas of production
- Is nimble and able to respond to change, supporting paradigm shifts from the designer, the director, rehearsal, or other areas of production or administration
- Seeks input and advice before it's needed—seeing the note before it becomes a note.

How is that done? The properties director has a responsibility to foster dialog up and down the hierarchy of any theatre operation. Communication with the artistic director requires active engagement in conversation about that person's vision and goals from a repertoire and presentation standpoint. This is *Big Picture* stuff, but it's important to understand what can be contributed to the collaborative endeavor at that level. What stories are important to this leader? How do they wish to take the audience on that journey? Where do they need help? Maintaining an open mind and understanding the artistic priorities makes everyone better partners in carrying out the "boots on the ground" work toward realizing the vision of the artistic leadership.

When working with the people the artistic director hires to conceive and tell these stories, articulately voicing concerns or suggesting alternative ideas to production design teams in a face to face meeting or via email requires not only creativity and positivity but also truth and diplomacy. Striving to meet the creative team's dreams in an environment of less than abundant resources can easily fall prey to negative dialog, and the resulting hit to collabora-tive relationships severely undermines trust. Adversaries cannot be partners. Advancing a true partnership with directors, designers, and performers often requires patience, clarity, and a willingness to gently educate.

Honest evaluation of project feasibility in a timely fashion is a must for fostering strong ties with the production director, who is doing the best to wrangle all the various shops and pro-duction numbers. Budgeting prop resources is more often than not a moving target, so frequent and detailed correspondence with production management, replete with options based on the realities of each situation, is essential to build trust and to get production management support in return. Functioning as an island is unhelpful when the connection to production manage-ment can be strengthened through clear and ongoing dialog about expectations, resources, and the individual unique challenges each project represents.

Trust and openness are paramount not only with artistic collaborators but also with senior management. From the production director on up to the senior administrative managers in each department, all of these folks are working to corral the resources allowing the prop shop to do the job and get paid for doing so. Using production management as a conduit to upper administrators can develop positive relationships within the company and secure invaluable resources. From trades of marketing materials (free tickets or program acknowledgments) in exchange for donated goods, materials or services, to investigating what that same marketing department might need from props professionals (a couple items from stock to make a window display more attractive or a televised behind-the-scenes segment resulting in increased ticket sales) requires keeping an open mind and honestly entertaining requests for assistance in a variety of ways. Likewise, the theatre's development department is a huge partner to produc-tion in writing grants funding anything from apprentice positions to specialized equipment vital to various aspects of creative work. Prop departments in turn have the ability to lend a hand with efforts benefiting the theatre's bottom line. Donating a spectacular or interesting prop to a fundraising auction, providing a behind-the-scenes tour or chat for a select group of donors, or assisting with décor for the annual gala are examples of productive cross pollination between the prop shop and development based on mutual respect of one another's strengths and abilities. When properties directors have a demonstrable track record of working "across the aisle," it cannot fail to attract positive attention from the executive director, from whom all numbers flow.

Communication among peers and lateral colleagues, while it may seem to go without saying and is perhaps an underlying assumption, forms the bedrock of teamwork within the production department. Each area has special skills to share and props crosses all boundaries on virtually every show build. Maintaining good humor and a sense of shared responsibility, helping others and allowing oneself to accept help, will earn respect and trust and strengthen connections with production colleagues. A strong collaborative relationship with other area heads depends on empathy as well as advocacy, and constantly reaching out to touch base is one way to keep those doors open.

The importance of observing, listening, and accepting input from the prop shop artisans and show run staff cannot be overstated. These people, individually and as a team, are a deep resource best cherished and supported, and the strength of these human assets is in direct proportion to the time and energy given to listening, acknowledging, sharing information, and managing their creative skills and attributes with respect and evenhandedness.

> *Creativity is seeing what everyone else has seen,*
> *and thinking what no one else has thought.*
> —Einstein

Creativity is the underlying quality defining everything done in the shop and is the basis of thought when approaching a new design. The prop shop must find or build all of the details of hand props from books, weapons, tea cups, and candlesticks to furniture and stage dressing enhancing the scenic environment. Ideas may evolve from a foundation based on historical research or may be something referenced obliquely from an actual object. Sometimes the designer has extensive research or drawings demonstrating what is needed, but often the information evolves from discussion, rehearsal notes, and input from many points of view and diverse artists involved in the process. Having a grab bag of solutions and a broad depth of experience in making things allows the prop "build" to become a rewarding and engaging process, delighting the designer or director who dreamed it up and strengthening the confidence of the actor who has to interact with it onstage.

Creativity is:

- Innovation—improving on a previous solution/experience
- Invention—creating something entirely new
- Imagination—to form images and ideas freely
- Improvisation—solving a problem within limited time or resources
- Curiosity—the insatiable desire to learn and explore
- Flexibility—willingness to adapt to new information or viewpoints
- Vision—seeing the "What if?" The roulette wheel of product and process

Brainstorming options to present to the designer that show different ideas and address the particular situation allows for an enormous pool of solutions to be offered. It might be a different way to build something, allowing it to match what the designer envisions within the budget and build time frame, or it might be a different or new product offering the desired finish, strength, durability, ease of working, or expense. Developing that particular reservoir of creativity relies on experience and investigation. These provide a foundation in problem-solving and a grasp of products: knowing what materials are available and comprehending the attributes those materials have so they can be used in various and different ways. The understanding and knowledge of many skill sets in building, sculpting, sewing, drawing, and crafting allows "riffing" on those processes, spawning different ideas. The ability to juggle it all to transcend traditional notions and create something new in a different way epitomizes the ideal trajectory of prop work.

This is the artistry of manifest invention. The option to build it, buy it, borrow it, or pull it from stock is often the initial step. But then one's imagination can run free, seeing beyond the "as-is" to envision the enhancements through which a prop might become better or different and how it might fulfill the designer's vision, the actor's need, and the director's wishes.

In the prop shop, both "brains" of management and leadership need to be present. While these seem to be similar, they are flip sides of the same coin. All too often the word management is seen with a negative definition, as in controlling, reactive, or procedure oriented, while leadership is seen as more "touchy/feely," with definitions like visionary and inspirational. But the necessity of being a good manager must fit hand in glove with being a creative artist who inspires. The theatre world works with the hard deadline of opening night and tight budgets of time, materials, and personnel. A good manager sets the boundaries of what is possible. An inspirational leader encourages the greatest solution to the seemingly impossible. A brilliant properties director aspires to both.

Hiring and inspiring prop artisans endowed with imagination, creativity, and experience of hands-on skills brings excitement to the collaborative and creative work process. Finding a balance within the structure of problem-solving while matching the design needs is the challenge. Given any one person's style of working with others, it is possible to come up with a management framework for running a shop and leading a build that

Figure 1.1 Leadership/Management Circles

allows for tremendous individual creativity, balanced with the hard reality of deadlines and budgets.

Mission: to lead a shop full of unique artists to transform a diverse array of objects and materials to become a cohesive artistic statement reflecting the stories presented to the audience.

Vision: to fluidly navigate the intricacies of imagination and manage the bedrock of real life limitations in order to produce the highest quality product with the greatest possible impact.

Values: to work and play in a generous, open, and truthful way, pursuing the highest professional standards of quality, and nurturing relationships across all corridors of our professional environment.

* * *

As properties directors, WE are listeners, educators, and advocates for the developmental process of creating and making props. WE support and foster the interconnectedness of all production elements in this messy brilliant creative endeavor called THEATRE.

Job Titles
and Duties

The prop shop lives in the hierarchy of the theatre accountability and responsibility structure. It is only one of the legs in the multi-appendage creature called *production* needed to mount a show successfully. Understanding the sense and sensibilities needed to work in the prop shop allows an appreciation for the people who fulfill that work. Depending on the size of the shop and the organization, job titles and the duties assigned to a specific position may vary widely. This is partly due to the nature of how the prop shop evolved.

The evolution of the properties position is murky, and it is only in the last few decades the status of having someone directly responsible for the props has been codified. In the past, all too often the props were left to whoever could scrounge together the list of items needed, and any "built from scratch" items were requested from the scene shop or costume shop, which worked it in around their other priorities. Sometimes stage managers were required to find props as part of their job in support of the rehearsal and performance process. Today, all that is changed. The professional prop shop is a separate entity working in close collaboration with its cohorts in costumes, scenery, electrics, and sound.

The person who manages the prop shop goes by various titles, depending on the organization itself. Many regional theatre properties shops are managed by the **properties director** and are accountable to the production manager for the on-time, on-budget, as-designed production of the stage properties to the satisfaction of the scene designer.

In theatre, the use of the "master" designation, as in properties master or master electrician, was commonly used when the technical director was the overall head of the technical production process. It also harkens back to the usage of master as a title given to an artisan or tradesperson demonstrating mastery of a skillset. Master was originally applied almost exclusively to men, but its meaning now has been extended to include women and is considered gender-neutral, since few women would be comfortable being called mistress, the traditional female equivalency of master. As the position has evolved, the usage of more professional

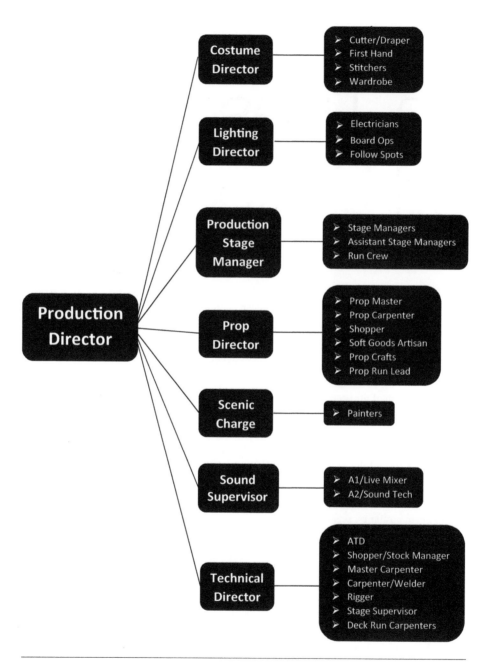

Figure 2.1   Production Hierarchy. Accountability and "hierarchy" structures may vary from organization to organization. Sorting out accountability lines (who can hire you, who can fire you) as opposed "to the satisfaction of" is helped by knowing the hierarchy structure.

business terms such as director or manager skirts the issue of gender altogether. The title of properties master as a "traditional" title is a nod to historical convention even when the job duties and accountability structure are identical to a properties director. In theatres with an **IATSE (International Alliance of Theatrical Stage Employees**, also called **IA**) contract for the running of the shows, the union prop run person might be called the properties master but would not be responsible for managing the prop shop or working on the actual build. In those cases, the person running the shop is generally called the **properties director** or **properties manager**, sometimes shortened to prop or props director or manager. It just depends on the particular person and theatre organization.

The movement to the properties director title for the person who manages the shop build and supervises the properties artisans is an evolution most dominant in the last decade, as the technical director became the person who managed the scene shop, and the larger managerial position overseeing the entire production budget, technical personnel, and production calendar is now commonly titled **production manager** or **production director**. The title of properties director acknowledges the separate and equal nature of the work between the prop shop and scene shop and the equal footing of the job with the technical director as a lateral collaborative colleague.

Some smaller companies have a different management structure, with a technical director still coordinating all the production areas; in those cases, the person who manages the prop shop might be called the **properties master** or **properties manager** for clarification of accountability.

Larger companies also utilize the **properties master** title to designate a person who is part of the prop shop staff specifically leading the build on one show or who manages the prop builds specific to one theatre in a producing complex with several stage venues. Shops in these companies are generally headed up by a properties director, and the properties master is accountable to the properties director. Since it is difficult for a person to be in two places at the same time, having a properties master in charge of a specific show/theatre space allows the properties director to keep multiple show builds going, communicate with upcoming designers and attend meetings, tech rehearsals, and design conferences while increasing the flow of information via the properties master to the shop. The properties master in this case guides the show from shop build through load-in, technical rehearsals and opening, as well as addresses any on-going show maintenance issues and final strike. The properties master and the properties director should have distinct roles defined, allowing for the artisans and other colleagues to understand the authority, communication path, and priority process to avoid confusion or feelings of split loyalties. Sorting this out will be specific to the individuals in those positions, depending on their own skill sets and preferred management practices. It is less about hierarchy than about clarifying what part of the pie each person takes on . . . It's all the same pie.

In recent years, the title of **properties designer** has evolved in acknowledgement of the highlevel of collaboration the prop shop has with the scenic designer in creating the complete stage setting. This title does cause some concern in the prop community, as many feel designing the props is a critical part of the scene design and cannot be separated from the overall visual scenic concept of the show. Unfortunately, props are often left to the last minute, as the scene designer is primarily focused on the "big picture" of the scenic elements. Occasionally, designers seem unable to define the props beyond the most rudimentary information. This is often exacerbated by the trend of increasingly curtailed residencies for out of town scene designers, necessitating a closer and in-person collaborative relationship between the prop director and the stage director in order to rapidly address fluid staging needs during the rehearsal process. Some scene designers utilize the properties director to complete the majority of prop decisions and to choose the details fulfilling the overall intention of the design. In the past, an assistant designer might have fulfilled those requirements, but for the sake of expediency, prop directors often end up propelling the design process, functioning as an assistant designer, and occasionally doing the design work when the scenic designer falls short. The properties director has the management and process skills necessary to move those design choices directly into the shop, while the assistant designer position can often just create another level of communication to manage within the production process. Out of this added responsibility and collaboration on the design, the title of properties designer has evolved to grant some level of acknowledgement for the work.

In some cases, this title and responsibility is defined from the start, and the properties designer works in collaboration with the scenic designer to conceive the stage properties as an equal part of the creative design team. Part of the process from the beginning by attending concept meetings with the director and other designers, the properties designer is an equal contributor to the development of the cohesive visual approach. During the rehearsal process, the properties designer also addresses any evolving changes, adds, or cuts to meet the needs of the particular scene/actor/script problem, considering the overall design of the show as set by the overarching design concept. Having the properties designer in-house as the head of the props area facilitates a quick response. This is especially true when a theatre company utilizes freelance scenic designers who may be juggling a number of shows or are working remotely, and are unavailable to make daily input into the design/prop build process.

The title of properties designer is also common in academia, smaller start-up companies who may not have scenic elements but utilize props to establish the setting, or in organizations lacking the money to appropriately pay someone so grant an elevated title in lieu of a decent salary. In rare cases, the title of properties designer may benefit a prop department head working with an IATSE crew, as rules governing who can complete work notes on stage may be more relaxed for designers than for non-union prop employees. Adding "designer" to a non-union prop department head's title enables dressing work and completion of fussy detail work on stage to unfold without delegation of those tasks.

Even when no properties designer is designated, it seems many scenic designers are relying more and more heavily on the properties director or prop shop manager to make design decisions based on an understanding of the overall look of the scenic design and in collaboration with the director. As creative artists, it is the nature of collaboration and creation to offer solutions, provide alternatives, and support the design process. Trying to find the line of design input in order to put a title on it is a waste of time and energy better spent on the creation of the work itself. Everyone designs as they problem-solve. Everyone designs as they build or engineer a prop. Everyone should be engaged in and connected to the design decision.

The position of **prop shop manager** is often found in larger theatres where multiple shows may be in the prop shop, requiring a mid-level shop manager to solve day-to-day shop priorities while the properties director juggles the overall management of all the shows. The shop manager runs the shop and assigns the work to the artisans, allowing for the various projects to be completed. The shop manager juggles the deadlines of upcoming shows against the time demands of producing the props and the efficiencies and needs of the staff. The prop shop manager title is also used somewhat interchangeably with properties master or properties director in some organizations.

In organizations with multiple producing spaces, having a shop manager to juggle the work flow through the shop may also be further assisted by having prop masters assigned to individual shows. With the properties director leading the overall management of the season, this allows for a scaling of priorities to be sorted out, giving the artisans focus on what has to be created first. It spreads the load of attending design meetings, technical and dress rehearsals, and production meetings while granting administrative responsibilities to a wider group of people; this allows multiple productions in various spaces to move forward, the information with stage management and show run staff to be coordinated more easily, and budget and calendar updates to happen efficiently. Defining job duties and having an open communication process for establishing priority and managing conflict is essential for this kind of inter-layered management style to succeed. This intermix of administration and supervision demands an open management style and a high level of communication to all levels in the shop. It works for some organizations and some people, but others may desire a more traditional top-down layering of responsibility and management, with a trickle-down information process and a pyramid of accountability and work process. Either method of management will work, depending on the people and the organization's needs.

SKILLS AND DUTIES: THE PROP SHOP

The **properties director** must have a strong background in management of a shop and staff, budgeting, and period research and be able to read, interpret, and draft the scenic designer's prop sketches into working drawings, utilizing appropriate construction techniques/materials to satisfy the production's particular needs; further, the properties director must be skilled in all phases of property construction and be a collaborative and effective communicator with stage managers, directors, actors, and other area heads. The properties director is ultimately responsible for maintaining the prop shop tools and equipment and keeping a wide variety of supplies in stock, from lumber, steel, plastics, and paint to sewing and craft materials.

Figure 2.2 Properties Director. Properties director Jolene Obertin, Seattle Repertory Theatre, confers with her artisans, James Severson, Angela Zylla, and Nicolette Vannais. Photo courtesy of Ruth Gilmore.

The properties director establishes and maintains the high standard of safety for work done in the shops and on stage. While each person in the prop shop and, indeed, in the theatre itself, is ultimately responsible for ensuring their own safety and making personal decisions about work processes and products used in the production of theatre props, the properties director should make safety a top priority. Beyond just the obvious desire to work in a healthy and safe environment, it's the law. The general duty clause of the **Occupational Safety and Health Act (OSHA)** states, in part, that the employer shall furnish "employment and a place of employment which are free from recognized hazards." The properties director has an obligation to maintain health and safety standards for the protection of all who work in the shop and to promote necessary tool/supply upgrades and shop maintenance needed to comply with safe working practices both to management and to the prop staff.

Most importantly, the properties director manages the build as it moves through the shop, adjusting crew assignments and determining priorities in response to rehearsal requests, availability of materials, changes in the prop list, difficulties in building a prop, and all of the juggling of whether some particular prop is built, bought, pulled, or borrowed from another company. Attendance at production and design meetings allows for efficient communication with all departments, including those overlapping into props such as costumes, scenery, or electrics. Acting as the point person in the prop shop, they direct necessary information to the properties crew about changes in specific props or projects, to stage management about status of projects and specific handling or use of props, and to the designer about requested changes or rehearsal adds. They also work with the production manager to balance the budget needs for the show and the personnel hires.

In addition to running the prop shop, the properties director is often responsible for the maintenance of the properties stock and managing prop rentals to community organizations and other theatres. The marketing and development offices often request assistance from the prop shop for back-stage tours, educational events, fundraising gala decoration, photo shoots, and other community and fundraising events.

In small theatres and especially at the university and community theatre level, the properties director is often a one-person shop. Obviously, the level of production must also be smaller given the limited number of hours in the day and the ability of one person to do the work accomplished by a full staff in other organizations. The one-person properties shop usually relies on strong local contacts for borrowing items and a realistic understanding of the limitations necessitated by budget, time, and availability of volunteers or other production personnel who may be able to help out if they have time available in their own production work. However, the passion and commitment demonstrated by these small shops remains the same for the dedicated properties director striving to put on stage the best product to support the play.

THE PROP STAFF

Most regional theatres and larger producing organizations have a staff to support the prop build. Assisting the properties director or the properties master of a show is a crew of **properties artisans**. They are responsible for the construction, acquisition, and innovative creation of all props used in a production. Small shops have artisans utilizing a large variety of skills, with the expectation that each person has the skills to move the prop from beginning to end through the shop. Generally, no title specialization is noted beyond properties artisan or properties assistant. Larger shops tend to have specialist artisans who work with a more specific area of expertise and are given titles such as soft goods artisan, props carpenter, crafts artisan, shopper/buyer, assistant prop master, or shop manager. The flexibility of duties associated with those titles is reflected in the skill set each individual brings to the shop. It's incredibly helpful to have a variety of folks with dual areas of expertise to collaborate and work together on projects. Even in shops where the title is properties artisan, the individuals tend to have skill sets connected to some level of proficiency and are assigned projects and the work associated with those skills. Hiring in a new artisan to replace someone who is departing is often a search for the skill set the previous person brought to the shop and usually

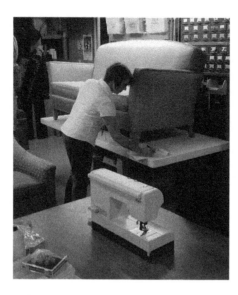

Figure 2.3   Soft Goods Artisan. Soft goods artisan Margaret Hasek-Guy at Milwaukee Repertory Theater.

requires a juggling of responsibility and redistribution of who does what as the shop adjusts. Considering the enormous variety of skills required to efficiently and effectively accomplish a show build in the prop shop, having the greatest diversity and overlap of skills is more than helpful; it's a necessity.

Properties artisans work under the supervision of the properties director but are expected to be self-motivated, creative, innovative, collaborative artists honoring the design intent while making the props stage-worthy and safe. The properties director may also delegate some responsibilities to the artisans, such as the maintenance of tools, purchasing of supplies, organization of stock/equipment/materials, management of rentals, assisting with marketing events, etc.

A **soft goods artisan** completes the patterning, draping, tailoring, and sewing of fabric-based projects. An understanding of fabric varieties, usage, and manipulation is a necessity, as is familiarity with hand sewing techniques and machine sewing processes utilizing standard sewing machines, serger, or a walking-foot sewing machine for larger projects and heavier upholstery fabrics. Upholstery projects utilize theatrical techniques duplicating traditional looks but often utilize many "costuming" tricks for fabric, interior lining, structure, and foam build up. Sewing skills are required to build the pillows, curtains, bed coverings, drapes, and all the various "soft" props needed. An understanding of fabric dyeing, painting, and distressing is needed to allow for appropriate aging and storytelling. Often working from sketches or research documents, the soft goods artisan must be able to estimate yardage and pattern

Figure 2.4 Props Carpenter. Props artisan/carpenter Jen Lyons builds a roulette table for the Skylight Opera production, *La Traviata*.

various projects to create appropriate fullness and drape matching the designer's image, understand usage of trims and construction techniques for finishing, and be able to interpret and design for rigging or manipulation of soft goods by the run crew or actors on stage. On shop built items, the soft goods artisan works in the design and construction part of the project to prepare the frame for the soft goods work in collaboration with or as part of the construction team.

A **properties carpenter** works to construct, restore, conserve, or alter furniture and other items from wood, plastic, or metal for the stage. Using construction techniques similar to theatrical scenic construction as well as traditional woodworking processes, prop carpentry skills must allow for the repair of damaged or fragile original pieces to a stage-worthy status, reinforce stock pieces appropriately to protect them for specific stage action, and modify existing pieces to create a designed or specific period silhouette and structure. Increasingly, properties carpenters also fabricate furniture from scratch to meet specific design requirements as an alternative to purchasing an expensive antique and attempting to strengthen the old piece for stage use. An understanding of finishing techniques and detailing is important, as are skills in metalwork and welding to construct reinforcing armatures or ornamental pieces. Understanding how to use traditional tools for woodworking, such as the table saw, lathe, drill press, mortising joiner, miter saw, or standard hand tools, allows for work on restoration and reproduction. Utilization of more modern tools—such as a 3D printer for detail work or a CNC (computer numerical control router) for designing parts on a personal computer and then cutting various hard materials from wood, steel, plastic, and foams—allows the prop carpenter to mechanize the production and duplication of complex shapes and layered projects with precision. Having the skill to take a period research photo or rough drawing and draft a construction drawing allowing for the specific needs of the show from actor use onstage to efficient scene change needs in addition to understanding materials and processes for building is at the heart of the work done by the prop carpenter.

Figure 2.5 Crafts Artisan. Crafts artisan Anna Warren preparing a mold to cast a bust resembling one of the actors for Milwaukee Repertory Theater's mainstage.

The **crafts artisan** is truly a jack of all trades and should possess a wide variety of skills, including casting and molding, graphics layout and manipulation, faux and fine art painting, floral arrangement, leather working, jewelry making, special effects, carving, and sculpture work. Larger theatres may have a person hired to specifically fill the crafts position, supplementing the specialty artisans who usually have crafts skills complementing their area of specialty. This position may be shared with another area such as costumes or the paint shop. The crafts artisan often is the designated finish artisan, utilizing faux finishes, glazes, paint, stains, dyes, or other techniques to tone and seal furniture, hand props, or dressing pieces. A rapidly developing area in the crafts specialty is in the creation of ephemera or paper goods for the stage using the computer. An understanding of software programs for graphics scanning, manipulation, and printing is essential for the creation of period newspapers, posters, letters, hand bills, or magazines. The computer also allows 3D printing and creation of small hand props or pieces for larger items, and knowing the programming and manipulation of images to manufacture objects with a 3D printer is an area expanding in the industry. The crafts artisan works closely on the creation of hand props and dressing, starting with pieces pulled from prop stock for adaptation to match the individual needs of a show, or may assist on a large project with other artisans to craft detail work once the initial construction is completed. This artisan may also be trained as a puppeteer and puppet designer, an area of growing interest and value, needed not only to create the puppet but to help train the actors or stage crew in the manipulation and use of the puppet in the show.

The **shopper/buyer** finds and procures the products, raw materials, requested items, or specific props needed for the build of the show. Good visualization skills and an understanding of process are especially important as this artisan must coordinate the acquisition of what needs to be purchased with the other artisans who are using those items or products to build

Figure 2.6 Prop Shopper. Prop shopper Dana Fralick prepares his shopping list and research prior to departing for his workday.

the props. Strong interpersonal skills help in negotiating purchases and setting up delivery of goods as well as in the discovery and purchasing of items. An understanding of budget management and accounting is important in coordination with the properties director who is managing the overall budgetary decisions. Strong computer skills for research and acquisition are especially valuable in this position, as the ability to find specific items or order materials has become more accessible via the web and eBay purchasing, making the entire world a prop marketplace. As more and more dependence on the web for procuring materials or for purchasing specific objects/props occurs, having a dedicated shopper to research, get information to the designer for confirmation, order, track shipping/delivery, and input budget information into the show budget track sheet eases the workflow in all other areas.

TITLES IN RELATED DISCIPLINES

Job titles across the various disciplines where props are utilized can vary given the history of the organization, the affiliation with IATSE, the accountability structure as defined by the particular company, or by tradition. Titles, in conjunction with written job descriptions, help define lines of comparable work within the larger structure of an organization and are utilized for promotion, compensation considerations, and duties. Job titles assist in clarifying the chain of accountability and understanding who establishes the priorities in production. Knowing the skill sets associated with job titles may help in assigning those titles to staff during the hiring and promotion process.

When considering prop work with **IATSE (International Alliance of Theatrical Stage Employees)** specifically, there are four primary inroads to pursue: applying for a house or tour

IA prop position which grants you union membership upon hiring, applying to obtain a position on the organizational or "stringer" list, joining an organizational effort within a specific theatre/venue, or applying to the IATSE apprenticeship program. In any of these situations, one can encounter a number of differing structures within which a prop professional might function. The IATSE is organized into local jurisdictions, which handle theatre labor needs within a particular geographic area. Within the pantheon of IATSE contracts and work agreements governed by each local, a vast array of definitions can be found for prop personnel. Each work situation is governed by the specific collective bargaining agreement that each local has with a specific theatre or organization. These unique agreements, when comprehensively written, cover everything from soup to nuts: meaning that the wages and conditions and even job duties are entirely up to each local to negotiate with employers and venues within its own jurisdiction.

An IA crew is traditionally organized into distinct departments: carpentry (including fly men, riggers and loaders), properties, electrics, wardrobe (which includes makeup), hair/wigs, and sound/projection. "Props" as used in IA parlance is a term potentially covering both construction and running crew, who are responsible for hand props, personal props, set props, set dressing, trim props, ground cloths, special effects including breakaways, mechanical effects, atmospheric effects (fog, fire, snow, etc.), furniture, floor coverings, and set up of the orchestra pit. Crews can be assigned on a four-hour, day-long, or long-term contract, and on production work or on show calls including theatrical events, concerts, trade shows, or extended touring shows.

A common division of labor for the IA prop crew is typically top down: the **properties head** has similar job duties as a non-union properties director. Beyond crew management and leading the prop build, the union prop head plans and manages the prop pack, load in, load out, and handles all onstage props notes. The **lead property master** is an assistant to the head of props, assuming all responsibilities in the absence of the properties head. They work with the stage manager and props run crew in running the show, including crew assignments, prop tables preparation and performer training for prop use. **Prop builders** are responsible to the prop head and lead property master, in order of hierarchy. Their job is to assist senior property employees in the construction of properties and perform basic duties as assigned including show run.

Other tasks traditionally assigned to props crew in an IATSE venue include doing support set up onstage and in the orchestra pit and general stage cleanup and maintenance.

In **OPERA**, there is often a division between regional or summer opera structures and more traditional large grand opera prop departments. Regional opera companies may trend toward non-union prop shops, functioning similarly to smaller regional theatres in terms of prop shop accountability structure with a **prop director**, **assistant prop director**, **shopper**, **carpentry lead**, **prop craftsperson**, **soft goods artisan**, **and prop run crew lead.** Smaller opera companies often employ a non-union **props coordinator** who gets all of the props to the theatre, be it by building or purchasing or pulling or whatever means are necessary. In these instances, the prop coordinator is largely working solo or with occasional hourly supplemental labor as needed. When the props are loaded into the theatre, they are handled by the IA **prop master** and his or her crew during tech rehearsals and performances. The ability of the prop coordinator to execute notes on props once the union crew has charge of them can often be limited in some union contracts. This may result in a bit of schlepping props back and forth on the part of the prop coordinator to work off site on larger notes that the IA prop run crew doesn't typically tackle.

In top tier **GRAND OPERA** companies, the prop department is frequently a fully union-ized crew responsible for procuring, building, modifying, rehearsing, and running all props and set dressing. Usually these prop departments have developed over many long years, so titles can be quite unique to the history of each organization. The **property master** runs the department, responsible for making sure all props exist and are where they need to be for rehearsals and performances. The **assistant property master** assists the prop master in all duties but may also help with accounting and purchasing, crew payroll, storage and inventory-ing, trucking, and "running the deck" as needed. Most large organizations utilize three **keys** or **leads**, a Stage Left (SL) key, a Stage Right (SR) key, and an Orchestra key. In general, the SL and SR keys are in charge of prop running for the shows and turnarounds (productions done in rotating rep, where two different shows will be performed in the same venue on the same day at staggered show times). They manage whatever rank and file union crews are onstage at any given time and are responsible for pre-setting all props. The Orchestra key manages seating in the pit, large instrument handling both in the opera house and trucking to off-site rehearsal or performance locations, backstage orchestra and instrument management during performances, and general pit equipment. The **out of house key** is responsible for the rehearsal halls, both the spaces and all props used in them. When rehearsals are running in more than one space at a time, a second and sometimes a third "key" are needed to support rehearsals and consequently foresee notes before they become problematic, communicating with the prop master as an "early warning system." **Backup keys** or **leads** cover when the pri-mary "keys" are unavailable. The **shop mechanic,** similar to the prop shop manager position, runs the prop shop and acts as the department head's right arm in organizing the prop build, retrofitting props brought in, and completing rehearsal and run notes. Any prop crew member not otherwise occupied reports to the shop mechanic for prop build tasks.

In huge organizations such as these there may not be enough work throughout a season for a prop member with just one specialized skill. The structure above, utilizing a group of highly experienced professionals with diverse skills, ensures consistent work spread out for everybody on the union prop crew. It's also helpful for the people building props and furniture to be the same people who run the shows. In this structure, the builders remain cognizant of what it takes to handle each prop on stage: when something can be taken apart, how much time for a scene change, whether a prop will fit smoothly through scenery mechanics to allow collision-free travel on and off stage through large crowds of performers, and a myriad of other prop builder-to-user situational challenges.

BROADWAY productions may list a house props position as **props master** or **produc-tion props master**. This is a union position and the person is in charge of prop pre-set, run, and security of the props at the end of the show. The person who actually builds the props and organizes the procurement of everything is often called the **properties coordinator** or

properties supervisor. This person is an independent artist who may or may not be affiliated with a production company, non-union or union, hired to provide the props for the show.

In **FILM**, the title given to the person realizing the production designer's creative vision is **art director**, although that is for all sets and locations as well as props. Furniture, wall coverings, street signs, and all that is essentially already on the set at the start of a shooting day is under the purview of the **set decoration department**. The **on-set dresser** or **set decorator** works on site to prepare the specific location or set with all the necessary props. On-set propping involves a lot of check-in and out of items, keeping track of all necessities, documenting continuity (especially in dining or food shots), and working with the location manager for each shot while prepping for the next. During actual filming, **standby props** works directly with the art directors to resolve any problems and carry out immediate tasks to allow filming to proceed. The **art department coordinator** tracks clearance and art releases as well as making sure vendors and the art department crew gets paid.

Working with the art director specifically in the properties area would be the **property master**, overseeing the entire property department in managing the prop build, procurement of props, and coordinating delivery of completed props for filming. The **production lead man** functions like a technical director, responsible for receiving drawings and budgeting the labor for the production team and coordinating with the property master. In the microcosm of the film prop department, prop staff mostly deal with hand props, weaponry, and other items handled by talent, both procuring and dealing with the items on set. **Production buyers** source and purchase props for set dressing as well as the materials needed to make props from scratch. A general title, **prop maker**, is used for those folks who do the hands-on building of specific hand props. A **charge hand carpenter** builds props such as furniture and set pieces. The **drapes master** produces and installs the soft furnishings, while the **greens men** use foliage, trees, and greenery to build the landscaping needed. The **props store men** care for all rented or brought-in props, collecting and transporting them to and from the filming site.

COMMERCIAL SHOPS build for corporate events, theatre, TV, film, concerts, sporting events, festivals, retail environments, and a wide array of museum displays and installations. The artisans working for these companies are often called **master craftsmen** and typically report to a **project manager** who is supervising a specific project or part of a larger project, or to the **shop foreman** who is leading the specific build on a project. Depending on the focus of the company, they may also incorporate the traditional titles from theatre or from film, and in some cases from the fine art world, and have corresponding job duties as well.

A good prop person is truly a "Jack (or Jill) of All Trades." Every hobby, interest, or experience adds to the body of knowledge informing the skill set of a props artisan. Just think of all the situations represented on stage and the various characters portrayed needing to have props to help them fulfill the action of their character or to define something about their person. Every day events coupled with an observant and curious mind can form a body of knowledge needed to replicate similar events on stage. The key is to assemble a staff having an eclectic,

HAND PROPS—SKILLS

- Calligraphy
- Model making
- Graphics layout and ephemera
- Molding/casting
- Additive and subtractive sculpting
- Body and face casting
- Puppetry
- Taxidermy
- Jewelry making
- Quilting/embroidery/knitting/
  needlecrafts
- Papier-mâché
- Leatherwork
- Musical instrumentation
- Painting—spray paint techniques,
  acrylics, faux, watercolors, colored pen
  & pencil
- Culinary/food preparation and handling
- Magic and breakaways
- Weaponry/pyro and FX techniques
- Computer—graphics, publishing, drafting

SET PROPS—SKILLS

- Welding/metal working
- Knowledge of tools, materials, techniques
- Basic rigging and engineering
- Furniture construction/restoration
- Woodworking
- Plastics construction
- Sewing
- Knowledge of fabrics, foams, trims, and
  underlayment
- Upholstery
- Draping/fabric layout/pattern making
- Fabric dyeing/distressing
- Faux painting—wood grain, marble,
  stone, aging
- Radio control/pneumatics/small
  specialty electronics
- Special effects

DRESSING—SKILLS

- Painting—acrylics/watercolors/
  portraiture
- Floral arrangement
- Sculpture/3D carving/foam
  carving
- Large scale and small scale
  pattern work
- Electrical construction/wiring
- Picture matting and framing
- Photography
- Shopping
- Internet protocols and tracking
- Pulling from stock to fit the show

Figure 2.7   Prop Skills

SENSIBILITIES OF A PROP PERSON

- **Organization**
- **Time management**
- **Flexibility in the work process**
- **Diplomacy**
- **Collaboration**
- **Creativity**
- **Eye for detail**
- **Flair for design**
- **Color coordination**
- **Textural sympathy**
- **Creative adaptability—seeing "What if. . ."**
- **Verbal and written communication**
- **Drafting/sketching/graphic communication**
- **High production standards**
- **Self-motivation**
- **Innovative thinking**
- **Research inquisitiveness**
- **Computer expertise—word/spreadsheet/drafting/graphics**
- **Memory for details/sizes/history/visuals**
- **Knowledge of period, styles, and architecture**
- **Safety awareness and compliance**

Figure 2.8   Prop Sensibilities

varied, and balanced group of skills, interests, and strengths, so no matter what is thrown at the prop shop to solve, someone of the group can step up and say, "Oh, I know how to do that . . ."

Beyond the hands-on skills, a good prop person must be flexible in their work process as priorities change and props get added or cut. They must be creative and able to see how to adapt and modify items to create something new or different. Prop people must have an eye for detail and flair for design, utilizing color coordination and textural sympathy in interpreting the designer's ideas. High production standards supported by an understanding of how things work on stage demands innovation and a passion for doing this very specialized work to create props meeting the design parameters, produced in a timely manner, and working within the budget restrictions.

* * *

While not all organizations have a separate and designated prop shop space, a staff of prop artisans, and a dedicated budget for props, the process of properties production remains the same. Regardless of title or job duties, it's about putting together the collaborative creative team in support of the show. No two prop shops run the same way or have the same balance of skills in personnel. Every build is different given the variables of when it falls in the season, who is designing, who is directing, what is available in storage, who is available to work in the shop, the budget provided for purchasing items and buying materials, etc. However, understanding the process and procedures in the following chapters should help any organization have an effective and collaborative properties production experience.

For information about having a prop career and contracts, salary/benefits information, networking, training, and internships, please see Chapter 11 in this book.

Working in Film

An interview with Melissa Woods, Freelance Assistant Art Director, Los Angeles, CA

How long have you been doing props for film, and how did you get started in this career?

I started out doing props for theatre and was doing that after receiving a wonderful education at the University of Wisconsin-Milwaukee. I was a prop artisan and then prop master, then I got my first feature film gig through a friend of my roommate in New Haven, CT. It was an indie horror film and on that set and under the guidance of a fabulous production designer Jeanette Andriulli, I learned set etiquette quickly and the fun of tracking continuity as an art director of a small team. It was through contacts I had and networking that I worked on a few other film projects, then decided to pursue my MFA in Scenic Design while continuing to pursue film. University of Arizona's Theatre, Film and Television program seemed like a good fit! After grad school I moved to LA, did a few web series and shorts and eventually got a union New Media series! So, I've never exactly done props for film, but I've worked closely with them as an art direction/production designer.

Melissa Woods
FREELANCE ASSISTANT ART DIRECTOR,
LOS ANGELES, CA

Film prop people are called by various names—different from theatre titles. What are the job titles and job responsibilities of each position?

Oh man, I could write a chapter on this, haha. Well, the department heads are typically Production Designer, Art Director, Construction Coordinator, Prop Master, and Set Decorator. Each of them usually have a team of set dressers, prop makers, day players, and drivers! Specifically, within the props department, there's typically an assistant prop master, a lead fabricator, propmakers, prop painters, prop department coordinator (usually handles vendors, insurance, shipping, etc.), prop buyers, prop carpenters, there might even be a prop welder! A gang boss usually oversees everything, but a transportation (which is a separate union) gang boss might be responsible for determining where trucks park on set. Sometimes there's a weapons or miniature/model department which might employ prop makers, prop maker foremen, plasters, sculptors, specialty prop builders, and there might be some graphics overlap. Each project is different!

What kind of union is available to people working in film, how do you get your "card," and what are the advantages/disadvantages of being union?

Most of the bigger productions, things you see on TV/in the theatre are union. Made-for-TV movies that I've worked on have all been non-union. With the benefits of being eligible for bigger projects, a pension, health, and dental insurance are all nice advantages. The union also negotiates for higher rates and better working conditions for people. There are countless perks including training courses, eligibility rosters, etc.

How is working in film different than working for the stage? How is it the same?

There's no such thing as "tech" in film, but the busiest time for us is typically the shoot itself. During preproduction, we're going on location scouts, planning builds, researching, and drafting. A theatrical production's build time is pretty much the same, but in a large film or TV show, instead of building a set in a theatre, the locations might be in different states or countries. Sometimes if a schedule is tight, they'll plan on doing pre-production and shooting simultaneously. Usually in that case, the prop master is prepping and the assistant or on-set props person is running things on site. Tracking continuity is a big task! Something you don't have to think about in theatre. Small props or dressing items that track from episode to episode or scene to scene need to be carefully tracked and accounted for. The bonus to working such long hours with such heightened responsibility is the paychecks can be pretty substantial. A typical shoot day is twelve hours, with a half hour for lunch. The perks of being on set include craft services (three meals and snacks) and the jovial company as well as traveling to new locations or working on a soundstage. Feature films and commercials can have 6–7-day shoot weeks but for a TV show, a typical shoot week is five days. Sometimes the locations can be far away from where you live, so with a commute (especially in Los Angeles, Atlanta or New York) you might end up doing several sixteen-hour days. Sometimes on low-budget shorts in remote locations, producers suggest staying on location to cut back on travel time. While I have found this a good idea in theory, there's usually a snorer. Or five.

How do you find work?

Combination of websites, social media, and contacts that I've made either on set or from theatre contacts! Looking for work is how I spend 100% of my time when I'm not on a gig!

What is the best part of the work you do?

I think after a show wraps and goes into post-production (which I typically have very little part in) and I get to watch the finished production, see what shots did and didn't make the cut, seeing how it all cuts together is a great joy. I also love meeting new people, learning about their skills, and what brought them to the industry. Everyone has some crazy celebrity story and it's really easy to talk to people about movies on a film set.

What is the most challenging part of the work you do?

Sometimes we're forced to create giant scale projects with very little time and very little money. Sometimes the "labor of love" projects have funding that falls out and work you turned down is filled by someone else and no longer available. So, dry spells do happen! Being able to budget from the busy season to the dry is an important skill!

What are the most critical skills for a film prop person to have?

Attention to detail, focus, ability to self-motivate and keep a cool head under pressure. Film is a very high-stress medium to work in. Sometimes prop people get blamed for the darndest things and are responsible for an insane amount of tracking. Being easy to work with is important as well. You need to be able to collaborate and quickly revise and share ideas with others, while taking and implementing notes. You can easily teach some new skills, but you can't teach positivity!

Describe your ideal day.

I think my ideal day would be spent rendering a set or plate for VFX, working a 12-hour day working on drafting/renderings. That is not typical, I would say I spent about one-fifth of my time doing that. Mostly, I spend my time budgeting and doing cost reports, graphics, and some shopping/returns.

If you were advising someone about how to start a career in film work, what would you tell them?

Don't be afraid to work for free! But be honest with your superiors about what you do and do not know. There's nothing more disappointing than hiring someone to do a job they say they are familiar with only to find out they're unqualified! If you're unsure of something, especially regarding safety, ask questions! In film, time is precious and an accident or a mistake can be a very big deal. Starting out as a production assistant is a very quick way to learn the ropes.

C H A P T E R   3

What Is a Prop?

Props live in the world of the visual design created by the scenic designer to establish the stage setting for the play. They are the details fleshing out the architecture of the stage setting to define the characters in the play, set the time period, support the action needed within the structure of the play, and complete the "bridge" between the characters on stage and the reality of life objects.

A good analogy to define "*what is a prop?*" has been likened to the real-life situation of when a person moves from one home to another. A moving van pulls up and all the contents of the home are loaded in the van and it drives off to be unloaded into the new house. The house is the scenery. The scenery includes the actual walls, floors, ceilings, doors—the architecture of the house. This does not move. It is stationary and permanent. The items boxed up, covered in pads, and carried out to the moving van when a person is changing residences would all be considered the props.

The props are all the non-permanent items. Think of what would be put in that moving van—dishes, lamps, chairs, books, pictures, furniture, blankets, drapes, rugs, letters, office supplies, appliances, lawn tools—all the "stuff" people need in their everyday living and utilize to furnish their homes. It can be either personal (a book on Egypt) or non-specific (a pillow) but every item says something about who owns that item. Even the non-specific pillow tells us something. Is it a bed or sofa pillow? Feather or foam? In a pillowcase or ticking cover? Clean or stained? Each item is a small clue into who the owner is, giving insight into the character of the owner. Finding or building those items is the prop person's job.

Clarifying who does what with colleagues in other production shops is somewhat fluid and dependent on a specific organization's history as well as specific personnel and their talents. This separation of who does what is examined in more depth in following chapters.

Props can be broken down into several easy categories, and most prop shops work with three categories—hand props, set props, and stage dressing.

Figure 3.1 Hand Props. Hand props (teapot with sand, cup, basin, small prayer rug) support the action and help establish character: *Songs from the Uproar*, Milwaukee Opera Theatre. Lisa Schlenker, ephemera & prop curator. Photo courtesy of Mark Frohna.

HAND PROPS

A **hand prop** is anything carried or handled by an actor within the action of a scene. It often helps define an actor's specific character such as a cane, cigar, liquor flask, lipstick, feather duster, floral bouquet, or sword. A hand prop might also help fulfill the action described in the play, such as a gun used to threaten another character, a fountain pen for signing a contract, a letter opened and read, or a piece of fruit eaten and enjoyed.

Making a hand prop list can be done specific to character or listed just as they appear within the play. The script might mention numerous props on first read through, but hand props are the one area that seems to change the most depending on the rehearsal process.

The "*adds*" of hand props arrive as the play is being blocked and worked through in the initial staging process. Actors will often make specific requests for a hand prop they need to help them in "fleshing out" their character. This is also the area that gets the most "*cuts*" in the final weeks of rehearsal and "tech" as the action of the scenes becomes more comfortable and the actors sure of their characters. Making an initial listing of the props and being able to analyze a script to find the props starts the prop build process. Read for both items and action.

In the example below from *Seven Guitars* by August Wilson, Act I, Scene 4, some of the hand props are called out in the character dialogue, while other props are simply implied.

LOUISE: *Ohh. Just the man I want to see. Give me one of them Old Golds. Hedley give me one of these old Chesterfields. Here I'll trade you the pack.*

RED CARTER: *Naw. I ain't gonna do that. I don't want no Chesterfield! I don't see how people smoke them things.*

From these two lines, the hand props would include a pack of Old Gold cigarettes, a pack of Chesterfield cigarettes, and possibly matches or a lighter to light the cigarettes (making them a consumable) and maybe requiring an ashtray.

When making the listing, it is handy to group items together which support a single action or character, even if it may not be called out in that particular scene or mentioned in the script. For example, if you have a character who asks for a cup of tea, the props required to support this single request might be as simple as a mug of tea. On the other hand, it might be a full tea service on a full tea cart complete with silver trays, serving teapot, cups, saucers, sugar bowl with silver tongs and cubed sugar, a small cream pitcher, tea spoons, waste bowl, and tea caddy. While the character only mentions a cup of tea, it may be appropriate to support the request in a more complete and visual way. Additionally, it is helpful to ask other questions: What fits the action? What fits the length of dialogue? Do they have time to make the tea? Should the tea already be made in the teapot? Is it appropriate for the characters to own and use a tea service? Or is this just a request for a mug of tea? The director or designer will need to answer these questions, so have a list with appropriate questions for the initial design conference. Some questions may need to be taken to stage management and solved as the play is rehearsed.

Figure 3.2 Set Props. Furniture pieces used to set the scene for Act II, *Ring Round the Moon*, University of Wisconsin-Milwaukee. Sandra J. Strawn, properties director.

SET PROPS

The **set props** are the large movable items used to help establish place that are not built into the set. Generally, this is the furniture or "sittables" and would include things like chairs, tables, rugs, appliances, barrels, trunks, or large rocks. But it can also include larger items like tents, a canoe, a car, or even a wrestling ring. Research photos showing style or finish and/or drawings for pieces to be built are communicated to the prop shop directly from the scenic designer. Their size and location are notated on the floor plan, showing the relationship within the stage setting and used by stage management to set up for rehearsal purposes. The initial description of the setting is often communicated from the playwright at the top of the scene.

It may be a sentence as simple as this one from *Proof* by David Auburn:

SETTING: *A back porch of a house in Chicago*

This description gives little information about the props needed or the time period. The details are placed throughout the script itself in the action of the characters needing places to sit or picking up objects and relating to items on the stage. In order to prepare for the first meeting with the designer, the properties director would need to read carefully to get an understanding of what set props might be required.

On the other hand, some playwrights give quite complete visual descriptions with specific prop information, such as in *Seven Guitars* by August Wilson.

SETTING: *The action of the play takes place in the backyard of a house in Pittsburgh in 1948. It is a brick house with a single window fronting the yard. Access to the room is gained by stairs leading to a small porch on the side of the house. This is VERA'S apartment. LOUISE and HEDLEY live on the second floor in separate quarters, which are accessed by steps leading to a landing and a flight of stairs alongside the building. The stairs are wooden and are in need of repair. . . . The yard is a dirt yard with a small garden area marked off by bricks in the downstage right corner where VERA has made a garden of vegetables and flowers. A cellar door leads into the basement where HEDLEY stores his gear. Off to the side and in the back of the yard is a contraption made of bricks, wood, and corrugated sheet metal which is where Hedley kills chickens. It couples as a grill for cooking and when it is not being used, it breaks down with a minimum of parts left standing. During several of his scenes HEDLEY builds or dismantles his contraption and stores its pieces in the cellar. There is an entrance to the yard through a latched gate to the left of the building. There is occasionally a card table set up in the yard with an eclectic mix of chairs. Several light bulbs, rigged by way of extension cords, run from VERA's apartment to light the table so they can sit and play cards on the hot summer nights of 1948.*

The prop list can be started from this description. Set props would include the card table, chairs (various), and the chicken killing contraption/grill. Time and place are defined specifically and even "use" is described to inform the choices to be made.

Both of these script examples are for plays set in the back of a house in the city, but the level of information provided on props varies considerably. The scene designer may use this description as the basis for the design . . . or may choose to completely ignore it, but at least it's a place to start in understanding what may be required to set the scene. Once the design

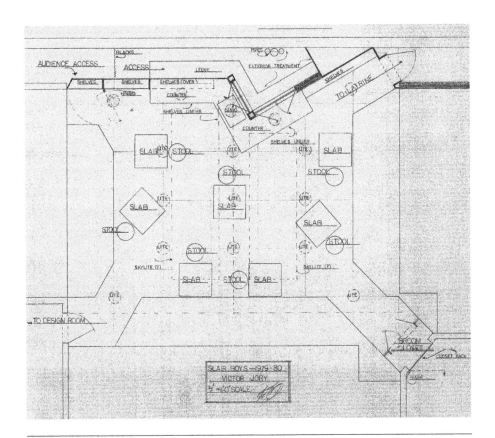

Figure 3.3 Floor Plan with Prop Notation. *Slab Boys* floor plan with prop notation for set props and dressing as well as scenic and lighting elements needing to be coordinated with the prop shop. While the furniture pieces are props (slab tables, stools) other elements such as the sink, counter, and shelving would need to be coordinated with scenery. The hanging lights would be provided by props but coordinated with electrics and factored into the load-in with scenery. Paul Owen, scenic designer, Actors Theatre of Louisville.

has been finalized, this information is often communicated to the prop shop directly from the scenic designer, and size and location are notated on the floor plan to show the relationship within the stage setting.

Set props tend to be fairly well defined early on since that information is needed prior to rehearsal starting. They may also take up the bulk of the budget and the energy of the build in many shows, so it's helpful to know this information as soon as possible from the designer to allow preliminary budgeting for the build to happen. Furniture pieces set time period and character quickly, and the prop shop must find the specific items requested by the designer for a particular look. The challenge lies in finding the piece with the right look that will also function well for the action as defined in rehearsal by the director. In addition, the pieces often have to be shifted and moved to show a passage of time or to allow for a scene change between places. Prop furniture takes a high level of abuse, and often the actions blocked on the furniture puts more stress on a piece than it would normally receive in a lifetime of normal use in a home environment. Appropriate reinforcement and finishes must be considered as items are selected or built.

Working from what is available in stock, designers may choose to have items built or altered specifically to fit the show. Utilizing photos or sketches, the designer communicates the "look" desired to the prop shop, and the prop build begins.

Figure 3.4 Stage Dressing. An example of how prop dressing can make a design visually complete. *Just A Little Critter Musical*, First Stage. Nikki Kulas, properties director; Lisa Schlenker, scenic designer. Photo courtesy of Paul Ruffolo.

STAGE DRESSING

Stage dressing (or **set dressing**) encompasses all the decorative items used to enhance the visual setting. These items are rarely moved or even touched by the actors and are mostly used to help the designer establish place or time period as well as character detail. Examples would include curtains on the window, books in a bookcase, hanging chandeliers, a moose head hanging on the wall, magazines and floral arrangements spread on a coffee table, or pictures arranged on a wall. While dressing may be mentioned in the script, it is rarely complete and is usually ignored as the designer determines the details to fit with the particular design being created for the specific production.

Stage dressing information usually comes from the designer and may be communicated to the prop shop in various ways. Often the designer communicates the look desired by simply describing what is needed and relying on the prop shop to fulfill expectations from that verbal description. This works best in relationships where the prop shop and designer have worked together enough to have a strong understanding of what the designer means and usually envisions. Understanding and getting "into the head" of the designer to *see* what the designer is seeing as the vision for the play makes the verbal design process easier.

It is sometimes easiest to talk about set dressing by utilizing the scaled model of the stage setting or from the front elevations. Some designers include highly detailed stage

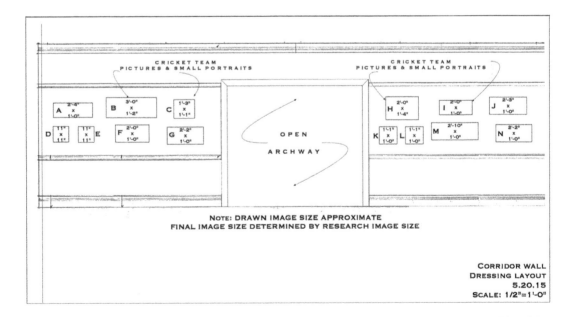

Figure 3.5 Front Elevation—Dressing. Front elevation showing wall dressing for *One Man, Two Guvnors*, The Alley Theatre. Frames and content are described in general terms/sizes and fulfillment is left up to the discretion of the prop staff. Hugh Landwehr, scenic designer.

dressing in their models. Others take front elevations and overlay prop detail onto the drawing showing size or placement of pictures, sketching in draperies, or showing other dressing detail. Working with the elevations or the model even while talking with the designer assists in clarifying what the designer is imagining. Knowing the dressing from the start of the build also allows the prop shop to work with the other production areas to anticipate where additional support may need to be added, where hanging pieces need to be rigged and how that might impact with lighting or other flying items, or to plan for a coordination of installation during load-in.

The smaller, detailed stage dressing is often just a conversation between the designer and the properties director about what might be placed around the stage. For example, if the play takes place in a modern apartment with a bookcase, coffee table, credenza, TV and stereo

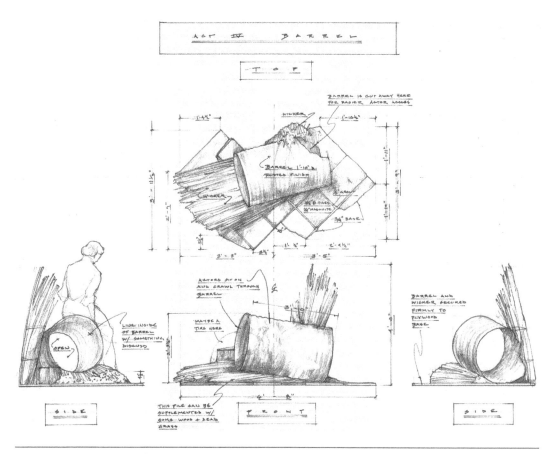

Figure 3.6 Designer Drawing—Dressing. Detailed top, side, and front view of barrel wagon showing proportion, texture, and finishes with information on usage for *The Marriage of Figaro*, Skylight Opera Theatre. Robert Perdziola, scenic designer.

WHAT IS A PROP? 39

Figure 3.7 Designer Research Collage. *Hot Mikado* design collage panels showing research, script notation on usage, and ideas on process from Sarah Brandner, scenic designer, Skylight Music Theatre.

cabinet, sofa, and other decor, the designer may call out for several specific items of decoration but will assume the prop shop would fill the bookcase with appropriate books and collectable items, dress the coffee table with magazines fitting the characters and season of the play, cover the credenza with a small decorative runner topped by a vase of flowers or piece of sculpture, file CDs and record covers in the stereo cabinet beside a remote control for the TV, pull throw pillows and a soft blanket for the back of the sofa, and otherwise make the setting appear like someone actually lives in the space. The actual selection and placement of those props is left up to the discretion of the props department, although most designers will "tweak" the final dressing to suit their personal vision.

Larger dressing pieces such as signage, curtains/drapes/blinds on windows, and paintings or mirrors hanging on the wall are such a critical part of the design that fairly detailed drawings to show scale, period detailing, fullness of drape, finish, color, etc. are usually provided by the designer to convey exactly what they envision. Some designers may choose to create a collage

Figure 3.8 *Gin Game* Model. Set model for *The Gin Game* showing furniture style and placement, suggestion of set decoration and foliage requirements, as well as color and texture choices. Paul Owen, scenic designer, Actors Theatre of Louisville.

Figure 3.9 *Hay Fever* Prior to Dressing. *Hay Fever* stage setting prior to set dressing. Note scenery delayed–missing molding and final floor painting. Kurt Sharp, scenic designer, University of Wisconsin-Milwaukee.

of photos to convey those choices and sketch pertinent dimensions or notes for clarification directly onto the provided photos. Either functions to provide the information and help the prop staff know what the designer wants.

Stage dressing can also include items such as trees, grass, bushes, or other landscape items, falling almost over into set props. These items might be considered scenery in some theatres. As in all things, negotiation and collaboration are essential in determining who is responsible for building the various parts of the production depending on budget, talent, and time.

Properties production, of all the areas on the production side of doing theatre, is probably the most collaborative with the designers and director. While some information is available from the drawings designers produce and from rehearsal, the prop shop often researches and creates much of what is placed on stage directed by their sense of the overall design

Figure 3.10 *Hay Fever* Dressed Set Shot. Preview set shot for *Hay Fever* with furniture in place, hand props pre-set, and completed stage dressing on walls and furniture pieces. Note dressing in backing areas of garden, front door, and upstairs hall. Kurt Sharp, scenic designer, University of Wisconsin-Milwaukee.

sensibility and an understanding of time period, place, and an interpretation of character from the rehearsal process.

* * *

Adding the furniture props and stage dressing is what brings the space to life. Props bridge the space between the actor and the setting, making it human and bringing it alive, giving it dimension, color, character, and offering clues to the world of the play.

C H A P T E R   4

Pre-Production and Planning

It all begins with the **script**. For props, the script defines the world of the play, establishing the setting, the characters, and the action. Reading the script or analyzing the libretto and score, in the case of a musical or opera, is the first entry into what the props might be for the production. The first read of the script enables a basic understanding of the story, revealing who the characters are and what is happening in the play. This read is critical to developing a framework for tracking the flow of action in the script and a summary of the plot and characters.

On the second and third read-through, finding and scrutinizing the details becomes more important. Where is the play set? (City, building, specific room, country.) When is the play set? (Season, period, time of day, holiday time.) Who are these characters on a deeper level? (Jobs, economic status, social status, relationships, passions, fears, religion, family group.) What plot complexities unfold in the play? (Actionable event, supporting events.)

For example, in Act II of *A Different Moon*, written by Ara Watson, the following scene occurs:

SARAH: (Entering) *I think maybe I better sit down in here for* . . .

RUTH: *Let me—*

SARAH: *I'm fine. I'm only* . . .

RUTH: (Leading her to sofa) *Well, of course you're fine. Now, you sit down right* . . . (seats her) . . . *there. Would you like a cold washrag?*

SARAH: *No, I'm really* . . . *It was just all the smells* . . . *made me* . . .

RUTH: *And I've had that stove on and it's hot in there* . . . *Would you like to lie down? I'll get you a pillow if—*

SARAH: *No. Thank you.* (Ruth makes a quick exit into the kitchen and re-enters immediately with a plate on which are two pieces of toast)

RUTH: *Here you go. You nibble on this and you'll feel a lot better.* (and later in the same scene—)

SARAH: *I like your house. You've got real nice furniture.*

RUTH: *Thank you. Mostly odds and ends. This table, though . . . I'm fond of this table. This one. It belonged to my mother. All hand carved by her brother.* (She touches it lovingly.) *And these two chairs are from her dining room. There were eight of them and we— my two brothers and my sister, myself—each took two. I got the two with the side arms.*

SARAH: *They're real nice.*

RUTH: (Moving to a picture) *This is my family.*

SARAH: *I saw that picture.*

RUTH: (Picks up the picture and moves to Sarah) *It was taken not long before my mother died. She was a really beautiful woman all her life, but . . . cancer.* (Looks at the picture and shakes her head, then more brightly.) *This is my sister Leah—she lives in California— and this is my brother Wendell—he lives here in Masefield, runs the post office—and this is Justin, my brother, he lives two houses down. I think Tyler looks just like him—same chin.*

SARAH: *Is that you in the back?*

RUTH: (Laughs) *Yes. I had everyone standing in front of me because I was eight months— It was right before Tyler was born.* (Putting the picture back in its place.) *I must get a new frame for this.*

These few lines pulled from the script give valuable hints into many things impacting the design and eventually, the prop choices. The kitchen is immediately adjacent to the living room since the toast can be so quickly fetched, and so the house is small. This size perception is supported by the comment about the heat from the stove. This will probably affect the scale of furniture and even require some "kitchen" dressing support seen through a doorway. The toast must be brought in on a plate (hand prop). The toast is eaten, making it a consumable. Some of the furniture is known now; the lines ask if she wants to lie down so whatever she sits on must be capable of also supporting someone reclining (a sofa or daybed), and the toast is set on an adjacent table easy for her to reach, so probably a side table or coffee table of some kind. From the next conversation, the furniture would seem to be hand-me-down but nice. It should not match. One table is quite specific in description requiring hand carving. Two of the chairs must be dining room chairs with arms.

The photograph (hand prop) in the scene is also quite specific. It is a framed family photograph with at least five people in the picture. Two of the people are men, three are women with one elderly woman and one pregnant woman. The final line suggests the frame may be "dated," but it could also simply be a way of changing the conversation and nothing is really wrong with it. Script analysis is not always a literal description. From these sixteen lines, the prop director can begin to see the characters and understand what their world might look like.

As the script is read, underlining or highlighting the props, making notations in the border, or writing questions about something occurring in the action that has an impact on the props is the start of organizing a way of thinking about the show and preparing to talk with the designers.

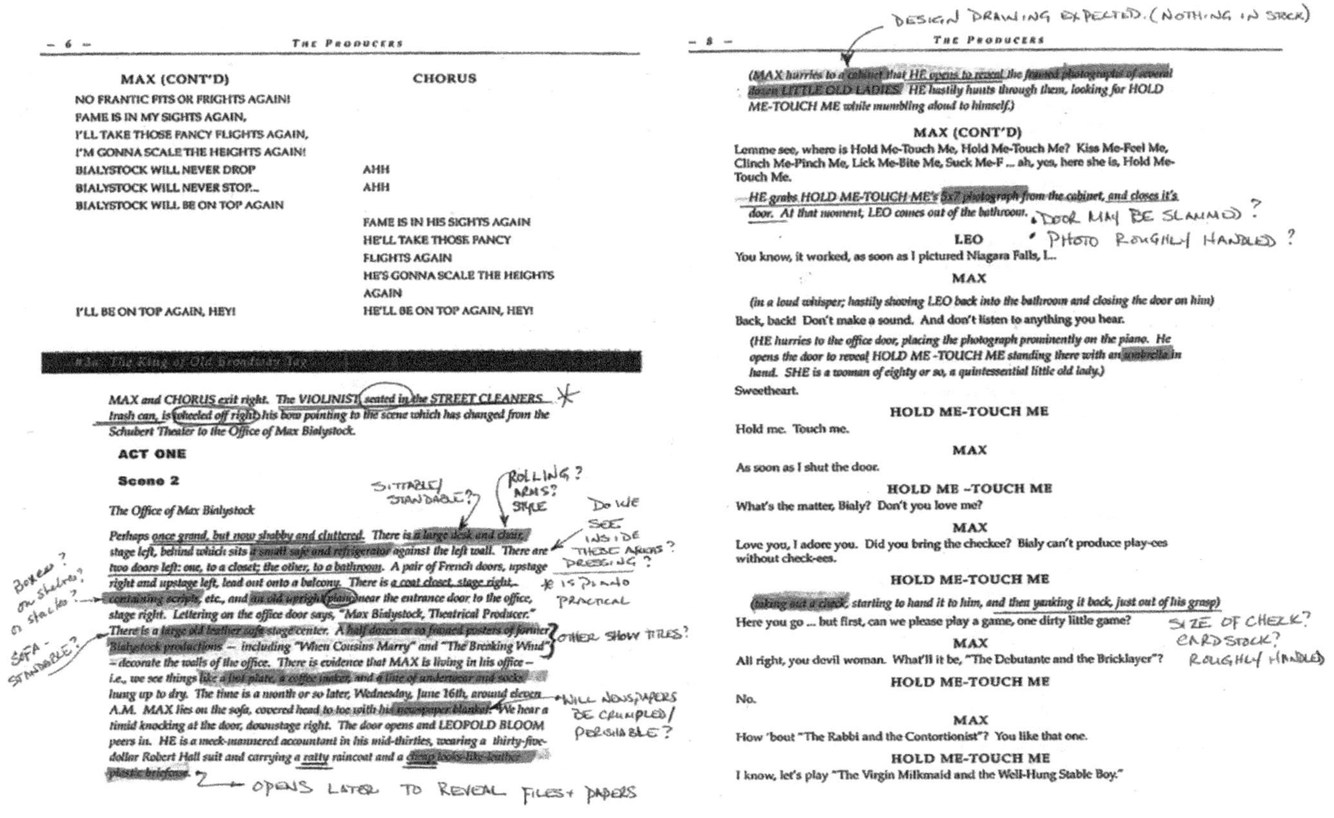

– 6 – THE PRODUCERS

MAX (CONT'D) | **CHORUS**

NO FRANTIC FITS OR FRIGHTS AGAIN!
FAME IS IN MY SIGHTS AGAIN,
I'LL TAKE THOSE FANCY FLIGHTS AGAIN,
I'M GONNA SCALE THE HEIGHTS AGAIN!
BIALYSTOCK WILL NEVER DROP — AHH
BIALYSTOCK WILL NEVER STOP... — AHH
BIALYSTOCK WILL BE ON TOP AGAIN

FAME IS IN HIS SIGHTS AGAIN
HE'LL TAKE THOSE FANCY
FLIGHTS AGAIN
HE'S GONNA SCALE THE HEIGHTS
AGAIN

I'LL BE ON TOP AGAIN, HEY! — HE'LL BE ON TOP AGAIN, HEY!

#3a: The King of Old Broadway Tag

MAX and CHORUS exit right. The VIOLINIST, seated in the STREET CLEANERS trash can, is wheeled off right, his bow pointing to the scene which has changed from the Schubert Theater to the Office of Max Bialystock.

ACT ONE

Scene 2

The Office of Max Bialystock

Perhaps once grand, but now shabby and cluttered. There is a large desk and chair, stage left, behind which sits a small safe and refrigerator against the left wall. There are two doors left: one, to a closet; the other, to a bathroom. A pair of French doors, upstage right and upstage left, lead out onto a balcony. There is a coat closet, stage right, containing scripts, etc., and an old upright piano near the entrance door to the office, stage right. Lettering on the office door says, "Max Bialystock, Theatrical Producer." There is a large old leather sofa stage center. A half dozen or so framed posters of former Bialystock productions — including "When Cousins Marry" and "The Breaking Wind" – decorate the walls of the office. There is evidence that MAX is living in his office – i.e., we see things like a hot plate, a coffee maker, and a line of underwear and socks hung up to dry. The time is a month or so later, Wednesday, June 16th, around eleven A.M. MAX lies on the sofa, covered head to toe with his newspaper blanket. We hear a timid knocking at the door, downstage right. The door opens and LEOPOLD BLOOM peers in. HE is a meek-mannered accountant in his mid-thirties, wearing a thirty-five-dollar Robert Hall suit and carrying a ratty raincoat and a cheap looks-like-leather plastic briefcase.

– 8 – THE PRODUCERS

(MAX hurries to a cabinet that HE opens to reveal the framed photographs of several dozen LITTLE OLD LADIES. HE hastily hunts through them, looking for HOLD ME-TOUCH ME while mumbling aloud to himself.)

MAX (CONT'D)

Lemme see, where is Hold Me-Touch Me, Hold Me-Touch Me? Kiss Me-Feel Me, Clinch Me-Pinch Me, Lick Me-Bite Me, Suck Me-F ... ah, yes, here she is, Hold Me-Touch Me.

HE grabs HOLD ME-TOUCH ME's 5x7 photograph from the cabinet, and closes it's door. At that moment, LEO comes out of the bathroom.

LEO

You know, it worked, as soon as I pictured Niagara Falls, I...

MAX

(in a loud whisper; hastily shoving LEO back into the bathroom and closing the door on him)

Back, back! Don't make a sound. And don't listen to anything you hear.

(HE hurries to the office door, placing the photograph prominently on the piano. He opens the door to reveal HOLD ME-TOUCH ME standing there with an umbrella in hand. SHE is a woman of eighty or so, a quintessential little old lady.)

Sweetheart.

HOLD ME-TOUCH ME

Hold me. Touch me.

MAX

As soon as I shut the door.

HOLD ME -TOUCH ME

What's the matter, Bialy? Don't you love me?

MAX

Love you, I adore you. Did you bring the checkee? Bialy can't produce play-ces without check-ees.

HOLD ME-TOUCH ME

(taking out a check, starting to hand it to him, and then yanking it back, just out of his grasp)

Here you go ... but first, can we please play a game, one dirty little game?

MAX

All right, you devil woman. What'll it be, "The Debutante and the Bricklayer"?

HOLD ME-TOUCH ME

No.

MAX

How 'bout "The Rabbi and the Contortionist"? You like that one.

HOLD ME-TOUCH ME

I know, let's play "The Virgin Milkmaid and the Well-Hung Stable Boy."

Figure 4.1 Script Notation. Making brief side notes in the script for prop discovery assists in preparation for the first meeting with the director and the designer.

Understanding the script prior to the first production/design meeting is critical to participating as a collaborative and supportive partner in the design and production process. While the director and/or designer may choose to move time period or alter the convention of presentation in other ways, knowing the initial script establishes the foundation for moving into a different interpretation.

Finding and reading the same translation or revision being produced allows effective preparation and will certainly change the prop list preparation, so it is always wise to ask for the specific script information, especially in the case of older shows where the play might have several translations or a revised version. Know which specific script is going to be used and work from that.

PRELIMINARY PROP LIST

After reading the script, the next step is to create a **preliminary prop list** compiling the prop information to use in the production and design meetings. Helpful information to include in a preliminary list would be:

- Act, scene and/or page number in script where prop is mentioned
- Prop item
- Description as mentioned in script
- Character who uses the prop
- Questions for designer/director.

Tracking the page number in the script allows easy communication when meeting with the director and designer so all are discussing the same prop or the same action/scene and can be accurate about what is needed or desired. Listing each item separately allows conversations to occur that cover each prop and prevent random jumping about the script; this ensures the prop director leaves the design meeting with the maximum amount of information to begin to prepare for work on the show. The preliminary prop list should include adequate information to assist in discussions with the director and scenic designer about how the prop will be used and what it looks like (size, shape, color, etc.), or to prompt inquiry into what may be a cross-over prop with another production area (e.g., does the floor lamp have to work, and if so is it controlled by the light board or completely actor operated? Do they turn the radio on, making it light up on the dial, and is music heard from the speaker? Do they eat the food mentioned? Does the gun come from a pocket or a holster? Are we using blood—if so, how much, how delivered, how to clean it up, and is the costume department aware of the blood effect?).

The furniture/set props may be described in the playwright's scene notes or may have to come from an analysis of what the characters are doing and how they relate to the space and each other. (If four characters are smoking and playing cards, it can be assumed four "sit-tables" and a table or playing surface of some kind may be required . . . as well as various

SKYLIGHT OPERA THEATRE PROPERTIES DEPARTMENT

2008-2009 SEASON

The Producers: Preliminary prop list with questions

Act/Sc/Pg	PROP	WHO	NOTES
	Act One Scene One: Schubert Alley		
1.1.1	NY Times Crate with newspapers	dressing	several other empty crates also?
	Schubert Alley dressing	dressing	built into the set? Portable/sittable/standable?
1.1.1	Usherette props:	choro	Flashlights? Pile of Programs? Anything else?
1.1.1	Programs and playbills	choro	number? Style?
1.1.2	Opening/Closing Night sign	technician	hand held
1.1.2	Ladder	technician	flips opening night sign over to reveal closing night sign
1.1.2	Newspaper	Max	script specific text P3. Perishable
1.1.3	Violin	blind violinist	Practical???
1.1.3	Cop props	choro	Gun? Billy Club? Other?
1.1.3	Newspaper Vendor props	choro	Satchel? Cart?
1.1.3	Grocery Cart	bag lady	contents: volume? Style? Just dressing, or handled?
1.1.3	Broom and trash can on wheels	street sweeper	trash can on a separate hand truck? Or just a wheeled version of a trash can?
1.1.3	Sandwich Board with show advertisement		worn? If so, by whom? Or does this just sit on the sidewalk?
	Act One Scene Two: Max Bialystock's Office		
1.2.6	Office Desk	set prop	Size, Style, Color?
1.2.6	Desk dressing	dressing	how much? How organized? What sort of look?
1.2.6	Desk Chair	set prop	On wheels?
1.2.6	Small Safe	set prop	On wheels? Size, Color, Type of door? Empty in 1.8
1.2.6	Refrigerator	set prop	Does it open? Practical inside Light? Dressing? Size?
1.2.6	old upright piano	set prop	Practical? Internal wireless amp and speakers for sound board control?
	Any Drapes on the Windows or French Doors?	dressing	
1.2.6	2 unframed show posters	dressing	When Cousins Marry: The Breaking Wind, etc.
1.2.6	Underwear on clothes line	dressing	Attachment points? Number of pieces?

Figure 4.2 Preliminary Prop List. Preliminary Prop List for *The Producers*, Skylight Opera Theatre.

hand props like a deck of cards and possibly gambling chips, beverage glasses, an ashtray, cigarettes, matches, score pad, or pencil.) Noting what is described even in a preliminary prop list allows for the discussion to be started prior to seeing the designer's floorplan with furniture notation. It can also prompt discussions detailing how the pieces might have to be handled in a scene change, or addressing special "action" anticipated in the blocking to suit a particular cast member.

Hand props are defined specific to character; they may be noted as part of the character description or can be found related to the action within the scene, such as in the card-playing example. Those hand props not directly embedded in the script should be noted but often are the first ones cut or changed, since they were specific to the production "recorded" when the script was published and may not be necessary in the present production.

Stage dressing will come directly from the specific design, so unless something is noted particular to the action (e.g., a painting of a character in the play referred to within the dialogue of the play), adding stage dressing to the prop list at this early point in the process is usually premature. It can be handy for prompting discussion with the director and designer, but these items are not retained consistently from production to production.

In any given show, one area that can become a sinkhole of expense is the **consumable** budget. A consumable, sometimes called a **perishable**, is any prop requiring multiples to be made/purchased because in the action of the play the prop is used in such a way that it cannot be reused. It might be eaten, torn, broken, gotten wet, set on fire, etc. It can be as simple as an envelope torn open each night, or as involved as the clock thrown on the floor and smashed in Chekhov's *Three Sisters*, which requires the casting of enough clocks for the technical rehearsal and run of the show. It could also be the entire kitchen full of set dressing, as in *True West* by Sam Shepard, which culminates in a typewriter being beaten to pieces with a golf club each night along with a large number of toasters. Beyond exploring the problematic safety issue for the actors and audience as bits and pieces of appliances go flinging off, the production and design team need to address the expense of finding enough toasters, typewriters, and golf clubs for the run and potentially dressing the set again following each performance due to breakage or damage.

Food is a consumable requiring appropriate and safe handling beyond just the expense of buying the food items itself. The odd piece of fruit or piece of bread can be easily solved, but some plays require food to be cooked onstage or meals eaten by the actors as part of the staging of the scene. Planning for this level of consumable must be accounted for at the preliminary stage in both budget and use, including pre-show preparation and post-show clean up expenses. Those items anticipated to be consumable should be notated in the preliminary prop list for discussion by all involved.

Research is formalized curiosity. It is poking and prying with a purpose.

—Zora Neale Hurston

RESEARCH

At the start of every build, just as reading the script and making a preliminary prop list informs the world of the show, doing **research** into what that world may look like is a helpful exercise. The pleasure of working in theatre, and especially in the specialty of props, is how the world changes with every production. For those few weeks of the build the prop shop "lives" in the time period, location, social rank, and economic status of the play. Who are these people and where do they live? Why do they do the things they do? The decisions made about what the props look like and the choices made to represent the furniture, stage dressings, and personal items of the characters onstage must reflect the script's parameters as well as the sensibilities of the artistic team. In a theatre season, one show can be an Irish political drama set in the 1700s and the next a modern New York comedy of manners set in an upscale apartment. Having a visual reference for those specific places and times is a good foundation for design collaboration and decision-making.

With the production team gathered together at the design meeting to talk through the show, the designer may present images or sketches reflecting some of the conceptual research done in creating the overall look of the play. Time period or place might be moved from what is called for in the script, or the creative team may choose a different and more specific viewpoint or style informing the decisions made about what the props look like. Some designs are modeled after specific art movements or even specific artist styles. Some designs are more skeletal or even abstract, and others almost photorealistic in the duplication of place and time period. Some designers may utilize researched images of furniture or props to show a range of choices fitting into the play motif to show color or general shape but with little regard to specific time period. All of these conceptual approaches challenge the properties director in solving the build process. Being prepared and knowledgeable about the look of a period and having an understanding of the shape, line, fabrics, materials, furniture, significant events, etc. appropriate to the play is essential. While the approach to the show may deviate from scripted specifications, having an understanding of the story grants the ability to pivot to the new interpretation more easily.

Research develops awareness of appropriate options and enables the properties director to offer suitable solutions. Ultimately, research simply presents the "actual" allowing the artistic process to move to the "desired." If the properties team has researched and knows the visual realities appropriate to the story, they can create fitting props to meet design and staging needs.

For example, the play might be set in 1920 Germany and the character is leaving home. How big is a suitcase in 1920 Germany? What kind of handles did they have? Did it have straps to hold it closed or just snap locks? What is the suitcase constructed from—cardboard, soft-sided fabric, metal? How were they covered—leather, cloth, edge bindings? Did they have rounded edges or square corners? What were common sizes? Getting answers helps define the "what does it look like?" question. Having an image as that starting point jumpstarts the evolution from what is "known" into the world of the designer's imagination and the reality of the play. Is the suitcase worn or stained? Is if from a previous era or location? Does it have travel tags or other defining character qualities? The prop shop does not try to reproduce a literal 1920 German suitcase. It builds a suitcase that when placed on stage and carried by an

Figure 4.3 Collage of Choices. Creating visual references of choices available from stock, to buy from a catalog, or to purchase locally at a consignment shop helps in the selection of pieces needed or can help spur the designer to clarify what they might be imagining. Mark Walston, properties director, Actor's Theatre of Louisville.

actor playing a man in Germany in 1920 "fits" into and does not detract from the scene. The viewer accepts it as a suitcase in Germany in 1920.

Many creative folk work best as visual responders. A verbal description cannot show as quickly what a few pictures can immediately illustrate. Pulling together an assemblage of images allows for specific discussions with the designer. After doing research to know what things might want to look like, it's helpful to gather images showing how the procurement of those items might happen. The prop director pulls together images of what is available to purchase, items in stock which can be used as-is or altered, and items available to be borrowed from another theatre or company.

This investigation shows the widest array of choices possible and allows for an active interchange strategizing how best to supply props compatible with the designer's viewpoint. Additionally, images help in the definition of fabrics, or color and finish on painted or uphol- stered items. They show scale and proportion in relationship to the set or the actors. They can jump-start the imagination of the design team, launching new ideas for problem-solving and innovation. All of these images create the foundation for the choices necessary to build the show.

Since the design team is not always available to do face to face meetings, it is helpful to have a way to share images and research. Online sharing platforms allow a group of people to post (known as "pinning" on sites such as Pinterest, Juxtapost or Vi.sualize.us) images or videos to a virtual board. Users upload images from their computer or pin things found on the web or on other boards. Most of these sites offer a way to search for images with similar content, so once an image of, for example, an eighteenth-century chandelier is pinned on the board, it's easy to click on the button for "more like this" to see dozens of similar images to select from.

Using Pinterest or other social sharing sites is as easy as setting up an account, creating your profile, and creating a new board to start saving images to and sharing. Be sure to check the Settings link once the account is active so e-mail notifications update. This can be turned off later if unsolicited emails start clogging the inbox. Pinterest has a "Pin It" button to add to any web browser to allow easy "pinning" when finding images on web pages. By clicking on the "Pin It" button, a screen will pop up asking the user to select the image wanting to be

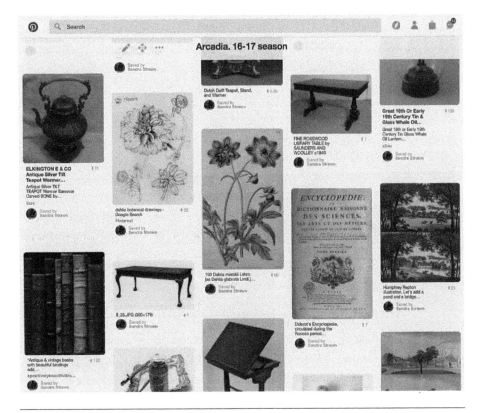

Figure 4.4 Pinterest Page. Using an image board such as Pinterest allows users to visually share images or video and browse through what other users have pinned. It allows the design team to share images easily and can be edited to delete images as the selection process defines the specific look.

pinned (if there's more than one photo on the page being viewed) and after selecting the image to choose which board to pin to and even write a short description if desired. When working on research for several shows it's best to create separate boards, allowing each show to have its own research board shared with the designers and director for that show and anyone else needing to see the information.

Another way of pooling research and other materials beyond simple image sharing is often a necessity. It's vital to have a site where floorplans, elevations, prop drawing, photos, prop lists, deadlines and schedules, or other information is available. Many creatives use file sharing sites like Dropbox, Google Drive, or Microsoft's OneDrive. Most providers offer a degree of free storage, but having additional space for photos and media is worth the small cost of an upgrade to more GB. These cloud-based storage systems allow easy sync between devices and shared users. Documents can be uploaded, allowing users to share, edit or modify documents, track the changes, and allow collaborative work to occur easily. The "owner" can let others share access to specific folders/documents and/or limit who can see, edit, or add files. By having one place for all the documents to live and opening access to all partners in the creative process, it is easy for the information flow to be transparent and fluid.

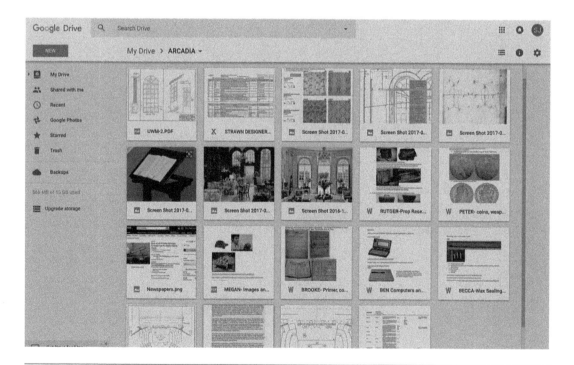

Figure 4.5 Google Drive Page. A cloud-based storage system allows multiple types of documents to be easily shared by all levels in the design and production process.

FINDING IMAGES AND DOING RESEARCH ONLINE

Doing research into a specific period is as easy as a click of the keyboard into the internet. Vast quantities of images are available through image search engines or on web sites. Today's image libraries, with clear pictures and multiple views, provide an easy and simple way of finding a plethora of sources for design and building decisions.

Most search engines like Google allow the user to specify between *Web* and *Images* on the top bar near the search window. If images are all that is needed, click on the *Images* icon and only pictures of what is requested will be found. If web pages of vendors who might sell items of interest are required, click on *Web* and the search will locate web sites. These web sites may contain pictures or drawings as equally helpful as the *Images*. Utilize both ways of searching if one doesn't seem to be giving good results.

For example, if the show being built requires a counter of extravagant desserts set in a French café, most designers will simply request a display of French pastries to dress out the countertop and not draw out specific desserts to be built by the prop shop. By typing "French Desserts" into the *Images* search window, thousands of pictures of various pastries, pies, cakes, donuts, and other yummy goodies are available for the use by the props craftsperson to create prop desserts.

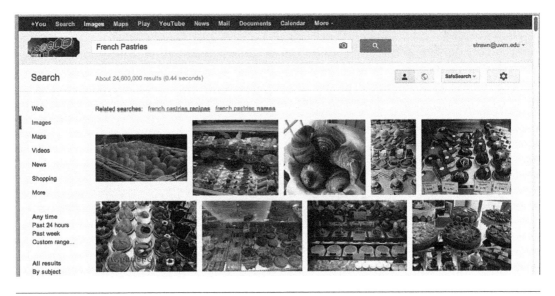

Figure 4.6   Images: French Pastry. Images link on Google search for French Pastries.

A couple of more clicks through the *Images* pages and a quick scan down each page shows numerous photos of French pastry shops with extravagant displays of pastries, showing how the display might be assembled, the style of the dressing, the various heights of the confectionary dishes, the dish styles, etc. Printing off these pictures and creating an assemblage of options allows the designer to select specific desserts or to define shapes, color, and textures to work with the overall design. This information is shared with the prop shop staff and becomes the inspiration for the craftsperson to work from in building the pastry display.

Typing in the same words into the *Web* search window, the listing becomes a long catalog of French cookbooks and recipes posted at online food sites as well as photos.

It is easy to peruse these for ingredients informing what the dessert might look like and it is often helpful to have these directions almost as a method of construction or, in the case of consumable props, to be able to cook the requested dessert. But if only fake desserts are needed, many website cookbooks lack good pictures. The image is usually more important for reference in the design process.

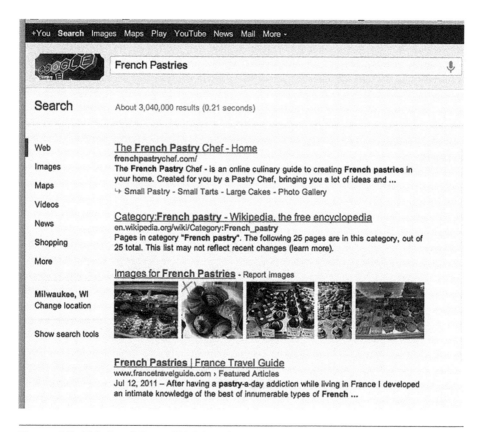

Figure 4.7 Web: French Pastry. Web link on Google search for French Pastries.

Using a search engine on the web also allows for quite *targeted* searching. It is simple to enter in a series of defining words and focus the search to match exactly with specific research needs. Entering in only "1950s, furniture," the results would be furniture all over the world from the 1950s as well as furniture built in the 1950s for sale on eBay, modern furniture reflecting the look of 1950s furniture available at local discount stores or national chain stores, furniture timelines including the 1950s, historical information about the 1950s, newspaper archives of the 1950s with furniture advertisements, etc. While fascinating, flipping through this can consume valuable research hours and fail to provide what is ultimately desired, especially if looking for something specific.

However, with no knowledge of the foundation of period and history of decor, it will be impossible to identify a "correct" image of a 1950s piece of furniture in any search. What comes first—the chicken or the egg? Prop directors must have a solid foundation in historical periods and decor to be able to utilize internet searches with accuracy and authenticity. Vetting web sources with non-web sources is crucial to a valid research process.

Typing in "1950s, metal swivel stools, American, drug store" delivers images for that *specific* stool type, including examples of American drug store interiors, reproduction stools from vintage stores, photos of people sitting on stools, and catalog pictures of contemporary stools, etc. By flipping from *Images* over to *Web* and keeping the same search window terms, it's easy to locate furniture vendors who sell reproduction 1950s stools, collectible shops selling drug store paraphernalia or an offering on eBay for a set of stools being sold from an old store. From there it is a simple step to "pin" the site to the show's board, take a screenshot of the vendor's page to send to the designer or print off the information/images to share with the designer.

On many builds, it is a combination of uses of the web to both find images and to locate materials. For example, in *Seven Guitars* by August Wilson, a rooster is brought on stage and beheaded in each show. It must have the appearance of being quite alive for the gruesome act to have full impact, and the actor uses the decapitated rooster's blood to mark a circle on the ground. To build this rooster (since an actual rooster being killed nightly on stage would be highly impractical as well as overly bloody and enraging to the ASPCA), the prop shop needs information on the construction of a fake rooster.

Going online and downloading various images of "roosters" is easy. Click on *Images*, type in "rooster" and hundreds of pictures pop up, giving close-up head shots, feet pictures, side-views, chickens in a yard, roosters on a fence, state fair champion roosters, etc. The prop craftsperson knows what a rooster shape, size, wing to leg proportion, coloring, etc. all look like, allowing the construction process to begin.

Next comes how to solve the "action" of the rooster, which needs to flop about and, more importantly, bleed on cue. Consider searching for "butchering chickens." YouTube offers a variety of short video clips showing people butchering chickens, which allows the craftsperson to understand what action will need to be replicated. Maybe it can be done as a hand-controlled wing flap. So, type in "puppet controls" or "ventriloquist controls" to start the search for various methods of rigging the wings to flap. Type in "Special effects, blood" to be taken to sites showing ways to rig a fake blood delivery system.

Meanwhile, the prop shopper is online searching "taxidermy, chickens" for feathers, fake feet, or feather pelts for purchase. *All* of this is available online. Today research is only a click away to discover what the chicken looks like as well as find a taxidermist living in Idaho with cured full-size rooster pelts and additional pads of tail and breast feathers for sale, available to be delivered by FedEx for the craftsperson to begin building the fake rooster. This technology is revolutionizing the props process, and the world is shrinking as the commercial listings open up to anyone with computer access.

Walking in with ideas to address the "rooster" problem (and there is something like this in almost every script!) with a ready solution or options for the designer and director to consider in those initial prop design meetings makes everyone's jobs easier and helps build a collaborative creative team.

The important caveat to single source internet research: while "quick and dirty" searches can rapidly turn up loads of imagery and may feel productive, the ability to evaluate the veracity of one's search results is crucial. Imagine being in a fantastic thrift shop packed with stuff. Close your eyes and reach out—you may latch onto an extraordinary treasure, or you may come up with Crazy Aunt Sophie's old white elephant gift—pure junk. As this analogy suggests, one will find a dizzying array of information on the internet ranging widely in value. It's all shades of grey. Information may wind up online for differing reasons, and in most cases, no one is required to approve the content before it appears for general public consumption. Stories, opinions, statistics, propaganda, and an astonishing number of actual facts all drift around in many shades of accuracy, truth, and reliability. It is the prop director's job to evaluate and substantiate the information found. Examine the sources cited on a given webpage—are they professional, credible, well respected, and verifiable? Seek confirmation from other sources, cross check with known facts, investigate secondary and tertiary sources of information. Think and view internet materials critically, rather than assuming on shallow glance the quality of what was found as unimpeachable. Curiosity, an awareness of things vastly predating individual experiences, the desire to understand history and philosophic movements, literature, and history of classes, manufacturing, society, and the changes impacting design and materials into product, evolution of eras and history—all this provides the solid foundation from which to evaluate one's research.

PROP LIBRARY

While researching on the web can be easy and fast, most prop shops continue to maintain an extensive library of books from general history of furniture and style books to collectable books on specific items such as perfume bottles or fruit crate art. These shop libraries provide a valuable hands-on trove of images and information, and knowing what is in the books makes them a readily accessible source. Having a huge wall of books, unorganized and unread, is a waste of space. Like all resources, in order for the library to be useable, it must be maintained, and the users have to know the contents and how to find the information/images without spending hours searching through book after book. Sharing the image can be done easiest by scanning in the information/photo to create a digital file and uploading it to the cloud-sharing folder or Pinterest style board. Just as with digital sources, verify the authority of the author and source of the information. Knowledge and understanding of period, place, and style is gained via study and exploration. Reading and studying the information beyond just paging over books for interesting pictures will create a better-informed dialogue in the design and production process.

One of the best resources is an old catalog such as those printed by Sears Roebuck, JC Penney, and other retailers. Mailed out since the turn of the century, each season new catalogs in homes across America illustrated the entire range of products available for purchase. These old catalogs are still found in junk stores or second-hand bookstores, and many prop shops have an extensive collection. Some reproduction catalogs are also available, and original catalogs come up for sale on eBay with some regularity. (Search under: Vintage catalog.) These catalogs offer a window into the everyday American world of clothing, household goods, farm implements, toys, travel, décor, and lifestyle. Detail in cost, availability, style, color, shape, trim, etc., is readily available through these books and the images contained within.

Other books of value focus on a specific time or items, such as Victorian English interiors or American Federalist furniture. These books often help in giving a sense of style and décor as well as offering images showing the variety of what is appropriate to that time for the props.

Modern books on interior design replicating a time period are also helpful as they tend to use many of the same theatrical shortcuts to interpret time or place that designers use. Lush photographs are often used to convey a certain look and can be a valuable resource in communicating an idea about fullness of drape, saturation of color choice, density of décor dressing, etc.

Photography books contain iconic images documenting time periods, events, people, places, and important historical events. Collections of photographs are published covering specific decades or about a specific topic, such as the American Depression. Time/Life Books offers a plethora of books filled with images devoted to covering a variety of topics.

Art books provide imagery for the time period before photography was common. By studying paintings, clues into how people lived are often revealed in the furniture, décor, clothing, and other items included in the artwork. Some designers choose to deliberately fashion a design in the style of a specific painter, often from the time period the play was written. Having a book with the paintings of that particular artist makes many of the prop choices obvious.

Books written for collectors also show many pictures and have specific detailed information about country of origin, size, manufacture, ornamentation, etc. that help to define a specific prop. These are available in highly specific topics such as dollhouses, Belleek porcelain, comic books, toy soldiers, Native American art, jukeboxes, etc. Used bookstores or junk shops are a great place to find these books inexpensively, and having them in the prop shop library is a handy way to access images on a specific topic quickly.

Public and school libraries, of course, offer an enormous resource of books available for checking out. Looking by subject matter such as "perfume bottles" may find a book on antique perfume bottles. If not, move beyond the obvious and look for books on collecting bottles, Czechoslovakian crystal, Tiffany, etc. It will take time and is usually no longer the first choice as a research method given the time constraints of theatre.

Depending on where you live, a local museum might also be a resource for research work. Most regional theatres operate in or near a major metropolitan city with fine art, natural history, decorative arts, and architectural museums available. Furniture, glassware, textiles, weaponry, and artwork are displayed for study and consideration. Take a step back in time in the permanent exhibits or explore a special collection relevant to the play. Most museums have an "education" department willing to allow special access; arrange for an opportunity to examine an object in closer detail or take a photograph for research simply by asking and obtaining permission. Having an actual object to take measurements from, to see the detail of joinery or finish, and to understand the fragility or weight of the item makes a trip to the museum worthwhile. Again, knowing the resource and having a contact to facilitate its use makes it valuable. Wandering around a museum hoping to find something relevant takes away priceless research time.

Research allows the prop staff to enter into the build process better informed about the era, the "look" of objects, possible pricing on available items, etc. Having done research before meeting with the designer and director allows the prop director to jump-start an informed build process, guiding the prop shop to work on completing the props with on-point visual references and period information.

* * *

Pre-production script analysis and research are the foundation for discussion and consideration during the entire build. As the properties director becomes engaged with the show and understands the particular interpretation and design statement determined for this production, all the information coalesces. This knowledge gives the properties director an armada of information with which to offer better choices and make appropriate decisions. As the prop shop begins the show build, knowing the script and understanding the historical and stylistic foundation, every choice becomes easier and the shop can make the decisions to best support the designer's vision.

Following the design meetings, with an understanding of what is needed from the director, based on the research of the prop shop and in reviewing the information/drawings from the designer, a working prop list is created that combines the preliminary prop list and all the information garnered from the production and design meetings. From the prop list the properties director is able to make a preliminary budget, anticipate specific production challenges, and start the organization of the show build. Organization is about efficiency: saving time and money. Get ready to get organized!

Getting Started

In the best-case scenario, design information is communicated with enough time to allow the budgeting and preliminary planning work to be completed weeks before the show actually enters the shop. Some theatres work six to eight months in advance of show build commencement, or sometimes even farther in the case of elaborate co-productions. This extended timeline is often the case for opera and musical theatre, where designers are contracted and designs must be completed to allow for the various next stages of planning, from the choreography and staging to the construction in the shops. Co-productions are a world all unto themselves in many cases, so please reference Chapter 10 on that subject.

In regional theatre, where the planning and rehearsal period is significantly more compressed, the designs for a show may dribble in with preliminary information available only a month or two out from start of build and final drawings arriving just in time for the build to begin. If designers could get the design process completed and submitted earlier, the results would be so much better! Unfortunately, in the contracting and scheduling world of the designer and director, the team is often not in place with enough advance time to give the opportunity for the design to evolve and the production team to respond and find better in-budget solutions or alternatives. As the "resident" position fades away from common hiring practices, the utilization of guest designers/directors has only added to the complicated juggle of collaboration on the show concept, including holding timely design meetings with all parties. Given those pressures, having firm deadlines established keeps the process moving forward in a supportive and respectful manner.

Ultimately, jump-starting the design process and establishing deadlines falls in the realm of the production manager. The design deadlines and important production dates are often communicated in a **production calendar** or **production timeline**. Individual theatres have timelines specific to the builds, but generally the timeline calls out the dates for design meetings/deadlines, drawing "due dates," first rehearsal, designer residencies,

Designer Dates		Production Dates	
4 months from 1st Reh.	Design Meeting 1 (on or by)		
3 months from 1st Reh.	Design Meeting 2 (on or by) PRELIM Sets/ Paint/ Props PRELIM Costumes/ Hair/ Makeup	Week after Prel. Design submission	Production response Sets/ Paint/ Props Costumes/ Hair/ Makeup
2 months from 1st Reh.	FINAL sets/ Paint/ Props FINAL Costumes/ hair Makeup	Week after Final Design approval Production Meeting 1	Begin PREP WORK/ ORDERING Sets/ Paint/ Props
1 month from 1st Ren.	PRELIM Lights PRELIM Sound / Video	8 weeks before OPENt	Costumes/ Hair/ Makeup Begin BUILD
1st Day of Rehearsal (5 weeks before OPEN)	FINAL Lights FINAL Sound / Video	Production Meeting 2	Sets/ Paint/ Props Costumes
	FIRST REHEARSAL Designer Presentations	5 weeks before OPEN Production Meeting 3	Sound Video
Build weeks	Production Meetings-if available (as scheduled)	4 weeks before OPEN Production Meeting 4	Wigs/ Makeup
Last week of Reh.	Designer Run Through	3 weeks before OPEN Production Meeting 5	
		2 weeks before OPEN Production Meeting 6	Prop Add Deadline
	SET LOAD IN / LIGHT HANG	14 days before opening	
	PROP CHECK-IN/ STAGE DRESS	10 days before opening	
	FOCUS	9 days before opening	
	SPACING REHEARSAL	8 days before opening	
	1st TECHNICAL REHEARSAL	7 days before opening	
	1st DRESS REHEARSALt	4 days before opening	
	1st PREVIEW	2 days before opening	
	OPENING	OPEN	
	CLOSING/ STRIKE	End of Run	

Figure 5.1 Production Timeline. Example of a production timeline showing the deadlines for design submissions, production response, start of build, load-in, tech, open, strike, etc. allowing production and designer goals to be clear to all parties.

load-in, technical rehearsals, and all other relevant production information up to opening night. The production timeline allows each shop to have expectations for information while holding the design team to specified deadlines. If the deadline is missed, the properties director can alert the designer and sort out what the difficulty might be or ask the production manager to step in to push the project along, explaining the budgetary and calendar consequences.

Keeping open communication with the designer during the evolution of design ideas and being proactive to advance the process—whether through finding pictorial research showing various options, pulling things for consideration from stock to be modified, doing sketches/ drawings for response from the designer, "swatching" upholstery/curtain fabrics for consideration and getting character fabric swatches from costumes to coordinate the look of things—is the responsibility of the properties director; whatever needs to be done to get decisions made, the

Designer Deadline Expectations

Scenic and Properties Design

Preliminary Scenic and Prop Design Information -all information needed to complete an initial material and labor cost estimate for the design. Package should include:
- ¼" or ½" scale Plan & Section
- Rough Model and/or Sketches
- Rough color/texture ideas
- Preliminary Prop List
- Research/Rough Drawings of large prop pieces /Furniture

Revised Design Scenic and Prop Design Information -information and revisions to complete a revised material and labor estimate for the design. Package should include:
- ¼" or ½" scale Floor Plan of the set with furniture
- ¼" or ½" scale Deck Plan
- ¼" or ½" scale Section
- ¼" or ½" Elevations
- ¼" or ½" scale Model
- Detail drawings and/or molding and trim information, as needed
- Information on special Rigging and/or Stage Automation Requirements
- Updated Prop List
- Prop drawings for built pieces

Final Scenic, Props and Scene Paint Designs shall consist of all information necessary to execute the design. This package should include (but is certainly not limited to) the following:
- Final Scenic Design Plans, Sections, Elevations
- Detailed Prop Drawings, as needed
- Prop Paint Renderings and/or Color Information
- Fabric Swatches
- Props and Paint Research
- ½" scale Paint Elevations
- Final texture information
- Color Swatches and/or Paint Number (Glidden Professional, Benjamin Moore or Pantone Preferred)

Note: Electronic drawings are preferred, in either AutoCAD or Vectorworks formats. Drawings done on paper should be originals or clear copies. Any drawings submitted in PDF format must include reference dimensions.

Figure 5.2 Deadline Expectations. Example of the deadline expectations for the scenic/prop designer for preliminary designs, revised information, and final design package. Example is a modified version of Alley Theatre Designer Deadlines. Karin Rabe Vance, properties director.

properties director should do. Deadlines are important to keep the show build on track, and the prop director often needs to nudge the process along.

Information about props should be submitted as part of the preliminary design ideas, with updates included in the final design package. Having preliminary prop information allows budgeting to occur in a timely manner in conjunction with scenery, and the entire package can be modified or approved by seeing the whole project.

Figure 5.3 White Model. The very preliminary white model shows, even at this early stage in the design process, basic set props and their relative scale and position onstage, giving a chance for designer and prop director collaboration on stock pieces, possible pieces to borrow or buy, and other options informing and assisting in the design process.

Figure 5.4 Final Model. In the final model the designer has refined the choices to represent the color, texture, scale, number, and 'look' of the props within the stage setting, giving the properties director more specific information to begin discussions.

Figure 5.5 Stage Shot. The final set props, hand props, and stage dressing come together to create the world of the play and the vision of the designer at University of Wisconsin-Milwaukee. Michael Gerlach, properties master; Sandra J. Strawn, scenic designer.

INITIAL PRODUCTION DESIGN MEETING

Once the preliminary prop list and research preparation is complete, a meeting with the designer and director is necessary to talk through options for all props listed. *When* this happens will depend on the availability of the people involved. The sooner the better in most cases, but at the very least this initial meeting should be scheduled several weeks before the start of the build. Some shops have the luxury of having these meetings months in advance, allowing for a well-planned prop build, while other theatres may not have the information available until the start of the rehearsal period. Stage management often attends the meeting to understand the considerations discussed and to learn how best to facilitate rehearsal needs.

Discussions revolve around all the details needed for the prop shop to begin the build. This is where initial decisions happen. For example: what do things look like? what is their anticipated use? what will need additional reinforcement? where does it come from? (out of a pocket, from offstage, flown in, out of a trap in the floor, from behind the proscenium, etc.) how is it shifted? (by stage crew, by actors, on wheels, on a rolling platform as part of the scenery shift, etc.) what color is it? etc. This information informs many of the additional decisions made in the following weeks of the build and where the collaborative exchange of research, photos, and solutions creates the foundation for the show build.

It is important to note this is just the starting point; everyone involved acknowledges the list will evolve as things get added, cut, or changed based on the rehearsal process. It is also at this point where the overlap between departments often occurs, depending on the priorities of budget, personnel, and talent. For example, what might have started out as a costume piece might slide over into props or vice versa, depending on who has the time, money, or skill to complete the items.

Preparing for the design meetings may have various levels of effort. Once you get to know a specific designer and how they work, it's easy to match the preparation to the need. Some designers will come prepared with detailed photos and scaled drawings of the props; others will have nothing but a general scenic plan and little idea of what is necessary for the props. It is helpful to know a bit about the designer and director before embarking on preparation. If the team in question is known for highly stylized approaches to their work, the prop director will have a very different set of questions to ask and parameters to explore. Researching teams and their past productions can be an additional necessity if the creative team is unfamiliar. Regardless, it helps to have done the basic research into the more important items and to have a grasp of the time period of the play. The research information and images provide a visual communication tool utilized with the designer to select what the prop might look like. Often designers will pick and choose pieces of images to create a specific "new" image. The designer may communicate this information through a specific prop drawing, a collage style representation, or simply via verbal description based on a review of the available research, leaving the actual documentation process to the properties director.

Compiling those images connected to a specific prop on the prop list gives the prop shop a way to direct the build on each item. It assists the budgeting process and defines the shopping priority for props needing to be bought or for defining the look of the fabric, trim, hardware, or raw materials necessary for an item to be constructed.

Most hand prop information is minimal at the preliminary deadline point since so much of that evolves during the rehearsal process. In some cases, the hand props are deeply imbedded in the script and might drive some of the work in the rehearsal, and the scene designer usually has a short list of those critical props. Having a preliminary prop list from the script written up by either stage management or the prop shop (as detailed in Chapter 4) helps by allowing an understanding of the scope of the build in balance with the "known" items from the designer. As information and decisions evolve, being able to see the entire build from the smallest hand prop to the largest set prop will help in the planning, organization, coordination, and eventual management of the build.

In the creative team/production meetings, reviewing and discussing the preliminary information allows the properties director to see the overview of the design intent for period, scale, number of pieces, how scenes will be potentially changed, color schemes, etc. The designer's prop list informs the preliminary prop list drawn up from the script, opening up the director and designer to decisions needing to be incorporated as the design moves to more of a final stage. Even rough drawings allow for a preliminary budget for materials and labor to be estimated. Most importantly, the preliminary information opens the floodgates to the mighty creative game of how to solve getting all these items on stage and fitting to the design within the budget allowed.

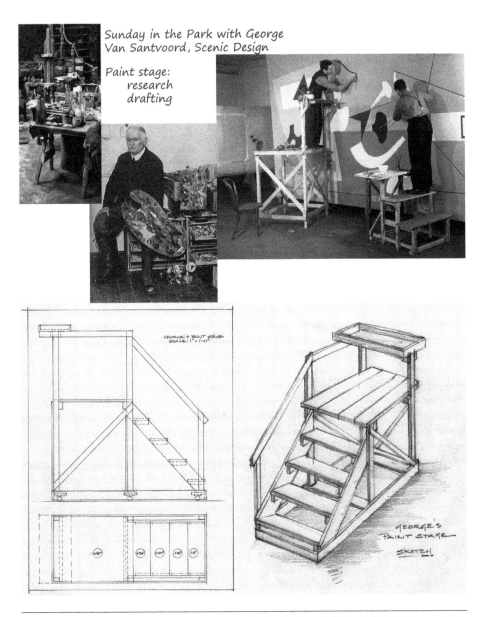

Sunday in the Park with George
Van Santvoord, Scenic Design

Paint stage:
  research
  drafting

Figure 5.6 Designer Information. Research and drafting for *Sunday in the Park with George* at Skylight Opera Theatre. Van Santvoord, scenic designer.

As the design process moves to "revised" and then to "finals," the process is a careful balance of offering solutions, products, and ideas to make the designer's dreams a reality. The creative communication between the shop and the designer continues as the prop list is developed and the drawings and elevations are delivered. As the build progresses and the rehearsal notes begin bringing new information to the shop and the designer to sort out, collaboration and creative problem-solving become a daily occurrence. The "final design" process culminates onstage as the show is loaded in, the stage is dressed, and technical rehearsals begin, demanding the highest level of collaboration between scenery, lights, sound, actors, and stagehands. The final prop design is never a "final" but merely a place along the way to opening night.

THE PROP LIST

Keeping track of all the props requested by both the designer for the visual appearance and by the director for the action of the play is the responsibility of the properties director. Some organizations have stage management involved more deeply in this process, but ultimately the prop shop has to have a detailed listing of every item needed so the build can be organized and managed. This is done through the use of the **working prop list**. The prop list is the organizational "brain" of the show build. Including all relevant information allows a "one stop shopping" location for any and all things related to the show.

Writing a prop list is highly individual to the organizational needs and level of complexity of the show. Several examples are documented in this chapter and demonstrate the various levels of organization determined necessary for tracking of information. Generally speaking, the prop list should have every prop noted as well as a detailed description of any details the properties director requires to track the prop or information about use or look. Using this simple form to enter the information allows the management of "adds" and "cuts" and is a quickly accessed organizational tool. The working prop list builds from the preliminary prop list but incorporates all the specific design-based information gained since that initial script-based list. Expect adds and cuts from the preliminary list as the working prop list is created to reflect this now very specific design-driven version.

FORMATTING THE LIST

Start off the prop list by utilizing a **show header** to make general notes about time period and place, listing the director and designer, notation about when the list was last updated, and other general show information. This is especially helpful in the middle of a design meeting when discussing period or specifics about a location and the mind goes blank! A quick glance at the prop list gets everything back in focus with no one the wiser. Placing that information at the top of the list on the first page allows the general show information to be available before diving into the microcosm of each scene. Adding specific **scene headers** throughout the prop list as scenes change and location or time period move and detailing the where and when or other general scene-specific information are equally helpful.

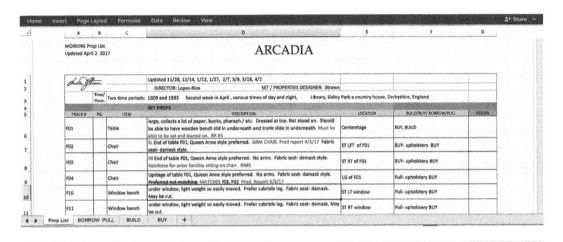

Figure 5.7 Prop List with Header. Using a header on top of the prop list gives general show information while bottom tabs allow easy access to the detail Build, Buy, Pull, Budget, etc. listings.

Most prop lists use column headers similar to this:

PAGE TRACK # ITEM/PROP CHARACTER/FUNCTION DESCRIPTION

and as the planning progresses, additional columns may be added for delegation of projects, projected solution for completion, or the progress of the prop using:

ASSIGNED ACQUIRE STATUS

Some prop lists track budgetary information on an additional column with both a **PRELIMINARY** and an **ACTUAL** column.

USING COLUMN HEADERS

The **page number**, just as in the preliminary prop list, connects the prop being worked on to the specific page in the script, allowing specific information to be quickly accessed. The page number reference is also a shortcut to finding how a prop is used when talking with a designer or in production meetings when the stage manager is giving notes about what has evolved in the discovery process of the rehearsal space.

The **tracking number** is a simple tool for organizing the prop list. Many regional theatres use a numbering system, assigning each prop its own number to allow for effective tracking of the prop on all subsequent communications from rehearsal reports to build notes, load-in sheets, run-sheets, etc. Working from the original prop list and known props, as props are added, each is given a number. Deleted props retain their number since they frequently return later in the process and can be easily added back in, but the prop and the number utilize a strike-thru to note its status. Non-duplication or reassignment of a number also prevents confusion, especially when prop lists are updated between the departments. Using a tracking numbering system is covered in greater detail later in this chapter.

The **prop/item** column is a simple listing of each individual prop such as broom, chair, knife, or digital phone. This prop name should be kept the same in all areas of communication. Sometimes when similar items are used, a more descriptive name is given to a common item, such as "wide-handled basket," to differentiate that particular basket more easily from the other baskets being used. That name tracks through both the prop list and stage management lists.

Connecting a prop to a specific **character/actor** or a particular **function/action** also helps clarify *which* prop the list is detailing. Entering the character name for a hand prop is helpful if the need to sort out hand props by individual occurs. For example, to find all the hand props for the character "Cyrano," the prop list can be quickly scanned for every entry in the column by character name. Then a list can be made of all the props used by "Cyrano," allowing easy organization for rehearsal use or prop check-in by character.

The classification of "function" includes information on how the prop might be used, if it's a "consumable" prop, as well as notes communicating any idiosyncrasies of a particular item; for example: "fragile" or "not structural" versus "sittable—standable—thrown." It is also a handy place to note when a particular actor known for his physical use of props will be handling the prop so special care can be identified.

A full **description** based on the information from the prop meeting with the director and designer (quantity, how it is used, color, size, detailing, etc.) and information on any research included in the "bible" should be notated in this column. Not all information needs to be included, but the listing should make the connection to whatever drawings, photos, research, paper tracking document, costume prop listing, or other finalized information is available. It is especially helpful to include sizing information as a quick reference guide instead of having to sort through the research pages for specifics when out shopping or in a meeting with stage management or others and a question comes up about a particular piece. Initially, this area might note any questions for the director or designer about the prop.

The prop list description also shows where overlap and collaboration with other departments occurs. For example, a chandelier might require the lighting department to run an electric cord for the needed power and the scenic department to rig a hanging line to suspend the fixture. The coordination of the project should be noted on the prop list to allow for adequate consultation between all areas. The prop list description area might have deadline dates noted for when it must be built for sending out to a specialty shop or when the piece needs to be in rehearsal.

As a management tool, the prop list also may have **assignments** for completion and a preliminary "guess-timate" of how the prop will be **acquired** (build, buy, borrow, pull). Putting artisan names to particular props allows the properties director to balance the load across the shop, see where collaboration is needed, or determine if a specialist/over hire situation is needed. Listing how the prop will be completed also shows where the shopper and the artisan must coordinate activity, the priority for pulling or finding props, and the obvious purchases the budget must allow. These definitions may change, but it gives a start to organizing the entire build. It is also easy to pull out each artisan's work list once names have been assigned or to create a BUY list for the shopper, a PULL list for the artisan going to prop storage, and a BORROW list of the things to be found in the community at other theatres or organizations.

ONE MAN, TWO GUVNORS PROP LIST

DESIGNER: HUGH LANDWEHR

ALLEY THEATRE, KARIN RABE Prop Director

NO.	PG	CHARACTER	X	PROP	NOTES	TO DO	WHO	DEADLINE	B/F/S	ESTIMATE	ADJUSTED	ACTUAL
				1:1 Charlie's House								
1102	7			Side table	SR of SR chair. Small, built. Is placed on top of chair seat for moving it, so any dressing would need to be attached.	Does this need dressing? - Karin talk to Hugh			built?	$ 150.00	$ 29.67	$ 29.67
1103				Buffet Table - fake top		attach tablecloth and food- Monday						
1106	7			Standing lamp	SL side of the window unit. Turned wood post, see photos.	•cover lampshade with new fabric and trim	Sarah	Tech	Stock	$ 150.00	$ 225.00	$ 228.11
1108	7			Framed Photo of Queen Elizabeth	at her coronation - SR of window on wall. See research photo for style and finish	•add hanging hardware and install	Erin	Set Dress		$ 50.00	$ 50.00	
1109	7			Family Photos	or other framed art - SL of window on wall. 4 frames, all of Pauline at different times in her life: baby with bonnet, 5 years old, 10 years old & in a late 50's outfit. Frames should be approximately 6" x 9" - one oval for baby, the rest rectangular. Arranged on the wall in a diamond pattern	Install photos	Karin	Set Dress		$ -	$ -	
1110	7			Window drapes	see Info from Hugh	Build	Jessica	Set Dress		$ 300.00	$ 190.67	$ 190.67
1110				Roller Shades	Manila colored, with pull rings	Install	Karin	Set Dress				
1113	7			Party Can of beer		•Label work- add words on two sides, maybe add in drawing using transparent paper •Open can	Sarah	Tech		$ 25.00	$ 25.00	
1120	9			Small plate with crackers	small plate with a couple of paper doilys on it and 3 or 4 remaining ritz crackers.	Attach crackers	Sarah	Tech				
1131				Overhead light	Hangs on ceiling piece	Install		Load in				
				1:2 Cricketers Arms								
1201	16			Pub sign	flown. See elevation. Maybe it has a seagull perched on top of it. Chain should be welded together so the sign doesn't swing. Sign should be made of a smooth surface and have thick paint texture added to it. Make sure it stays thin to fit in overhead space	•make seagull sit on top •Hugh will do paint work Monday	Tomoko	Load in	build?	$ 200.00	$ 200.00	$ 30.55
1210	16	Francis		Orangina Bottle	has Orangina colored water in it. Is consumable	ordered- build label		tech		$ -	$ -	
1213	17	Stanley		Big Trunk - Stanley	built - see photos of London & Berkeley. Should be strong enough to withstand abuse, but not too heavy. Both should be similar in look, enough to be confused, but should be different. This is done with different fabrics. Opening style like: a foot locker, but look of a steamer trunk. Will need false bottoms in them and pockets for items (frame, diary, etc.) Will build 3 - one openable (Rachel and Stanley) for future scenes.	•Cut out luan and cover with fabric- install. Make sure to ease edges of luan •Cut strips of edging •remove hardware from real one to put on fake one	Eric	rehearsal		$ 750.00	$ 500.00	$ 298.04
					needs to roll pretty quickly. Wire style. Should be squeaky. May have wireless speaker in it. Brown paper bags enough to fill the cart and filled with brown foam shapes, good enough fake stuff with							

PROP LIST-SCENE PLOT | SET DRESS | FURNITURE PLOT | EXPENDIBLES LIST | COSTUME PROPS | PRACTICAL LIST | WEEKLY CHECK LIST | +

Figure 5.8 *One Man* Prop List. An example of a different way to utilize headers and tabs to organize a prop list. Courtesy of Karin Rabe, properties director, Alley Theatre."

Lastly, it's helpful to have a **status** column notating when a prop has been sent for use in rehearsal, what stage of completion it may have reached, if ordered and being shipped, etc. A quick scan of the prop list allows the properties director to know when the prop has been used in rehearsal, resolving many of the difficulties arising from first time prop use before even arriving onstage. Similarly, a notation of "Waiting on fabric" or "Paint" tells where the particular prop is in the process of the build and gives the properties director some leeway in reassigning duties or motivating the process. The prop list is often updated in this way at the beginning of the week in an informal meeting with the artisans to set weekly goals, sort out new shopping needs, and solve any problems in the build process.

USING A TRACKING NUMBERS SYSTEM

Using a numbering system allows a quick code to help in organizing the prop list. This is only one method of numbering and not all prop shops use a numbering system . . . or they are unable to convince stage management to utilize it, so they only have it for their own organization and peace of mind. Regardless, having some way of identifying props other than by description is helpful. Depending on whether it's a hand prop, set prop, or dressing, a different code can be used.

A method easy to understand and implement for hand props is to use a 4-digit number, with the first digit standing for the Act number, the second for the scene number and the last two for the prop number. Hence, the first prop listed in Act I, Scene 3 would be 1301. If it had been in Act II, Scene 1, then it would have been 2101. Having more than ninety-nine props in a given scene would be extraordinary, so the system works. By simply looking at the prop number, it's easy to tell when the prop is introduced onstage.

The working prop list only notates the prop the *first* time it is introduced, regardless of how many other scenes it plays in. If a prop repeats, stage management may need to track it as utilized in multiple scenes, but it will track with the number from when it FIRST appeared onstage. Therefore, the stage management tracking scene sheet may have props using different act numbers even in the final scene of the play.

The numbering system also allows an understanding of what works with what. For example, if you had a suitcase brought in during Act I, Scene 2 and it was the sixth item added in that scene, its number would be 1206. This information is placed in the prop list along with the item name and whatever information is available. The listing for the suitcase might look like this:

1206   Suitcase   Hard sided, brown, with leather straps, 22" tall, 30" wide, 8" deep

If that suitcase was then opened in Act II, Scene 4 and had some items of clothing removed from the suitcase, the "dressing" would get its own number, and it should have a notation to connect it to the right suitcase so the props people know *which* suitcase gets the clothing. On the prop list, since it is seen for the first time in Act II, Scene 4, it might look like this:

2401   Suitcase Dressing   Placed in 1206, one pair of pants, one shirt (male)

This kind of detail becomes critical when a request comes in for the suitcase in Act I, Scene 2 to be stood on by the actor and needs an interior brace that will have to be removed during the scene change and clothing added. Then the listing would be:

1206   Suitcase   Stood on in I,2 by actor- add interior bracing (removed I,3 and replaced with 2401). Hard sided, brown, with leather straps, 22" tall, 30" wide, 8" deep.

Or if the switch can't be made, then the suitcase has to be duplicated with an identical one for Act II.

2402   Suitcase   Identical in appearance to 1206, dressed with 2401

The suitcase dressing should have its own number because it may require specific information to track with it, such as whether it is male or female, has some particular look to it, or color. If something particular is requested, such as a pair of red high heel shoes to be worn or thrown after being taken from the suitcase, and is to be included as part of the dressing, then, for instance, those red shoes should get assigned their own number:

2403   Red Shoes   Placed with 2401 in 2402, female, high heeled pumps, thrown (action), then put on and worn by actor.

It's helpful to leave spaces between assigned numbers when making up the prop list initially, in anticipation of props being added. It's also acceptable to simply list the props in order of their being defined, and assign *added* props the next number in the scene listing regardless of their relationship to another prop. The numbering system allows connections to be made regardless of either method used.

Assigning a numbering system to furniture and set dressing is helpful, especially when tracking items in a multiple set show. Some lists use a listing simply by *place*, utilizing an abbreviation to notate the location and then a number for tracking. The number does not need to utilize the same act/scene/number breakdown as used for hand props. The "place" identifier is usually enough.

In a scene placed in a kitchen rotating with a scene in a bedroom, the prop list might look like this with K (Kitchen) or B (Bedroom) and a designation of F (Furniture) or D (Dressing) followed by the number.

Set Props

K F 1	**Table**	**painted, seats four (KF2)**
K F 2	**Chairs**	**4 identical, painted, matches K1**
K F 4	**Refrigerator**	**1950s, white, 32" wide**
B F 1	**Bed**	**Twin bed mattress and box spring, jumped on**
B F 2	**Headboard**	**Painted black, goes with B1, must be strong**
B F 3	**Side table**	**Wooden, 20" tall, one shelf, one drawer**

Dressing

K D 1	**Clock**	**Cat clock, tail wags—(Practical—ELECTRICS)**
K D 2	**Curtains**	**Spring rod in doorway, floor length, floral**
B D 2	**Venetian Blinds**	**Never opened, distressed and dusty**

Several props of the same item may each have their own independent numbers. For example, the four chairs described above could be K F 2, 3, 4, and 5 or could use subheadings like K F 2-a, b, c, and d to designate they are part of a group but have a separate identity number. This is especially helpful when tracking maintenance required on matching pieces and members of a group. If the show report says KF2-c is broken, the prop shop will know which chair they are talking about by referring to the storage list for post-show strike and can easily access the right chair without having to examine all the chairs.

On a unit set the items can be simply listed as F (for furniture) or D (for dressing) with a number for tracking following it.

F 1	**Chair**	**Side chair, upholstered, turned legs**
F 2	**Table**	**36" long, wooden, will be stood upon**
D 1	**Chandelier**	**Black metal, hangs center (Practical—ELECTRICS)**

Some lists break the numbering down, similar to the hand props, with coordination between Act and Scene using the F or D simply before the number. The ultimate goal is to do whatever works most easily and allows an organized build coordinating all the props.

Some prop shops do not utilize a numbering system because the builds are small or do not require this level of organization. *Do what works for you.* If the numbering system helps, work with stage management to make it a useful organizational and communication tool. Decide how numbers will be assigned and communicate all information by making it part of the rehearsal notes and tracking system for prop run. This is simply another tool to bring clarity and organization to the production process.

Depending on the organization, maintaining the prop listing/description portion might fall to stage management or be retained in the prop shop. The critical part of this choice is how the updates are communicated between the areas. Regardless, the list is the start of organizing the build.

MAKING A PLAN

From the prop list, the properties director plans what might be built, pulled from stock and possibly modified, borrowed from another theatre or from a store, or bought in whole or in part. Part of this process is the consideration of what has to happen to complete each prop. Armed with whatever information is available, the properties director must ask:

- What does it want to look like?
- What does it look like now?

- What does it need to do? (Satisfying script/actor function/designer look/other production area interaction)
- How much/many are needed?
- Who handles it or makes it work?
- When does it need to be done?
- What talent is available to do it?
- What materials are available or can be obtained in the time allotted?
- What can be negotiated to change?
- How much money is it going to cost?
- How much time will it take to do it?

Most of these questions won't be answered at first review, and input from artisans on materials or time estimates may be needed. The properties director needs to make a "best guess" on what will work to begin the process of estimating the budget and accepting the design as "do-able." With experience, the multiple variables of how to review the list and decide what the best solution is within the constraints of the build allows for more accurate estimates of labor and materials.

Often the prop list is broken down into **process lists**. A process list is a division of the prop list into the individual ways the prop might be completed—built, bought, borrowed, or pulled. Many times, it's a combination of those choices. As the build progresses and decisions get made, the viability of those options change and the process lists change.

For example, to build a table for the show, the buy list must reflect the materials needed, such as wood, fasteners, specialty router bits, finishing stains, etc. But if a table is found in the stock of a furniture company willing to rent or lend it out, then all the lists change. It is now being pulled. The builder no longer has to build the table and the shopper no longer needs to buy materials but must instead arrange for the transportation of the table from storage to the theatre. Or, the designer might find a table in stock that would work but he wants a tablecloth made to disguise the top. This takes it off the build list for the carpenter artisan, but the buy list gets fabric and trim added to it and the soft goods artisan gets the add to build the table covering.

Each prop director will individualize the utilization of list breakouts from the primary list. For example, the bottom tabs may break down the build with a single detailed "to-do" list incorporating all the various levels of the build, buy, pull process instead of making it into four separate lists. One tab might be a "document tracking" list. Another might be for "practicals" or "weapons." The tabs are simply a way to focus the prop list into organized and specific subgroups. What tabs are used will often be reflective of the specific show or of the way a shop has to function given the limitations of time, money, and skill set available.

Creating and utilizing the prop list should reflect the individual management style suitable to the show and the organization. It is, ultimately, simply a tool to keep things on track, insuring all of the items needed for the show will be done. The prop list is a fluid, ever-changing

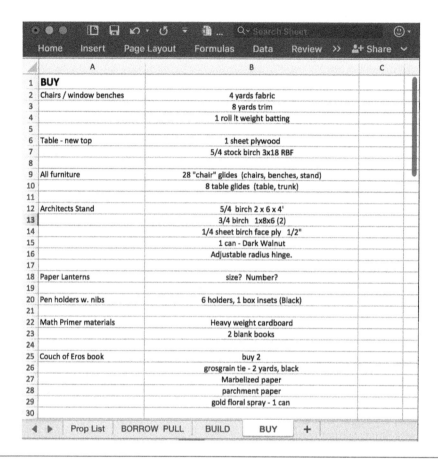

Figure 5.9 Buy Sub-tag. BUY process list for *Arcadia* tracking individual props and what needs to be purchased to allow for the build to progress. By moving through the other tabs it's easy to see what has to be built, or if something will be pulled/borrowed.

document reflecting the various choices and discoveries made in the rehearsal and build process. Every decision impacts what is done in the shop and how the props move to completion.

This is where the mighty juggle between the budget of time and personnel begins and the consummate skill of the properties director is needed most. The closer it gets to tech and opening, the more complicated it all becomes. Utilizing the prop list to coordinate the show build is covered in more depth in following chapters.

As a management tool, keeping the prop list up to date is mandatory, and communicating changes between all the involved partners is essential. But the prop list is only one part of the information the properties director maintains. The prop list is informed by all the drawings, photographs, research, fabric samples, sketches, director/designer discussions, and other information communicated during the initial design and production coordination process.

AROUND THE WORLD IN 80 DAYS

NOR	x	PROP	NOTES	TO DO	WHO	DEADLINE
		FURNITURE				
5	1	Chairs	set of 6 used throughout the play / See Hugh Research. Shop built. / •used as the sledge & the elephant. / •needs to hold the weight of 5 people. / •moves on glides	•add highlight on upper and turnings / •dust underside of seat (dust covers) with a color to give them a little contrast. See Hugh for more.	Eric	Low Priority
6	2	Table - Elephant	•dark wood painted grain finish - plain (no inset) top.	•Finer grain on top of all surfaces painted in this manner (table, globe, ottoman). Top grain should be more like the podium grain. See Karin or Hugh for more	Courtney	High Priority
7	2	New Reform Club Table	added. On casters. Finish stays as is / 36" diameter.	•One of the casters is sticky or not allowing the table to roll straight. It's spinning as they roll it. Please replace the bad caster.		High Priority
8	3	Globe Bar	•Should have the countries as they were in 1872 in different colors / •opens with rack that holds a brandy bottle and brandy glasses / •is used in final wedding scene to hold bouquet & small bowls of flower petals. / •painted finish to match elephant table / •30" diameter globe, 36" diameter stand. / •castered with 2" diameter wheels / •inside painted midnight blue to match the stage	•Finish exterior paint treatment / •Build flower platform / •Add a simple detail on the latitude arc - see Hugh for details / •add round rosette details to the blocks on the top and bottom. Do this after finessing paint finish. Rosettes may be brass or gold. / •open up the recieving bracket for the globe top, so that when they close it they have a bigger spot to aim for. I think we can just spread the sides of the current one open into more of a V.	Eric	High Priority
9	5	Life Preservers x6	•they will hang either on the railing, archway or ships wheel. / •30" in diameter. / •Canvas bands will be different colors for each. / •Ships names are: The Mongolia, The Rangoon, the Carnatic, The Tankadere, The General Grant, The Henrietta / •ropes around preserver should be cotton, not nylon / •all will be aged to different amounts / •build hangers for arch way and railings	•add 5 pointed stars in white to canvas wraps on General Grant ring. See Hugh for scale / •distress all life preservers - please see Hugh / •change out bolts on swinging hangers / •look at hangers with Hugh to see about adding a ball or some other décor on the end of the end of the arm / •gunk up the hinges on the swing arms or something else to slow down the opening of them. / •add stronger magnet latches on the swing arms	Tomoko	High Priority
10	7	Opium Den Screen	•See Drawing. / •top round sections light up internally to look like lit paper lanterns. / •printed silk panels with dragon design to be translucent. / •will over paint and grunge up screen	•new larger lanterns have been ordered. Install when they arrive / •add age and stains - glazes on frame and overpaint the gold and dirty the fabric. See Hugh for more	Tomoko	Medium Priority
11	8	Podium	See Drawing / •clerk bell on right side top, stamper on left side top, ink pad in middle / •Run crew will switch the clerk's bell for the gavel block and back. Both need to be magneted on / •needs to be as lightweight as possible. / •painted finish to match elephant table	•Touch up front bottom where MDF chipped away. / •paint inside of the bottom glossy blue like the upstage floor.	Tomoko	Low Priority
12	10	Ottoman - Fogg's House	•needs to be standable	•add rubber under fee to stop slippage		
13		**HAND PROPS - ACT 1**				
14	1104	Brandy Snifters	with fake brandy in them, the middle size (of the 5 sizes we have in stock	•work on color a little more. They're still to orange. It looks like they need a touch of green in them.	Sarah	Low Priority
15	1113	Carpet Bag	•fairly sizable / •will need a flat board on the bottom to help them sit and hold them open / •Pocket on the front for snow	•carpet bag has arrived / •Add a pocket to the front in the same fabric. / •darken handles - medium to darkish brown. Something to kill the red in them. Hugh suggests trying thinned out black leather dye on them / •build an insert for the bottom of the bag to hold 2 tea cups, the scene, the teapot / •sew the interior pockets shut	Karin	Medium Priority

PROP LIST-SCENE PLOT | TO-DO | SHOPPING | LOAD IN | PRACTICALS | DATA | Florida Rep Prop List | Sheet2 | Act Scene List | Budget | +

Figure 5.10 Prop List Example. TO-DO tab of the *Around the World in 80 Days* prop list. Note tabs on bottom showing organizational divisions for tracking of information. Karin Rabe, properties director, Alley Theatre.

SHOW BIBLE

To keep track of all the information, the properties director often gathers all the information from the design and production meetings and creates a file to hold everything and to track all the changes occurring during the building process. This file, or **show bible**, as many call it, keeps all the show information in one place for easy reference.

Laptop computers, handheld tablets, and cellphones have become standard management tools in the prop shop, and the "bible" is transitioning away from a physical notebook into a digital resource with images scanned in and calendars, budgets, rehearsal reports, prop lists, and such kept in accessible files and available electronically. Most of this information is now being communicated via the computer anyway, so keeping it as an electronic file makes sense. Having this information available electronically is especially helpful if available from "the cloud" or similar accessible online method of storing it. It is easy to update and track changes on the computer and send responses to stage management, the production manager, or other production shops via email and is especially helpful when responding to rehearsal reports so everyone is part of the conversation. As the basis for managing the build, it makes all information readily available in meetings attended, while shopping for the show or with the designer, for an artisan who has questions, to track communications between the shop and rehearsal, to review drawings for specific information, and to resolve any questions that might arise. Receipts can be scanned in, allowing originals to be processed to bookkeeping as necessary. Artisans can access the information easily and print off copies or download information to their personal electronic devices, study the designer's notes or research, and read rehearsal report comments about how a prop is used to clarify their thought process as they work on the show.

The prop bible uses tabs (if the paper version) or digital folders to organize the information, allowing information to be quickly accessed. Common folders might be: budget, calendar, drawings, email/communication, prop list, purchasing, rehearsal, research, or photos. Setting up folders digitally and putting them on an accessible cloud allows all contributors to access the information. The individual folders can have interior folders to create further organization. For example, a *budget* folder could hold interior sub-folders for receipts, personnel timesheets, and budget tracking sheets. Or the *research* folder could have interior sub-folders with one for hand props, one for furniture, and another for the dressing research . . . or one for designer research and another for the research done by the prop shop expanding on what the designer sent. The *reports* folder could have interior sub-folders for schedules, rehearsal, performance, production meeting, etc. Personalize, organize, and label the folders to match individual preferences and mode of thought and create an efficient, easy-to-update, and easy-to-access arrangement of all the show information.

Controlling access to the folder is often done in the privacy settings or by invitation to the site/folders. This allows folks at different levels of "need to know" to manage who is seeing what on the shared site. For example, if keeping the budget information discreet is necessary,

SHOW BIBLE - INFORMATION TO INCLUDE:

Contact information sheet-phone, fax, email, and address

Calendar/Schedules

  Designer deadlines

  Rehearsal/Load-in/tech/dress schedule

  Performance schedule

  Weekly work/build schedule

Communication/E-mail:

  (TO and FROM) – Designers, Director, Stage Management
    and all other production areas.

  Rehearsal reports

  Production meeting reports

Prop Lists

  Preliminary - with questions/answers

  Designer listing for design

  Working Prop List with updates

Drawings

  Floor plans and Elevations

  Prop drawings from designer

  Shop/working drawings

Research

  Photos and Documents

  Stock

  Borrowing availability

  Purchasing - local/online

Budget

  Show budget - working expenses

  Preliminary budget

  Seasonal/overhead budget

  Personnel/Hire/Timesheets

Borrowing forms and Insurance coverage forms (as needed)

Performance

  Run crew and Cast list

  Program listing information/tracking

    Prop personnel – how they want to be listed, bios

    Acknowledgements

    Special Thanks

  Performance report/Maintenance notes

Strike plan

Figure 5.11 Show Bible

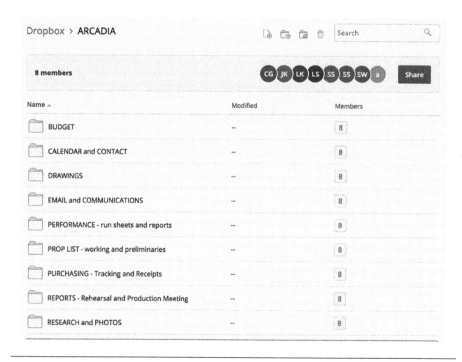

Figure 5.12   Dropbox—*Arcadia* Main Folder. A screenshot of an online Dropbox for *Arcadia* showing the various folders shared with collaborators.

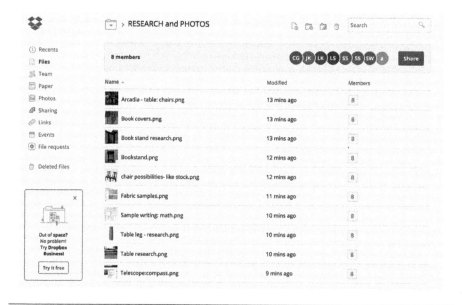

Figure 5.13   Subfolder—Research. An example of a Dropbox—Research sub-folder showing photos and research information.

its access can be limited. Some sites also allow "invisible" folders to be utilized so only those folks who have been invited can see them. An intermediate step utilizes a *View Only* status for team members invited to join by the particular administrator in charge, so folder contents can be available but not altered or removed. As a personal management strategy, it's up to the individual group of collaborators to determine who has access to what, but it would seem, in this highly collaborative method of creating theatre, the most productive and inclusive way of working would also be the most transparent.

Information can be printed off as necessary, but the three-ring binder "bible" is quickly becoming a relic of the past. Keeping it up to date was a big job that took valuable time away from the build. If the information is hard copied and kept in a physical notebook, juggling

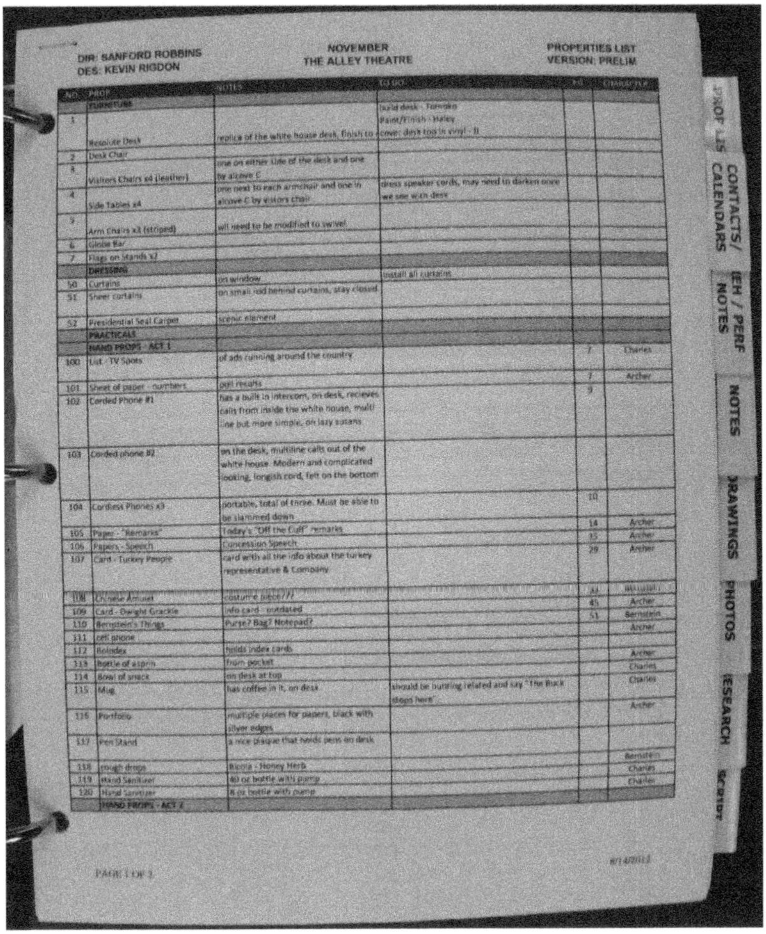

Figure 5.14 Hard Copy Bible. Example of a traditional hard copy bible. Note tabs on side to allow for quick access to different organized areas. Karin Rabe, properties director, Alley Theatre.

keeping the information secure and updated is somewhat more difficult. However, if your artisans do not have access online to the digital bible, having a hard copy in the shop becomes essential.

Some organizations utilize this method when their digital infrastructure is lacking. Even organizations using a digital bible might retain show research along with the designer's notation and any in-progress shots pertaining to the props in a physical prop "bible" for documentation of the build. This is helpful for those shows which may be re-mounted at another theatre, sent out on tour, or for those seasonal shows remounted annually, such as *A Christmas Carol*. Having the source material makes additions to the show, replications in case of breakage or the need for duplicates easier. It also allows the evolution of a prop to be tracked over several seasons when a different director uses the same scenic design for a seasonal show but needs to alter the props to fit the newer version. For archival purposes, having a hard copy of the prop list, budget, designs, and prop run paperwork secured in a safe and dry location will be helpful should the show be remounted or transferred later to another organization. Keeping all the information only in "the cloud" may not guarantee its availability in the future. Back it up.

Usually, the properties director manages the "bible" (electronic or otherwise) and all changes are tracked and noted so the information is up-to-date, creating a single source for all questions. Regardless of how the information is stored, the shop bible is a critically important organizational and management tool for the build on any show.

* * *

Getting organized utilizing a prop list and a prop bible insures a way to track all the changes and information flowing into the prop shop on any build. Keeping the information up-to-date and communicated to all collaborative partners keeps confusion minimized and allows for a smooth and stress-free build as it moves from preliminary planning and design through to the rehearsal and build process.

Working in Regional Theatre

An intervview with Mark Walston, Actor's Theatre of Louisville Prop Director, Louisville, KY

How long have you been doing props, and how did you get started in this career?

I've been doing props for 29 years. My first experience as a props master was on *My Fair Lady* when I was a senior in college. My college theatre advisor thought I should try props. I really loved both the creative part of it and the organization. Before I graduated I also got to do *Fiddler on the Roof*. More learning and experience came in summer stock before I got my first professional job in regional theatre.

Mark Walston
ACTOR'S THEATRE OF LOUISVILLE PROP DIRECTOR,
LOUISVILLE, KY

You've been at ATL for many years. You've worked as a Co-Prop Master, Props Master, Props Designer—describe how the titles encompassed job responsibilities and advantages/ disadvantages of each.

At Actors Theatre, we've always had two props masters because of the number of overlapping productions that we do. When I moved into the job, the other props master and I were both young and not nearly as experienced as the people that we replaced. The strategy was that we would do big shows together and work as Co-Props Masters, each of us handling the projects we knew best. This worked very well, but wasn't necessary as we gained experience. We still do it occasionally for big shows like *A Christmas Carol* that are only rebuilt every ten years or so. The title of Props Designer was one that was used for many years in our programs. The job itself was basically the same as the Props Master job. A few years ago, this was examined and the designer designation was discarded. Every Props Master that I know does their best to bring the vision of the set designer to life on the stage. As head of the Props Department here, my title is Props Director. When I am doing a production, I'm the Props Master. I think that these two titles describe what I do in the most accurate way.

You have productions returning annually in the repertory at ATL. *(Dracula/Christmas Carol)* **What special considerations do you have for those plays as opposed to a regular build/ normal show prep?**

The main consideration for these shows is making sure that they are stored safely in a way that keeps items in good condition. Both of our annual productions are stored in the basement at the theatre in dry, dust free rooms. We spend more time putting things away than we do in getting them out. We always take note of extra wear on various pieces so that we know what will need some repair before it is used again.

You have worked with Paul Owen as the resident designer as well as working with many guest designers. What are the advantages/disadvantages of both?

The big advantage of working with a resident designer is their familiarity and knowledge of what is available in our stock and what the strongest talents of the artisans are. After repeated experiences with the same guest designers, they often have some of this knowledge too. With new guest designers or a designer that doesn't work here frequently, extra time is spent in sharing our resources and talents. A major disadvantage of not having a resident designer is the physical absence of that person during the build. Emails, calls, and photographs are helpful, but not as helpful as seeing a piece evolve in person and having a face to face conversation with the artisan who is building it.

ATL has two primary producing spaces and a third black box theatre for very small shows and showings. How do you juggle the priorities of producing multiple shows in several spaces, keeping everyone happy, communicating up and down the food chain, and being ready for tech?

My main priority is focusing on the show that opens first and tackling things in order. If it is possible to get a jump start on the second or third show because it is easier or decisions on it have been solidified first, that works well too. I also use the tactic I learned in driver's training of looking at the big picture when I'm in the driver's seat and not just the little details. This kind of focus takes practice and a willingness to learn and try new ways of organizing. It also takes time to gather all of the information in order to make good decisions.

ATL is known for its exploration of new American plays. How is working on a new play different from a play that has been produced before?

New plays are still changing. Sometimes they are perfect, sometimes they need work. Remembering that and being as flexible as possible is the key. A dangerous path with new plays is to judge the imperfections and develop a negative attitude about what you are doing. I do my best to give the director and designer what they want to see. In the end, every production is a learning experience for everyone involved and a success for the creative team and the audience.

How is the shop/staff/management process/timeline different (or the same?) for the New Play Festival when you are building, tech-ing, opening, running multiple new plays?

I think that the main difference is that we are working on several productions at the same time with limited time. Being smart about how the time is used is the key to a good outcome.

What are the most critical skills for a properties director/master to have in managing the shop, working with designers, and bringing a show in as designed, on time and under budget?

I think organization, communication, and commitment. There is no room for laziness here!

Describe your ideal artisan.

Someone with multiple talents, commitment to working with others, a good attitude, and a drive to succeed and learn more.

If you could be doing anything else and be guaranteed successful at it, what would you do?

I love my hometown of Detroit, Michigan. I also love architecture. I'd like to be in Detroit rebuilding the neighborhoods and helping the people and the city find prosperity and harmony.

Budgeting

Following initial design meetings with the scenic designer and the director to talk through the preliminary hand prop list and study the elevations or scale model for all the set props and dressing, the properties director now has a listing and the "big picture" array of information. The question is, "Can we afford it?"

Most commonly, budgets are set far in advance by senior management, either at the production director level or by the executive director in consultation with the production director, who in turn gathers input from all production department heads. Season budgets are approved by the board of directors, to whom the executive director reports. Budgeting production needs far in advance of design meetings can be a tricky process of best-guess estimating, and a careful review of the script for red flags is critical. Factors such as time period, number and type of locations, essential specific props called out in the script or stage directions, even the number of actors in the cast all have implications on a dart board style estimate prior to design team involvement. While some theatre administrators generate these budgets in a vacuum, leaving the prop director to live with the budget and make it work in the design phase, the best-case scenarios involve the prop director in an initial read and script/score assessment in order to advise the production director on department-specific areas to look out for and appropriately budget.

Most designer contracts specify the production budget figures available on a given show—a practice allowing the production director to set the budget bar, taking the onus off of the production department heads to act as the heavy on financial matters. Negotiation is rarely an option, but can occur in more affluent companies with strong artistic director influence over budget priorities.

Even the best laid budget plans do sometimes go awry, of course. If a creative team turns in a package wildly over the estimated resources allocated, some wiggle room is vital for balancing the numbers with the needs. In theatres where budgets are set over a season long arc and designs for all shows are submitted well in advance, prop directors may have the control to reallocate money from one show looking smaller than anticipated to another show which is headed for an overage. As long as the end of season bottom line for the prop department meets the number set by management, this practice is accepted. In leaner times, when a theatre may be living the equivalent of paycheck to paycheck, or when designs filter in throughout a season rather than planning in advance, this approach is untenable. Sticking to individual show budgets is mandatory in these situations. Constant communication between the prop director and production director on expected expenditures makes the budgeting process run more smoothly, aids in securing supervisor back up, builds trust, and avoids unpleasant surprises for management.

In situations when management sets budget numbers seemingly unrelated to a given show's requirements, production department heads must formulate an appropriate response with suggestions on more realistic numbers based on research and experience. How does a prop director calculate this estimate?

PRELIMINARY SHOW BUDGET

To answer that question, a preliminary show budget must be created. The **preliminary show budget** estimates the cost of materials for items to be built, modified, or purchased, as well as the "labor" estimate for the build or alteration of each piece. Each item on the prop list should have a "cost" associated with it given the preliminary supposition of how it might be completed. Every properties director knows this preliminary budget is, at best, a wildly optimistic (or pessimistic) first guess. The juggle done in the prop shop on *how* any one show gets built can be completed in a multitude of ways, depending on what stroke of fortune allows the right fabric to be found for pennies on the dollar, what furniture can be borrowed or found in stock, and how accurate the prop list remains to the first listing. Making a preliminary show budget can often feel like an exercise in futility but, frankly, it is done as a means to begin defining the show and the resources it will take to build it as designed.

In the evolving culture of department heads being held responsible for supplying the bulk of requests from the designer and director throughout the process, all within the resources laid out by production management, assessing costs ahead of the crunch time of the build and rehearsal period is a matter of enlightened self-interest. Sometimes it will all work out just fine, but for those shows brutally larger than the existing resources, this is an essential check and balance in the communication process. These preliminary prop list estimates become a vital tool to identify the best production department home for sometimes ambiguous projects, especially those "crossover" elements such as moving vehicles, masks, or other assorted pieces sometimes floating into the world of props. In situations when other department heads are equipped with more preliminary information in the design process, creative teams often default to moving budget overages from costumes or scenery into props, historically one of the later technical areas to see drafted out designs. A prop director who comes to meetings equipped with a reasonable preliminary materials and labor estimate can save the frustration of feeling buried right out of the starting gate and will be better able to guide the design team to pursue creative solutions early on. With a budget based on the props known at the time and a healthy contingency fund to cover the "what ifs," it is possible to give the production manager an assessment of the expected budget impact and negotiate changes based on anticipated expenses and build times.

In a large shop, the properties director may request information from the properties artisans who will be completing the work on a specific project or prop. Chairs needing upholstery should be measured to figure yardage and furniture from stock assessed for any necessary restoration or structural additions to fit the staging. Furniture to be built must have board feet estimated. Delegation to and involvement of the entire prop build team can make this process highly fruitful, reducing pressure on the prop director, and increasing problem-solving and ownership by all shop staff who participate. Smaller props shops will more likely rely solely on the prop director to estimate and calculate at this stage in the process. These preliminary figures, organized as simple lists, can often provide structure for a later more in-depth construction or assignment step list, and serve as an asset when estimating labor as well. Any prop being built or modified can, on some basic level, be broken down into a **materials estimate**. Completing a written estimate helps keep the projections organized. A simple materials breakdown might look something like Figure 6.1.

Finishing supplies such as paint, trim, molding, hardware, etc. not available in stock should have quantity estimated and sources identified and priced. Items being modified from stock should account for whatever needs to be purchased to complete the modification. Items to be purchased should be researched online or in stores for availability and pricing. Allowances for shipping expenses should be included in the budget. Labor time to do physical in-store shopping should be factored in for those local source items, antiquing, or thrift store ventures. Rental payments, when purchasing is not an option, might also be a factor in the overall budget estimate. When a show is set in a particular style or period, an allowance should be built into the budget acknowledging the difficulty of reproducing or purchasing items to fit that style. Additionally, in each budget a **contingency** amount (often as much as 20%) may be added to account for the additions, changes, cuts, and unexpected events occurring during the process of production.

Perishables necessary to supply during rehearsals and the run of a production can be incorporated into the general show materials budget as well, though in some large shops with extended runs the perishables line will have a separate budget to estimate and track. For example: a ten-week run of *Sweeney Todd* may include some early rehearsal props such as dough, and some consumables appearing only at early technical rehearsals, such as blood. Perishables to be defined by quantity of rehearsals and performances might include ingredients for Mrs. Lovett's dough to roll out on her pie shop table, edible "meat" pies for Sweeney and the pie shop patrons (chorus), stage blood for each murder, mashed potatoes tinted with food color to put through Toby's meat grinder, blanks for Anthony's revolver, batteries for the insane asylum lanterns, dish washing and sanitary supplies, food storage paraphernalia, gun

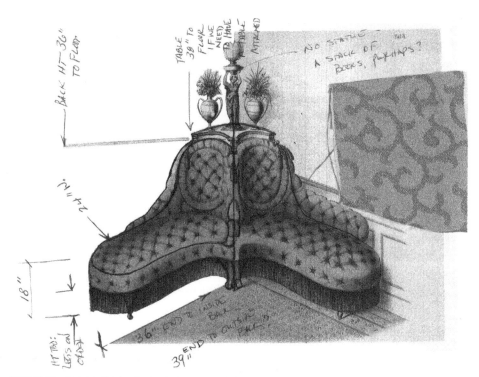

PRELIMINARY MATERIALS ESTIMATE: BUILD OF TETE A TETE FURNITURE PIECE

Part/Process	Description	Source	Cost
Standable deck	Plywood ½ paint grade maple	Bliffert Lumber	$ 80.00
Curved structure	3/8" bendable ply	Alpine Plywood	$125.00
Armature/structure	poplar 5/4 stock	KM hardwood	$129.00
Prefab furniture legs	8 @ poplar queen anne	Adams Wood Products	$ 96.00
Finish	Stain – cherry	Ace hardware	$ 12.00
	Satin varnish	Ace hardware	$ 18.50
General Supplies	Sandpaper, fasteners, shop rags, wood glue	Shop supplies stock	$ 27.00
Upholstery supplies	Urethane foam FR2835@ 2"	Active Foam products	$109.60
	Supreme cotton batting	Active Foam	$ 88.00
	Muslin, welt cord, tufting twine	Shop supplies stock	$ 35.00
	12 yards Fabric – designer swatch	LZ Textiles	$188.00
	Button blanks	Rowley Co	$ 15.00
	Fringe – 12 yards	LZ Textiles	$ 72.00
Contingency	rough 10 %		$ 100.00

TOTAL $ 1095.10

Figure 6.1 Materials Estimate. Preliminary designer research, with preliminary materials budget figures from prop director. Tête-à-tête project, Skylight Opera Theatre.

cleaning supplies, etc. As with any prop materials budget estimate, these expenses can be laid out in preliminary fashion to help decision-making and allocation of financial resources at the start of the planning process. Review and revisions are always necessary as consumables are cut, added, or changed in response to staging decisions, allergies, dietary restrictions, on or offstage clean-up requirements, impacts to other departments such as costumes, scenery or electrics, or other factors unknown at the outset of the planning process.

Prior to rehearsal the prop list is only a rough guideline, and it will change throughout the rehearsal process, sometimes impacting a budget severely. As a properties director becomes familiar with designers and directors, this contingency figure may need to increase or might be decreased based on those prior production experiences. Some directors and designers are less able to think through all of the script needs until the production parts are assembled and onstage, and some projects may follow highly developmental trajectories throughout the rehearsal and tech process. In these instances, props are often an area called upon to "fix" whatever difficulty is created, whether it's finding a different piece of furniture due to an unforeseen shift problem, adding foliage to cover a bad seam where scenery comes together, or adding more dressing to disguise a sight line. Contingency figures also help cover when

SWEENEY TODD PERISHABLES CALCULATOR (8 shows/week x 11 weeks)

Category	Items	Quantity	Per Unit Est.Cost	Total Estimated
Flour/Dough	1 pound whole wheat flour (Woodman's) & water	13	$3.98	$51.74
	salt	2	$0.89	$1.78
	shortening	2	$2.85	$5.70
Edible "meat" pies	pie crust mix	11	$2.19	$24.09
(ingredients per batch of 6 pies)	fruit pie filling	11	$2.98	$32.78
	caramel food coloring paste	1	$7.00	$7.00
	baking spray release	1	$3.70	$3.70
	muffin tin	1	$8.95	$8.95
	zip lock food storage bags, gallon	2	$4.50	$9.00
Shaving	barbasol sensitive shave cream	6	$2.17	$13.02
Stage Blood, washable	Glycerin, gallon	5	$23.00	$115.00
	Red Food color, powder, 5 pound	1	$45.99	$45.99
	blue food color, powder, 1/4 pound	1	$1.99	$4.99
	Hershey's chocolate syrup	2	$2.35	$4.70
	Blue liquid laundry detergent, 1.5 gallon	5	$7.97	$39.85
Toby Meat grinder "product"	instant mashed potatoes, 26 oz.	11	$4.05	$44.55
	Knox gelatin	22	$1.84	$40.48
	condensed milk	11	$2.39	$26.29
	(Stage Blood)			$0.00
Lovett sweets (#265 for run)	bon bons, gluten free, box of 50	6	$33.50	$201.00
Toby's Revolver	.32 cal blanks, box of 50	1	$39.95	$39.95
	gun cleaning solvent, 8 oz.	1	$8.99	$8.99
	cotton gun patches, 1 bulk bag	1	$6.84	$6.84
Fogg's Asylum Lanterns	9V batteries, 4 pack	11	$15.89	$174.79
Clean up & Hygiene	baby wipes	11	$4.99	$54.89
	unscented laundry detergent, 1.5 gallon	3	$8.50	$25.50
	Oxyclean laundry booster	1	$7.59	$7.59
	Dawn dish detergent	1	$3.99	$3.99
	dish sponges, 4 pack	1	$4.99	$4.99
Total			$267.02	$1,008.14

Figure 6.2 Perishables Calculator. *Sweeney Todd* perishables budget estimate for entire show run.

the cost of materials fluctuate. For example, plywood often increases in price and availability during a severe hurricane season, and steel prices fluctuate frequently based on industrial supply, demand, and sourcing.

Reviewing the prop list, it is easy to run down the list assigning a "cost" to each prop based on a preliminary judgment of how it will be completed. Once costs are projected for each prop, a preliminary prop materials budget can be completed. This can be a simple matter of creating a summary sheet combining the preliminary prop list with the individual item estimates the prop director has researched, or can be as in-depth as expanding those lists into a multi-tab spreadsheet itemizing each material, supply, and labor hour for each prop. For preliminary estimating when providing numbers for discussion with production management and the creative team, it is better to be concise and use a summary format.

It is important to remind the production and design team that *props are a constantly evolving area.* Like Dr. Doolittle's pushmi-pullyu beast, changes during the staging and rehearsal process usually require continual reevaluation of budget and priorities. Compromise and negotiation of fiscal priorities will continue as the build moves closer to technical rehearsals. The collaborative process with the designer is all important in making decisions that utilize

SKYLIGHT OPERA THEATRE PROPERTIES DEPARTMENT 2011-12 Season; Preliminary Prop Budget - 9/11/2011 *THE RIVALS* Director - Dorothy Danner; Scenic Design - Lisa Schlenker			
Est.	**P/S/B/A**	**PROP**	**NOTES**
		Salon - Act One Scene One	
NC	Stock	Chandelier	practical, flies. Blue glass arms and crystal bobiches and drops
$160.00	Purchase	2 pair of sconces	salon walls - one sconce on each side of mirror centered in faux panels per rendering. See design research. Source: chandeliers.com
NC	Alter stock materials	pair of mirrors	over tables between sconces. Mirrors are not "real" reflective. Prop silver surface. Inset into stock mirror frames.
$150	Build. Limited budget	Salon swags	Sheer pink with damask pattern. See designer fabric swatch - LZ textiles. Tiebacks and bows from stock satin ribbon, 2"
$20	Purchase	wall mounted coat hooks	positioned on either side of pocket doors
$200	Build	pair of wall mount tables	positioned on either side of pocket doors, attached to curved walls securely.
NC	Alter stock	pair of flower arrangements and pair of ferns	one on each table
NC	Stock	several stacks of stacks of leather bound books	on lower shelf of each table, as well as a taller stack on the tete table
$1,086	Build	tête-à-tête with quarter tables attached	upholstered unit- tufted, breaks into two parts. Standable. Jumped upon in boots. Table has magnet attachments to aid in keeping alignment and position when together.
$25	Alter stock	pillows for tete x 2	Pink velour with gold fringe to match hassock fabric. Re-cover stock down pillow forms.
$145	Build	Ottoman	Sittable by 2 demure sopranos; standable. Gold damask with fringe
$75	Build	Hassock	smaller than ottoman. See design drawings and swatch - pink velvet with cording, gold fringe and single button tuft.
$150	Purchase pots	two rolling potted palms	stock palm foliage & casters
$150	Build	rolling easel with guest list, floor plan, etc.	with pointer? Magnetized place cards? More detail necessary on use
$125	Alter Stock	pair of side chairs	Louis VX. Reupholster in pink velvet with French gimp

Figure 6.3 Preliminary Prop Budget. *The Rivals* preliminary prop budget following design meetings and collaborative negotiation on options of stock items to use vs. building or buying.

the best choices in spending the money wisely over the entire build and enabling the props to have an equity in completion. Props added at the last minute must be considerate of the money remaining to buy the item or the materials needed to build the item, as well as the labor available to complete the addition.

Another equally important area to budget, beyond the actual cost of building or buying materials, is the cost of personnel/time to do the work of researching, planning, finding, getting the materials, building, painting, sewing, etc. This second budget should accompany the materials budget, estimating the hours available and/or needed for the build. One labor hour is one person working for one hour.

Labor estimates serve two purposes beyond just informing administration of the anticipated time allowance needed. They allow the artisan to break the project down into specific process steps and determine the products needed to accomplish the work, honing a specific plan for building. Secondly, examination of the process allows discovery of other options available to save time or money. While a useful tool, this is often only done in the case where a number of large projects need to be juggled for priority in the build or where the properties director needs to negotiate with the designer regarding other options or alternative solutions.

Other considerations in the labor budget might include estimating additional outside labor to be hired in on a project larger than the full-time staff can accomplish or on a project requiring specialized skills. Just as in the materials budget, a contingency should be allotted to give some leeway in the estimate and allow for sick days, difficulties with a project, or changes coming from rehearsal that force a change in the design and build of a prop.

Creating a labor estimate and show budget requires a broad understanding of the processes and products required to fulfill the production of properties. Much like an expert cook who can throw together delicious dishes in a staggering array of ways with changing ingredients, an analysis of the prop list and all the possible ways it can be solved almost makes this a "best guess" scenario. While scenery may be able to budget labor based on the normal and usual process of building stock units of platforms or walls, it is a rare thing in props to duplicate a process is a similar fashion. With experience and hands-on practice, it is possible to make a reasonable expectation for labor to accomplish some specific task, such as to reupholster a chair or to build a table. But, of course, every estimate is impacted by the variables of the skill/experience of the person doing the work, the availability of materials, the difficulty of the final "look," and what other things also need to be accomplished in the same space by the same worker. Each build and each designer demand a level of specificity that makes highly detailed timelines from previous shows moot. However, it's helpful to make a "first pass" even if it's only to help in the prioritization of project work and assist the shopper in knowing *what* needs to be in the shop and *when* the multiple items are going to be required in the process. It helps in defining whether the workload is possible during any given build and assists the properties director in creating a calendar and deadline schedule, both vital to a calm, organized, and successful build period. It also gives a perspective on how to prioritize the decisions cropping up in every build. Some things can be negotiated . . . others cannot.

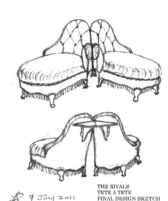

THE RIVALS
TETE A TETE
FINAL DESIGN SKETCH

The Rivals Tete a Tete <u>Step List</u>

<u>and Labor Estimate</u>

Carpentry & Framing work, total hours: 20

➢   Cut & frame standable deck sections – 4h
➢   Install legs – 2h
➢   Cut armature for backs and arms & install to decks – 3h
➢   Make full size pattern for bendy ply backs on armature – 1.5h
➢   Cut and install bendy ply backs and arms – 3h
➢   Lay out tufting pattern & mill holes for tufts 1.5h
➢   Pattern full size facing curves – 1h
➢   Cut Bendy ply facings and install – 2h
➢   Pattern table curve to back of tete pieces - .5h
➢   Cut and route table top & support brackets – 1.5h

Finish, total hours: 7

➢   Finish sand legs & table pieces – 1.5h
➢   Assemble table halves to their brackets - .5h
➢   Stain & seal legs & table pieces – 5h (dry time between coats)

Upholstery, total hours: 26

➢   Make buttons x 12+ spares – 1.5h
➢   Transfer tuft pattern to urethane foam inside back padding - .5
➢   Cut and mill foam for tufting – 2h
➢   Apply Batting and tuft upholstery- inside backs & arms in <u>real fabric</u> – 8h
➢   Paper pattern seat facing and backs, & cut foam pcs – 3h
➢   Apply urethane foam, batting and muslin upholstery to seats – 3h
➢   Apply batting & muslin upholstery to facings – 2h
➢   Cut seat, facing and back patterns in real fabric – 2h
➢   Stitch flanged cording to facing fabric – 1h
➢   Apply real fabric to seat, facings and backs – 3h

Trimmings, total hours: 5

➢   Apply French gimp to back seams - 1
➢   Apply fringe to bottom edges - 2
➢   Stitch on tassels under arm points - .5
➢   Measure, mark and pierce fabric on back for table attachment   points - .5
➢   Attach table halves - .5
➢   Photo for stock database - .5

PROJECT HOURS TOTAL = 58 h + 6 h contingency = 64 hours estimated X $15.00/ hour = $ 960.00

Figure 6.4   Labor Estimate. Preliminary labor estimation worksheet and step list for the Tête-à-tête project, *The Rivals*, Skylight Opera Theatre.

The preliminary material and labor budgets are shared with the production manager and designer for any negotiation in possible design changes required to bring the show in on budget and completed by opening. At this point, negotiation between departments might occur with another department either offering to pay for part of a project materials expense if the work is completed by the prop shop, by sharing labor resources inter-departmentally, or agreeing to take on the entire project as part of the other department's load. In extreme cases, it may mean the designer making substantive changes to the design or the production manager using contingency funding to help cover some of the budget overage or to hire in extra workers. Knowing the potential "costs" at the start of the build is essential to help everyone to make better choices.

SPREADSHEET TRACKING

As the build begins, all purchases are tracked in the **show budget spreadsheet**. Working closely with the shopper, the properties director keeps a worksheet that allows the expenses on a show to be monitored and anticipated. As purchases are completed and estimates become reality, the budget is juggled to allow choices to be made with an understanding of the overall impact each decision creates. For example, the designer may be given a choice between prioritizing one project over another. Buy the $40-per-yard fabric for the chairs and use a table in stock or buy $15-per-yard fabric for the chairs and buy a new table, or lumber to build a table matching the design better than the stock table. Each choice is correct depending on what resources are available and create the strongest image of support for the play. Each choice "costs" in a different way: one is more labor intensive and the other weighted toward purchased items. The management of financial resources and priorities and what is best for the design is a constant juggle and requires close collaboration between the shop and the design team.

The **budget spreadsheet** can be a simple accounting of what has been purchased, or one can divide it by project and identify purchases specific to each project. Some prop directors utilize a column integrated into the prop list itself to track expenses related to each prop, while others track it using a show-specific spreadsheet, making informational notation as necessary. The value of itemizing each item purchased against a specific prop allows the final cost expense to be determined at the end of the build. It's also handy to have a method of tracking what has been spent on specific projects to assist in future budget projections, but often the data entry of information is problematic and time consuming. Some properties directors have the prop shopper or the prop shop manager, if they have one, enter this information in the spreadsheet. As a management tool, a budget spreadsheet can be as complex as time allows, creating a searchable database for many purposes.

Most shows require only a simple spreadsheet that shows what has been purchased, from whom it was purchased, what it cost, when it was purchased, and how it was purchased. A simple description might be added to help jog the memory of what it was used for or to notate

	THREE SISTERS		SHOW BUDGET			
Date	Vendor	Item	Description	Cost	How	2,500
22.2.12	PayPal	Tray	antique hammered brass samovar tray	$50.00	Visa	$2,450
26.2.12	PayPal, ThinkFastToys	Top	spinning/humming	$13.04	Visa	$2,436.96
23.2.12	American Science and Surplus	Bottle, cork	cologne?	$0.48	PC	$2,436.48
1.3.12	World Market	Misc	Bunny, tumblers, frame, 18" toss pillow	$62.94	Visa	$2,373.54
3.3.12	PayPal,	Kerosene Lamp	Antique 1880 German Kerosene Oil Lamp	$76.19	Visa	
3.3.12	Michaels	Flowers	false flora	$14.79	Visa	
3.3.12	Menards	Stove materials	carved rubber, crib, canopy kit, 6" finishing	$23.93	Visa	$2,349.61
6.3.12	PayPal	Clock	Vintage Holland Electric mantle	$41.00	Visa	$2,308.61
11.3.12	Target	Bathroom	waste basket, pitcher and washbowl	$60.97	Visa	$2,247.64
13.3.12	Furniturebuy.com	Desk	Pulaski Accents Paulette Desk	$438.90	Visa	
13.3.12	Menards	for Heater	misc. parts	$52.51	Visa	$1,756.23
14.3.12	Home Depot	Lumber	for chairs, desk, and screen frames.	$223.93	Visa	$1,532.30
19.3.12	Furniturebuy.com	Desk	Pulaski Accents Desk – BACKORDERED	$438.90	REFUND	$1,971.20
21.3.12	Etsy; TomsBarn	Camera	Hand prop	$37.50	Visa	$1,933.70
22.3.12	Vogue Fabrics	Fabric	Grey, possible chaise slipcover	$35.91	Visa	$1,897.79
24.3.12	PayPal, Western Bid, Inc	Cup Holders	Russian Samovar glass holders	$62.98	Visa	$1,834.81
26.3.12	Bazaar	Fabric	for bench and chairs	$329.81	Visa	
26.3.12	Calico Corners	Fabric	for screen sides– act I	$107.93	Visa	
26.3.12	Jo-Ann Fabric	Fabric	for screen sides– act II	$58.54	Visa	$1,338.53
26.3.12	Paper Mart	Tissue paper	for leaves	$81.87	Visa	$1,256.66
7.3.12	PayPal, Overstock.com	Goblets	Wine glasses, champagne flutes; crystal	$124.63	Visa	$1,132.03
27.3.12	World Market	Glasses	shot type, for vodka	$41.85	Visa	$1,090.18
28.3.12	Utrecht	Various art.	Newsprint, B&J cleaner	$28.49	Visa	
28.3.12	Broadway Paper	Paper	Packaging (for tea box) and tissue/wrap	$58.13	Visa	$1,003.56
29.3.23	World Market	Bottles, glasses	For perfume/cologne, for vodka	$21.67	Visa	
29.3.23	TJ Maxx	Home items	Kitchen item, stationary, domestics	$29.54	Visa	
29.3.23	Jo-Ann Fabric	Trimp	For footstool, JC Penny chairs, etc	$75.28	Visa	$877.07
31.3.12	Elliot Ace Hardware	Various	cabinet lock, epoxy, barge cement, glaze,	$87.42	Visa	$789.65
2.4.12	Jo-Ann Fabric	Stencils	For screen painting	$114.91	Visa	
2.4.12	Jo-Ann Fabric	Toweling	For bedroom	$41.68	Visa	$633.06
4.4.12	Chattel Changers	Kitchen	adornments	$50.68	Visa	
4.4.12	Menards	Hardware	glides, hinges	$18.25	PC	$564.13
5.4.12	Hahn Ace Hardware	Various	Lamp supplies, tape, water putty	$38.43	Visa	
5.4.12	The Paint Shop	Paint	faux wood	$32.35	Visa	$493.35
9.4.12	Jo-Ann Fabric	Trims	ribbon, gimp	$19.16	Visa	$474.19
10.4.12	Home Depot	Hardware	hinges, corner braces, felt pad	$31.50	Visa	$442.69
12.4.12	Jo-Ann Fabric	Fabric	for x-backed chairs	$43.33	Visa	
12.4.12	Target	Various	candy', tape, crayons	$27.47	Visa	$371.89
13.4.12	Precious Ceramics	Clocks	cast and fired	$96.00	PC	$275.89
14.4.12	Menards	Liquid nails	stove "iron" attachment	$29.56	Visa	$246.33
18.4.12	Menards	Cake supplies	Silicone caulk, power grab	$23.16	Visa	
18.4.12	Walmart	Glasses	for samovar cup holders	$24.67	Visa	$198.50
19.4.12	Utrecht	Paint	for screens	29.64	Visa	$168.86
20.4.12	Winkie's	Misc.	Wrapping paper	13.66	Visa	
20.4.12	Winkie's	cardboard	for screens	6.33	Visa	$148.87
24.4.12	FleetFarm	Lamp	chimney for kerosene lamp	5.06	Visa	$143.81
25.4.12	Jo-Ann Fabric	Pen	Gold leaf pen for screens	7.14	Visa	$136.67
29.4.12	Pick'n'Save	Cs	olives, peanuts, instant tea, bread	34.95	Visa	$101.72
29.4.12	PayPal, Overstock.com	glasses	backups	52.50	Visa	$49.22
				FINAL:		**$49.22**

Figure 6.5 Spreadsheet. Show budget tracking of all purchases made for the prop work on the show. Note it is "search-able" by any of the headers, allowing information to be found quickly and for an overview to be seen of the decisions made as the show progressed. Courtesy of Meredith L. Roat, properties master, UW-Milwaukee theatre.

a specific amount or other potentially important information. This is particularly helpful when, in the future, it's necessary to track down where something was purchased because it's needed again and all that can be remembered is it was acquired for a particular show. Go to the budget, scroll down through the items purchased, and the information is there—job done!

Setting up a standard spreadsheet and working with the shopper to be sure all invoices and receipts are entered on a timely basis keeps the properties director current on what has been spent and allows decisions on anticipated buying to be relevant to the remaining budget.

It is helpful to track *how* supplies were purchased, especially in the event items need to be returned or if a problem occurs with the item. Most theatres use a credit card for the majority of their purchases, and the credit card companies will assist with problems when items are purchased using their credit card. Additionally, the credit cards can be "coded" specific to a shop and used for all purchases in that area. Some shops have multiple cards allowing each card to be specific to a budget line such as show budget, overhead, vehicle, etc., or to allow more than one person to be shopping. Some theatres still work with purchase orders or have accounts set up with particular vendors. Lastly, cash transactions are utilized in some instances.

If using **petty cash**, it is crucial all receipts are safeguarded until recorded and submitted for reimbursement; otherwise, you're just out the money. Most theatres use a standard reporting form to itemize purchases made with petty cash, and the receipts are submitted along with an accounting of what budget to charge against. In some organizations, the prop shop is advanced a set amount of petty cash at the start of the season to accommodate purchases requiring the use of cash, such as flea markets, individuals, or small businesses when either the vendor is unable to accept a credit card or the amount of the purchase is too small. By submitting receipts, the petty cash advance is "replenished" as the season progresses and the advance is turned in at season's end by either reimbursing the amount as cash or as a combination of cash and receipts.

KINDS OF BUDGETS

In addition to the show budget, the properties director often has several other budget lines to manage. Size of organization and kind of administrative structure will determine who controls what budget and how they are reported.

The **overhead** budget (sometimes called **supplies** or **shop perishables** budget) is used to purchase bulk supplies for an *entire season* of shows. This allows better pricing on materials and keeps the shop supplied so work is not dependent on the arrival of materials purchased on an "as needed" basis. Items purchased on the overhead budget may include: muslin, foam rubber, upholstery batting, sewing sundries, staples, sandpaper, hardware (nuts, bolts, nails, angle irons, pop rivets, casters, etc.), brown paper for layout, glues, white and black paint, spray paints, tints, brushes, sealers, latex gloves, dust masks, hearing protection, office supplies, etc.

The overhead budget purchases those consumable items used in the building of props over the entire season and cannot be easily attributed to a single show.

A **tool and shop maintenance** budget is utilized to buy new tools or to fix/replace broken tools. This budget purchases those items used over *multiple seasons* and builds. Items purchased on this type of budget often include ladders, rolling carts, storage units, computers, software upgrades, new tools, etc.

Some organizations keep this budget at the production management level or even higher administratively in a "facilities" budget, viewing these expenses as a capital improvement. In that case, the properties director must work to ensure administration understands the importance of providing funding for replacement and maintenance of shop tools as an immediate need while planning for future improvements and anticipated larger item replacements. Depending on the accessibility and openness of the relationship between production and administration (usually a reflection of the size of the organization), this structure of control over the budget and how it gets spent may work as easily as having a designated prop code within the facilities tool maintenance budget.

Some development departments undertake specific fundraising events to support the renovation of production spaces and the upgrading of equipment or seek out donors with a special interest in the production side of theatre to underwrite the purchase of a special tool outside usual budget considerations. Similarly, the marketing department will sometimes offer show tickets or advertising in the program in exchange for materials and services supporting production work. Getting the folks in these offices to understand and appreciate how their promotion of the production areas generally benefits the bottom line will open the door to all sorts of ways to support the theatre and the shops.

Most regional theatres have the commitment of the theatre administration, backed by the marketing and development offices, to budget for large ticket items and shop renovations at the "facilities" level, balanced with a tool and maintenance "seasonal" budget managed by the properties director in order to keep tools maintained for safe operation and to replace small ticket items on an as-needed basis.

Some organizations have a single budget line for both overhead and tool/shop maintenance. It is handy to have the budgets split, even if only internally, to enable the properties director to see what is used in show production versus the overall production costs for tools and shop maintenance. This understanding is especially helpful when working with estimating budgets in collaboration with the production manager. It is important to track how the overhead budget is spent since a single show can consume more than its fair share of the supplies bought to cover the season. Understanding the support the overhead budget can give to a particular show might illuminate budget planning for upcoming seasons with similar shows. Higher budget adjustments should be made to compensate for the additional expenses the overhead budget covered.

Some theatres may require the properties director to manage other budgets for expenses ancillary to the production process. These might be part of a larger facilities budget held at the administrative level with special coding for each area to utilize, or a specific amount might be budgeted to each area with management granted to the area head.

The **vehicle/travel** budget often covers the maintenance of a company vehicle, personal reimbursement of mileage when a member of the prop shop uses their own car for business such as prop shopping or moving items from prop storage to the theatre, expenses for rental vehicles, gas and tolls, and/or parking expenses. Some organizations use this budget to cover travel for the properties staff when attending conferences or when it is necessary for a properties staff member to travel to another city when working on a co-production or for design meetings.

A prop **storage** budget may account for any expenses associated with where the props are stored, including monthly rental fees, heating or cooling, purchasing of carts and moving equipment, and any space maintenance issues. This budget might also be just a smaller budget to cover things like light bulbs, cleaning supplies, and moving equipment and materials (e.g., boxes, moving pads, carts) and the actual rental or facility upkeep is covered at the administrative level. It is tracked separately from the overhead or shop tools/maintenance budget in order to track expenses related specifically to the props storage areas. Those organizations renting out their prop stock or selling their stock also benefit from having a separate budget line tracking the *income* so it can be turned in to the theatre or used for a special project. Some theatre companies simply put the money into their overhead or maintenance budgets, indicating it as an income line item. In many cases, prop rental income goes directly to the theatre's general bottom line in the general ledger. For the prop director, use of a tracking spreadsheet for prop rental income is highly useful, as is detailed record keeping of actual costs related to maintaining a prop stock. This documentation is the best tool to use in negotiating with management on how prop rental income is allocated and can often justify significant improvements to stock resources when management is on board with safeguarding stock assets to defray future prop production expenses. Purchase of new storage racks and materials handling equipment or labor to maintain frequently used rental items can be offset by this rental income line.

Another area usually maintained by upper theatre administration (i.e., managing director or production manager) is **personnel** hiring, even when it is an over-hire situation, including hiring, payment, taxes, and withholding. The prop shop, however, will need to track hours and time used from their allotted budget of money. Those prop shops utilizing over-hire personnel may have a variety of folks hired as specialty artists or to assist when a load-in or strike requires extra hands. Depending on skill level and how long the person has worked at the theatre, pay will vary. Determining who is hired and how much they are paid is often left to the discretion of the properties director. The properties director contacts the potential over-hire artisan and then processes time sheets or a weekly reporting of hours to administration, allowing an accurate tracking of people hired, and money remaining in the over-hire budget. As with any budget, the properties director should occasionally confirm the accuracy of those figures to insure the shop figures are in agreement with administration and to alert upper management if a deficit seems likely.

BOOKKEEPING AND REPORTING

The level of bookkeeping and reporting often is reflective of the size of the organization and the level of accountability to the various administrative units over the production area. While some theatres view this as administrative oversight and control, other organizations prefer to simply assign a lump sum and allow the prop director to manage the budget for the season, reporting in as necessary or on a set schedule.

Generally, show budgets are reported to the production manager, while the other budgets reflecting entire seasonal expenditures are reported to either the production manager or the managing director. The properties director may get reports from central bookkeeping of the theatre to justify accounts on a monthly or seasonal basis. Some organizations use online reporting systems to track all purchasing, which allows the production manager to have an up-to-the-minute view of where the budget is on any given show or account. Shared budget spreadsheets on a central server are a handy way of keeping transparent financial records for department heads and production director alike, and eliminate time spent communicating

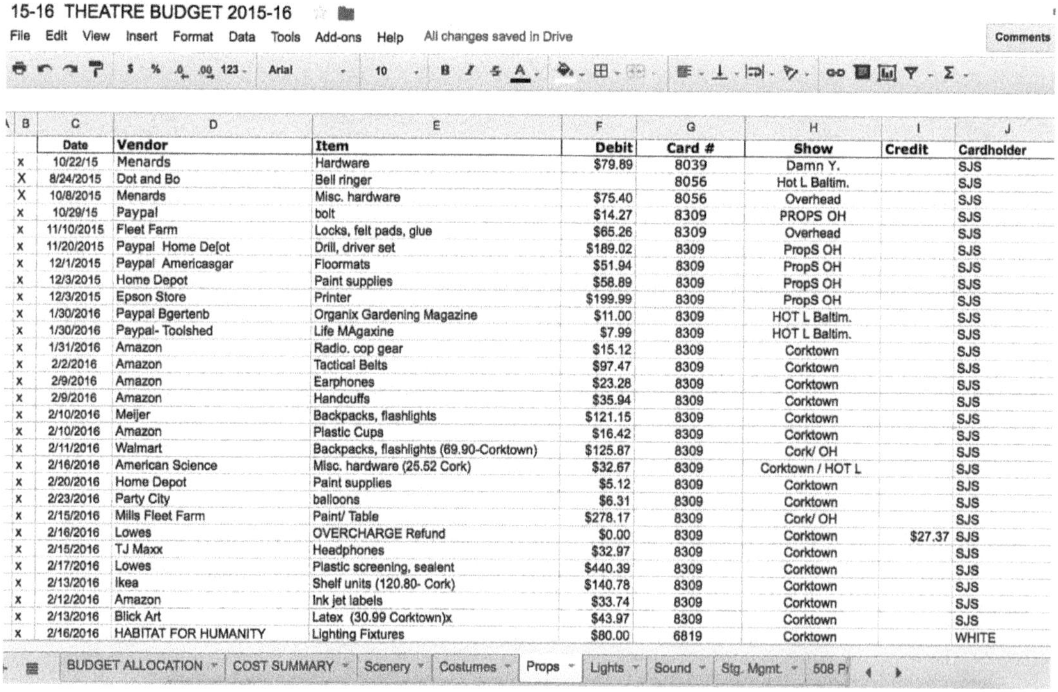

B	Date	Vendor	Item	Debit	Card #	Show	Credit	Cardholder
x	10/22/15	Menards	Hardware	$79.89	8039	Damn Y.		SJS
X	8/24/2015	Dot and Bo	Bell ringer		8056	Hot L Baltim.		SJS
X	10/8/2015	Menards	Misc. hardware	$75.40	8056	Overhead		SJS
x	10/29/15	Paypal	bolt	$14.27	8309	PROPS OH		SJS
x	11/10/2015	Fleet Farm	Locks, felt pads, glue	$65.26	8309	Overhead		SJS
x	11/20/2015	Paypal Home De[ot	Drill, driver set	$189.02	8309	PropS OH		SJS
x	12/1/2015	Paypal Americasgar	Floormats	$51.94	8309	PropS OH		SJS
x	12/3/2015	Home Depot	Paint supplies	$58.89	8309	PropS OH		SJS
x	12/3/2015	Epson Store	Printer	$199.99	8309	PropS OH		SJS
x	1/30/2016	Paypal Bgertenb	Organix Gardening Magazine	$11.00	8309	HOT L Baltim.		SJS
x	1/30/2016	Paypal- Toolshed	Life MAgaxine	$7.99	8309	HOT L Baltim.		SJS
x	1/31/2016	Amazon	Radio. cop gear	$15.12	8309	Corktown		SJS
x	2/2/2016	Amazon	Tactical Belts	$97.47	8309	Corktown		SJS
x	2/9/2016	Amazon	Earphones	$23.28	8309	Corktown		SJS
x	2/9/2016	Amazon	Handcuffs	$35.94	8309	Corktown		SJS
x	2/10/2016	Meijer	Backpacks, flashlights	$121.15	8309	Corktown		SJS
x	2/10/2016	Amazon	Plastic Cups	$16.42	8309	Corktown		SJS
x	2/11/2016	Walmart	Backpacks, flashlights (69.90-Corktown)	$125.87	8309	Cork/ OH		SJS
x	2/16/2016	American Science	Misc. hardware (25.52 Cork)	$32.67	8309	Corktown / HOT L		SJS
x	2/20/2016	Home Depot	Paint supplies	$5.12	8309	Corktown		SJS
x	2/23/2016	Party City	balloons	$6.31	8309	Corktown		SJS
x	2/15/2016	Mills Fleet Farm	Paint/ Table	$278.17	8309	Cork/ OH		SJS
x	2/16/2016	Lowes	OVERCHARGE Refund	$0.00	8309	Corktown	$27.37	SJS
x	2/15/2016	TJ Maxx	Headphones	$32.97	8309	Corktown		SJS
x	2/17/2016	Lowes	Plastic screening, sealent	$440.39	8309	Corktown		SJS
x	2/13/2016	Ikea	Shelf units (120.80- Cork)	$140.78	8309	Corktown		SJS
x	2/12/2016	Amazon	Ink jet labels	$33.74	8309	Corktown		SJS
x	2/13/2016	Blick Art	Latex (30.99 Corktown)x	$43.97	8309	Corktown		SJS
x	2/16/2016	HABITAT FOR HUMANITY	Lighting Fixtures	$80.00	6819	Corktown		WHITE

Figure 6.6 Online Spreadsheet Tracking. Some organizations have active online reporting so administration can have access to the spending progress on a show and be able to sort out any coding or funding stream issues. This example has bottom tabs to move between the overall seasonal cost summary page to specific production areas. Individual areas track purchases, noting critical information in a searchable format to be able to pull out show-specific spending or other budget details.

routine numbers and budget status. Many spreadsheet programs exist for this sort of application, from basic stalwarts like Microsoft Excel, Apple Numbers, or Google Sheets to super-power accounting industry programs such as Sage.

In some cases, more than one accounting platform may be used within the same company—one in Production, another in the Finance Department. This can create a reconciliation headache between the two programs, and is at the very least a time-consuming process to justify figures regularly. A good basic accounting program shared throughout the company will enable users to link budget spreadsheets together for cross departmental ease of instant reconciliation. Pages can be password protected or view only, which gives added layers of security to those who need control over those particular budgeting workbooks, or those budgets holding sensitive information.

Entering the information in the prop shop budgets so the account is up-to-date can be part of the shopper's job or may fall under the responsibilities of the properties director. By using shared budgeting spreadsheets, data entry can be standardized and assigned to a variety of prop shop personnel to spread out the load, or allow staffers to take on certain projects from concept through final product, including the administrative aspects of the prop. Accurate reporting is critical, and those who manage and allot the company finances appreciate accurate and timely budget oversight. All things are possible with good communication from the prop director across all levels of the prop shop staff, from prop director up the chain to the production director, and back again.

* * *

When sound financial management is demonstrated in the prop shop, administration can trust the estimates and decisions made knowing the money is well spent to the benefit of the show and the theatre itself. The prop build can begin with an informed view of the known costs, allowing the inevitable changes to be managed efficiently for the on-time, on-budget goal of meeting the designer's vision. On to the build!

The Build Process

Once the prop list is updated and all the information from various sources compiled, the build in the prop shop can begin in earnest. The properties director, in close advisement and collaboration with the rest of the prop artisans, navigates the intricacies of how to complete each prop depending upon what is in stock, the availability of items in the community from other organizations or theatres, what is within the skill of the prop shop personnel to build, the advisability of altering stock pieces, the availability and expense of materials to build the props, the necessity of having the item in rehearsal quickly, and/or the expense of purchasing the item and getting it shipped and available in the time frame allowed. Every component of the decision-making process can and will change as the prop build progresses.

THE JUGGLE

Solving the variables of that decision opens up four options in analyzing a comprehensive prop list, regardless of whether it's set props, dressing, or a hand prop. Each prop may be completed in one or a combination (usually) of the following:

PULL   BORROW   BUY   BUILD

PULLING FROM STOCK

First, looking to see what is in the prop stock and can be pulled offers a fast and usually less expensive solution to finding the prop. Many theatres maintain a large inventory of items used recurrently in productions, and with slight modification most objects can be made specific to each show. Having a prop stock saves thousands of dollars in hand prop procurement alone and can still offer a variety of choices. Many items such as kitchen pots or pans, china, glassware, period magazines, ashtrays, garden ware, tablecloths, office equipment, and decorative objects can be used repeatedly on stage for a variety of projects even without alteration. Paper props like newspapers, magazines, or letters built for one show, when saved in stock, are a quick pull when dressing is needed for the next show. Stock picture frames can have new photos added. Greenery and floral arrangements can be rearranged and reused. Blankets, bed sheets, pillows, or other linens need only a quick washing and they're ready for the stage.

Frankly, as the seasons roll by, the ability to generate a deep stock of items available for reuse in future production of shows saves not only money and time but creates a diverse collection of items supporting whatever a designer might dream up as well as parts and pieces able to be combined into a plethora of objects. It's not just the common items of teapots, books, table lamps, or old phones—it's also Russian samovars, fake wedding cakes, taxidermy animal heads, mummy coffins, or even body parts!

Figure 7.1   Prop Storage. Glassware/kitchen hand prop storage for Actors Theatre of Louisville prop shop. Mark Walston, properties director.

Figure 7.2 Fake Body Part Storage. Alley Theatre prop shop storage area of body part castings from brains to bones and all parts in between. Karin Rabe Vance, properties director.

Having a stock of furniture is where the largest savings benefit the theatre. Storing and maintaining a furniture stock might seem costly, depending on the location of the stock, but it will save a theatre thousands of dollars in time and money over multiple seasons of use. Selecting furniture and reupholstering it or making slight modifications to the "look" allows the designer to make the choice specific to the show and saves having to build from "scratch" or buy new items. Owning certain classic silhouettes of furniture means they will be used repeatedly with a simple change of the fabric or frame color or by combining the items in different configurations to create a new look. Even if all the pieces cannot be pulled, often the savings offered by using some stock furniture allows investment in a specialty piece to complement existing stock pieces and enrich stock for future productions.

Analyzing the research information from the designer for shape, form, period detail, finish, etc. and using the research photos or descriptions to help identify stock pieces for consideration creates a collaborative dialogue about what possible pieces from stock might satisfy the look the designer desires. As possible options are selected and stock photos and critical information are sent, the winnowing process of selection becomes easier. As the rehearsal process moves forward and pieces get added, the ability to take the designer's previous selections as well as the initial research to extrapolate "the look" simplifies the process of selecting pieces from stock to fulfill the requested add.

Having a **computerized inventory** of furniture stock has become increasingly common as a management tool. Many designers are not in residence, and being able to post photos and

Figure 7.3 Prop Stock. Prop storage at Actors Theatre of Louisville. Mark Walston, properties director, ATL.

Here's some research for table legs and armchairs. They're from "Furniture Made in America 1875 - 1905", by Eileen and Richard Dubrow, Schffer Publishing Ltd., 1982.
Page 58: Side chair candidates: #5 in the bottom row is ornamental but rectilinear, with some ornamental interest; same idea for #2

Page 69: Table legs: Bottom row, center table- this is what I meant by chunky. Page 172: #176 Desk: another version of chunky legs.

   Page 53: #54; Fogg's armchair candidate: simple, rectilinear;

#55 below it: a cushy version of same but still rectilinear and eastlake-y.
Page 55: No. 9 and No. 3: These appear to have higher backs, which is also a possibility, as long as they don't obscure Todd (which unfortunately may not be possible anyway).

I hope these are helpful. I've sent Mark an email asking for a talk about the questions we came up with today. Hopefully, I'll her back from him soon and pass on the results to you. ~ Hugh

Figure 7.4 Designer Research and Comments. Scenic designer Hugh Landwehr formulates initial set prop information to give to the prop shop, helping them to visualize the style and proportion of furniture pieces for *Around the World in 80 Days* at the Alley Theatre.

Figure 7.5 Stock Design Choices. Options from the prop stock are selected based on the designer's research, including pieces to re-upholster or alter as well as table leg possibilities to use on a built piece. Karin Rabe Vance, properties director, Alley Theatre.

dimensions on a website for the designer to view stock pieces under consideration allows for quick communication of available pieces.

Using software to create an inventory with pictures of each piece of furniture along with information such as dimensions, upholstery, finish, physical condition, previous show use, time period, etc., allows for items to be easily "searched" in the database by the entry of any particular characteristic—such as "bench" and "wooden" to find all the various wooden benches in stock. Various file management platforms such as Filemaker Pro or Microsoft Access are available, but they are focused more toward managing a "business" inventory and tend to be clunky for the kind of information accessing, updating, and review of stock needed to manage a theatre's collection. The need for this kind of specialized inventory management tool is gaining traction within the software development industry, and a few programs—StageStock, for example—have been introduced. Some theatre companies keep their entire inventories online, while others prefer to select options and create a "cloud" Dropbox online for the designer to see the selected group.

Keeping the inventory updated and accurate is critical. As pieces are bought or stock items changed, updated photographs and information should be added to the computerized inventory. This is often assigned as part of one of the artisan's job responsibilities during strike.

A: 2' 7" x 1' 10", 2' 4" high

E: 3' 6", x 3'6", 2' 5" high

I: 2' diameter, 2' 3" high

M: 3' diameter, 2' 3" high

B: 2'1" x 1' 8", 2' 2" high

F: 3' diameter, 2' 5" high

J: 2'2: diameter, 2' 4" high

N: 1'8" diameter, 2' 2" high

C: 2'4" diameter, 2' 4" high

G: 2' 1"x 1' 6", 2' 4" high

K: 1' 8" diameter, 2'2" high

O: 2'6" x 1' 9", 2' 5" high

D: 1'11" diameter, 2' 4" high

H: 3' diameter, 2' 5" high

L: 2'6" diameter, 2'4" high

Figure 7.6 "Added" Table Options. When a set prop is added at the last minute, the properties director can save the day by reviewing the period, style, scale, and finish on previous choices made by the designer, going into stock to find options matching the needs of the rehearsal request as well as the look of the show, communicating the options with relevant sizing information, and emailing the designer to make the final selection. Karin Rabe Vance, properties director, Alley Theatre.

Figure 7.7 Prop Online Inventory. Online inventories allow designers to view stock items and select possible pieces for use in the design, to see size, condition, upholstery, or finish available, and to communicate precisely with the properties director about "look" even if not using any specific piece in the inventory. Jim Guy, properties director, Milwaukee Repertory Theater.

The digital inventory for set props and large dressing pieces is useful for selection and easy viewing, especially when the storage site is away from the main theatre space or the production studio. Having a bar-scan or method of identification by number or label allows the actual pulling and transportation of the pieces to be delegated with the hand-off of a list of the items requested or needed.

Creating and maintaining a similar inventory of hand props would be helpful but impractical. There are literally thousands of hand props in most companies' storage and maintaining that filing would be a full-time job alone. Managing the hand prop stock and keeping it organized is an intensive and time-consuming project without even attempting to track all the changes, adds, and breakage coming with producing a season. Simply going to prop storage and selecting what will work best or collecting several options for the designer to choose from is a quick and easy solution to start the process. It's kind of fun to just walk the aisles and "shop" for what is in stock. Sometimes the most amazing possibilities present themselves, or spur the imagination to improvise.

When pulling, it is important to keep an open mind about what discoveries might occur as props are sorted, chosen, and set aside. Often times it is possible to discover something that

Figure 7.8 Hang Tag System. Aisles are lettered and individual storage bays are numbered allowing a system of finding and storing props in the large warehouse. Hanging files replicate the online page for each item, giving specific information about each prop without having to pull it out to do measuring or check condition when onsite. Mark Walston, properties director, Actor's Theatre of Louisville.

might be easily modified or utilized as part of a built piece. Fabric sewn as curtains for a previous show can be modified into a bedspread or dyed a different color to work in the present show. A wooden box can be covered in fabric and with leather straps added would transform into a period trunk. Almost anything can become a lamp. A letter handwritten for one show can become a proclamation with the addition of a gold seal and some ribbon. Look with fresh eyes and think about the possibilities of what can be done, how it can be altered, the "what if" of pulling an item and using it in a different way.

Pulling dressing is an adventure into character analysis. Think *who* is this person? What are their hobbies? What kind of books would they read? Do they garden or enjoy cooking? Where have they traveled? How old are they? What is their religious affiliation? What is their favorite sports team/artist/recording artist? Answering these questions can help define what items to select for shelf decoration, to hang on the walls, to fill the niches and spaces around the set needing prop "fill." When pulling dressing, it's common practice to grab a wide variety of items for final selection on set dress day. Remember to include different shapes, colors, textures, and patterns unless the design is a specific palette or look. *Variety creates interest.*

Once the pull is completed, items are moved to the prop shop for alteration or finishing. This may include additional reinforcement to support the specific action of the production, a change in upholstery to fit into the color scheme, or a simple clean and polish to restore the original luster of the finish. In more drastic cases, a stock piece may be significantly altered to create a different silhouette, to lower the back or extend the length of a piece of furniture, or may be disassembled to use parts to create an entirely new piece. This choice usually lies with the properties director, working in collaboration with the artisans and the designer to prioritize what can be done on the budget allowed, within the limitations of talent and time.

Any alteration or modification of stock items invariably requires some materials to be found or purchased, whether it's wood, upholstery supplies, paint, trim, or craft supplies. The artisan/s involved in completing the project must determine what is needed and communicate the quantity to the properties director. Working with the shopper/buyer to determine pricing and availability within the budget limits, the material list is prioritized and becomes part of the "buy" list. In smaller shops, the bulk of this process may fall to the prop director.

BORROW

Those theatres fortunate enough to have other organizations within a short driving distance often have a relationship allowing the sharing of stock items between their companies. Storage space is always critical and while having a stock available is very handy, the necessity of maintaining stock is always limited by the availability and accessibility of the space it is stored in. Establishing and maintaining a mutually beneficial loan agreement allows theatres to use what is available at other companies and not need to buy/store the same items.

Some *non-theatre* organizations such as furniture or "antique" stores are willing to lend out items from their floor stock for credit in the program or for a small rental fee. Borrowing an item from an individual is also a possibility; finding the person who has a personal collection of whatever specific item is needed is like finding a gold mine. In all cases, those relationships must be guarded with great care and stewardship. It only takes one instance of a damaged or lost item to sever a relationship with an individual or organization, so extraordinary attentiveness and consideration must be given to anything borrowed.

Having insurance coverage for *every* borrowed item is mandatory. Many organizations have some kind of insurance policy covering items lost, stolen, or broken, but many items being borrowed fall under the deductible and, in the case where something gets damaged or lost or stolen, then the full expense must be covered. Hopefully the loss would be covered under a "contingency" budget, but it might come out of the props budget and can be a costly unanticipated expense. All too often, theatres seem willing to take the risk for those items falling under their insurance deductible, believing it is "cheaper". Since many deductibles are in the $500 or even $1,000 range, many borrowed props would not have a viable claim against the insurance policy anyway since they cost less than that to replace or repair. But when a loss occurs, the full impact of the replacement of repair will then have to be borne by the theatre company and, most often, the prop budget itself. Ouch!

Determining if an item should be borrowed must always be measured against the potential for it to be damaged. Using a borrowed item onstage requires notification to stage management and anyone who handles the item of its value so all appropriate precaution can be exercised. It is especially important to inform the production manager in cases where borrowed items are under a greater risk of being damaged. This allows anticipation of what could be an additional expense and acceptance of the potential for budget "overrun." This mentality often justifies the expense of *not* borrowing an item but finding a different solution, especially when the risk is high that the item might be damaged. Many organizations are reluctant to loan out props if they know they will be shifted or used in a way that potentially endangers them. If there is a possibility for damage, it's probably better *not* to borrow an item rather than risk losing a borrowing source because an item was damaged in the show.

For items at low risk and appropriate for borrowing, a standard **borrowing form** is often used to help document ownership and value as well as the expectations of how the object will be used, stored, cared for, and returned safely during the length of its use. The form may also call out special thanks requirements and/or program or lobby credit.

This is especially important for those items *qualifying for coverage* under the theatre's insurance policy, as most insurers require some kind of documentation for reimbursement. Please check with the theatre's risk management person for details on insurance coverage and appropriate policy requirements. Check *before* bringing a borrowed item into the building and certainly before putting it on stage or into rehearsal.

Any borrowed items should be cared for as if they were the theatre's own property, or better. When borrowing furniture, be sure to arrive on time and in an appropriate vehicle, complete with moving dollies and moving pads to protect items while in transit. If borrowing glass items or fragile pieces, come prepared with appropriate boxes and packing materials.

All items should be safely stored, maintained, and cared for with the highest regard. Stage management and the run crew should be given all appropriate information on how to handle the borrowed prop and informed of any special considerations for its safe-keeping or use. At strike, if any alterations were done (with the owner's permission), they should be restored to the original basis before returning unless explicit permission not to do so has been given. Any fabric items should be dry-cleaned or washed. Furniture should be wiped down, vacuumed, or cleaned as needed. Hand props should be properly cleaned and

Theatre Prop Borrowing Form

LOANED TO:_____ CONTACT:_____

ADDRESS:_____

PHONE: (_____)_____   DATE PICKED UP:____/____/____

PRODUCTION:_____   TO BE RETURNED:____/____/____

The Theatre Properties Department is loaning the following items for use in your production/ workshop/ class as listed above. You personally, and for your organization (when applicable), by accepting these items and signing this loan form, agree to the following conditions:

1. Appointments must be made with the Props Master to look thru props storage, for PICK-UP and RETURN of props. If an appointment is missed by more than 15 minutes, it must be rescheduled at the discretion of the prop shop.
2. All items will be kept in a safe and secure location at all times.
3. All items will be returned in the same condition as they left prop storage, excluding **normal** wear and tear.
4. If modifications are desired, permission must be obtained from the Properties Manager in advance. Any "modifications" made without prior permission will be viewed as damage to the specific item, and repair charges will be accessed.
5. All repairs to damaged items must be completed by the Theatre prop shop (based on an hourly fee plus materials) unless other arrangements are made with the Properties Manager in advance of any actual repairs being started. REPEAT: Repairs done without permission will be considered "damage".
6. The borrowing organization is responsible for the stated value of any item that is lost, stolen, or damaged beyond reasonable repairs. Damaged items remain the property of Theatre even when total replacement cost is accessed.
7. The Theatre Properties Manager must be notified A.S.A.P. after any item is damaged. Please do not wait until the end of your rental to let us know.
8. All items are to be returned on or before the date specified on this form. Props must be checked in by the Properties Manager at the time of their return. REPEAT: If an appointment is missed by more than 15 minutes, it must be rescheduled at the discretion of the prop shop.
9. Renter is responsible for all shipping fees, moving and pick up arrangements. Items must be insured for stated value if returned by shipment

CONTACT _____

Returned: Donation due: [   ]

Notes: paid: [   ]

Item	Description	Value	Fee
Checks should be made out to: THEATRE COMPANY		TOTAL DUE:	

Figure 7.9 Borrowing Form. Creating a borrowing form to document all information and to have a written policy as part of the form allows everyone involved to understand desired protocol for the process. Completing the information allows for accurate tracking of valuable stock items out on loan.

wrapped in storage boxes for transportation and delivery. It is always wise to call ahead and arrange for prop return to guarantee that the props can be handed off with a minimum of inconvenience for all involved.

In the worst case, despite all precautions and planning, when something has been stolen, broken, or damaged, notify the production manager or risk management office so the insurance coverage process can begin. This may mean repair to the item or complete replacement. When replacement is impossible, then full reimbursement will need to be made to the owner for the cost of the borrowed item. Equally important is notification of the original owner who lent the items to explain what happened, the extent of the damage, and what is being done to rectify the situation. *Never* wait until you are returning a borrowed item to tell the person who lent it that something happened to it. Nothing will ruin a relationship faster than returning damaged items. Be honest. Apologize. Tell them how the problem will be solved and how the prop is going to be repaired or replaced.

BUY

Shopping is a necessary part of *every* build. Within every good prop person is a shopper just waiting to discover an incredible bargain! Best of all, it's using someone else's money!!! Sometimes it might be the procurement of materials to modify stock items or various components needed to assemble into a prop piece, like furniture legs to alter a stock table. It might be buying specific items particular to the production requiring no or very little modification, such as a game or specific book. Some things are a quick trip to the nearest lumberyard for lumber and glue while other items require the shopper/buyer to spend days tracking down a requested item with a particular look or specific function, such as a pearl-inlaid accordion from the 1950s. It also means buying perishable and consumable products, usually food or paper products, during the show run as well as supporting the shop's ongoing maintenance needs for getting tools in for repair or picking up replacement parts or supplies.

Creating the shopping list goes beyond noting specific props to be purchased to identifying parts and pieces for items being built or restored. Working from the designer's drawings for built items, a listing of materials and supplies can be generated from the dimensional lumber for construction down to hardware required to facilitate movement or handling such as hinges, castors, handles, etc. Creating a shopping list of needed materials starts with the artisan making a plan for construction, communicating needed materials/supplies to the shopper, and getting the product in the shop quickly so construction can begin. The prop shopper should utilize the artisan most closely connected with the build and finishing to generate the listing of what needs to be purchased, the quantity needed, and any other information impacting selection, and confirm all lists and plans with the prop director before heading out on errands. Hopefully much of this analysis was done at the budgeting stage and things can move directly to the purchasing stage.

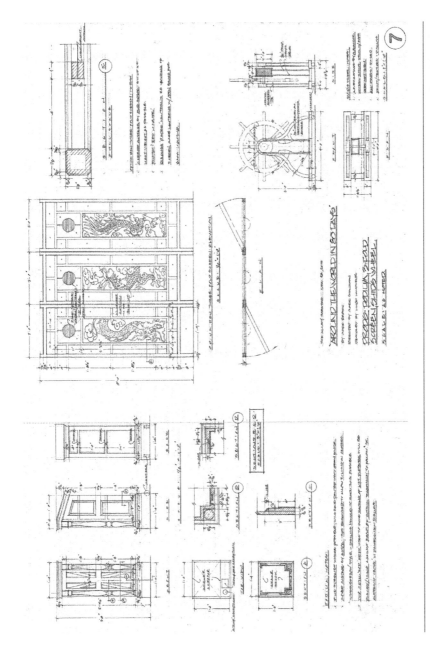

Figure 7.10 Designer Drawing. Prop plate of set props to be built for *Around the World in 80 Days* at the Alley Theatre. The wide variety of materials (lumber, paint, fabric, hinges, rope, stain, etc.) needed, as demonstrated in this plate of drawings, shows the challenge given to the shopper and the need to prioritize what should be purchased first, supporting the artisan's process of building, and allowing finishing products to filter in at a later point for completion. Hugh Landwehr, scenic designer.

Analyzing renderings for color and detail will also generate clues to fabric choices, paint colors, decorative flourishes, or other finish details. For some built items, having options for experimentation might be desired, and the necessity of purchasing several different possible solutions, such as different weight of muslin, different castors, or a different hinge mechanism, allows for some flexibility in the problem-solving process of the build. Some items may need to be returned if not utilized, but often pieces purchased for one show will simply go into stock for use on a future project.

Figure 7.11 Designer Rendering. Having some samples of various weights of muslin or similar fabric to do experimentation of paint treatment for the screen inserts would allow for final selection based on translucency and durability, since the screen must be back-lit for the desired lighting effect but also moved onstage and set up by only one actor. Hugh Landwehr, scenic designer for *Around the World in 80 Days*, Alley Theatre.

In the instance of fabric selection, getting a swatch of the fabric, taking a photo of the fabric bolt to show "repeat" or other detail, noting the cost per yard and estimating how much yardage is available is only the first shopping stop. Returning to purchase the fabric can only happen *after* the designer picks the fabric in consultation with the props director, who will be juggling budget as well as many other considerations. Providing a variety of options/ swatches/price ranges allows a "best choice" to happen, but this may involve more than one trip, so patience is a virtue in the prop shopper.

On any production build, local resources play a part; having a deep knowledge of vendors in the immediate driving area and a rolodex of sources to call eases the search. But now the prop shopper's marketplace has grown far beyond what is available locally with global reach to distant countries, souks, arcades, regional artisans, and specialized shops previously unavailable or unknown. Utilization of the **internet** for specialty shopping sites online, coupled with express delivery services, has dramatically changed the way the prop shop functions and increases the ease of finding things. The internet makes shopping convenient and opens the entire world as the market for procuring items. With easy "search" links, the ability to find even the most absurd request becomes increasingly possible.

Shopping on the internet requires a few simple security rules to safeguard the credit card and other personal information. Many sites require the buyer to register and set a password while also requesting delivery and credit card information. It's best to create a corporate identity and password so purchasing is separate from any personal shopping/identities. Be sure to write down registration identities and passwords in a secure place so accessing the site in the future is easy. Online web sites may be the portal for a large company that also has retail sites, but it is more commonly a shop with no local footprint. It's not possible to simply drive there and see the product; one must trust the description and photos available online. Some sites offer reviews or ratings from previous purchasers and it's helpful to look those over, but know some history of "fake" reviews and skewed ratings has been reported, so trust them only as far as comfortable. A healthy grain of salt goes a long way toward making good online purchasing decisions. If a deal seems too good to be true, be wary!

Even for companies with a physical footprint, the selection offered online may be larger than what they carry locally, so checking online can open more choices as well. Most of these companies offer free shipping to the local store for pickup there. Shopping online saves time as well as the expense of driving to the store, but shipping costs can add up quickly. Buying into a service such as Amazon Prime, which gives unlimited free two-day shipping on many eligible items, is a bonus. Shopping online at trusted sites with written return policies and a proven shipping department makes the process simple and safe. Always check to confirm the company's return policy. Some companies allow returns to a store even when the items were bought online, saving return shipping and handling fees. Newer online companies, while unknown and perhaps lacking a retail store, can be equally safe, but it's best to review their buying policies and be sure a full refund is possible if the merchandise is unacceptable. Many sites have contact information with a phone number allowing a way to contact the seller and talk to someone, or offer a "live chat" feature on their website so information can be confirmed prior to purchase.

Be aware of *where* the site is located and delivers from when placing orders. With the internet, the entire world is open for business but placing an order in a foreign country often results in a long shipping delay, customs expenses, and difficulty should a return be necessary. With enough time allotted however, delightful purchases are available from anywhere on the globe, and finding just the right oriental statue, a tea set from Ireland or a newspaper from Russia to help with set dressing is the extra step bringing a level of completeness to the design. Take the time to know where the item will be sent from and look for an estimated delivery date before hitting the "purchase" button.

A number of "re-sale" and estate sales sites are available online, allowing a kind of online flea market exchange direct from one person to another. eBay and Etsy are common sites for this kind of shopping. Everything But The House (EBTH) is a great example of the auction style online business format, where deals can turn up on a staggering array of estate goods for widely varying prices depending on who the competing bidders might be on any given day. Review the customer information to get some handle on the person's history of reliable selling, delivery costs, and specific information about the item. Many people on these sites offer a way to ask questions about the items prior to the sale or to negotiate the price. But as in all things, let the buyer beware.

When placing an order online, be sure to review all the information, checking for amount, color, size, shipping information, billing information, etc. Photos can be misleading, so really take the time to understand the written description and product information. Once certain it matches what is needed, only then proceed with the sale. Most sites will confirm the entire order before asking for a final buy button to be pushed, completing the sale. Print off or save to a folder the receipt and any information about anticipated delivery dates or seller contact information. Most online sites operate using order codes that allow an update on shipping or where the order is in process by going to the website and typing in the code. Once the item has been shipped, many companies will send an email with a tracking number to follow the shipment. This is especially helpful if working against a deadline and the package doesn't arrive in a timely fashion. Some shops utilize a **purchase log** to track what was bought, shipping information, registration information, etc. As items are selected and purchased, the shopper enters the information and can even set up alerts in the calendar when a package is overdue to allow a connected response to what is arriving and when.

Before entering credit card information, confirm the site is a registered secure site. Often these sites have a "lock" image in the corner as well as language confirming the site has appropriate protocols to keep credit card information safe from hackers or others who may want to access delivery or billing information. While most credit card companies offer fraud alerts and protective coverage in case credit card information gets stolen, it is the responsibility of the credit card holder to monitor activity on the card by scanning statements for unauthorized purchases and alerting the company when something is wrong. Policies vary

ORDERED - SHIPPING / TRACKING LIST   PROP SHOP 2016-2017

Columns may be sorted to find specific date, or to group all items from one source, or by how being shipped, etc.   Click on arrow to sort

DATE ORDERED	ITEM	ORDERED FROM	DUE DATE	NOTES
3/7/17	Paracord	Paypal	3/11/17	USPS, arrived 3/10
3/11/17	Corks	Northern Brew	3/16/17	UPS - Backordered
3/11/17	Grommets	Upholstery supply	3/13/17	FED X - arrived
3/12/17	Rhinestones	Amazon	4/8/17	Backordered. Will ship on first of month.
3/12/17	Checkers	Paypal	3/16/17	USPS - Arrived 3/15
4/1/17	Soynuts	Amazon	4/10/17	In route
4/1/17	NY cups and ink	Amazon	4/6/17	Preparing to ship
4/3/17	Checkers	Patchplugs	4/8/17	Preparing to ship

Figure 7.12 Purchase Log. As items are selected and purchased, the shopper enters the information and can even set up alerts in a calendar program for when a package is overdue, which allows a connected response to what is arriving and when. Keeping emails with order numbers and tracking numbers in a folder allows quick access for confirmation.

for cardholder liability, so check out the fine print in those agreements to know specific card exposure.

Before the internet, having a large resource file was critical. The properties director, or in larger shops, the shopper artisan, was known for the depth of the card file filled with resources, knowing where to find any item or having a person in the community known to the shopper/buyer who can connect to the needed item. Even today, maintaining a long list of resources both locally and via the internet is critical. It's always helpful to "know somebody who knows somebody" when trying to solve a particular prop problem. And as is often the case in theatre, shows are repeated. Someone has done the show before or has solved this particular problem. Knowing whom to call can cut down on a lot of time-consuming research and development. For prop directors, the most direct route is to put the question out on prop building/production/theatre websites. If a member of **SPAM (Society of Properties Artisans/Managers)**, it is easy to email the question to the group, and within hours someone in the group (and often several, if not many) will reply with a solution. For more information on SPAM, please go to the webpage: http://propmasters.org.

A prop shopper quickly becomes familiar with the local resources available in the immediate shopping area. A quick online search for local resources can narrow down the leg work and good telephone communication skills can quickly determine what is available and worth pursuing. As purchasing relationships develop and the shopper's knowledge of where to buy and what is available grows, the ease of shopping for many supplies becomes easier. Knowing where to find things in the community is critical to successful shopping, and strong "people skills" are necessary to maintain relationships with the shops and companies the theatre frequents for supplies. Getting discounts or special pricing as a nonprofit organization can save hundreds of dollars over the season, and repeat customers are more likely to get these accommodations. These businesses are also often willing to "hold" an item while a designer is consulted based on previous positive business experiences.

Resale shops and consignment stores are good sources for set dressing and used furniture pieces ready to updated, reupholstered, painted, and styled for the stage. Do an online search using "consignment shops" for a listing. Many shops have an online inventory, allowing for easy viewing of available pieces, and a phone call can confirm pricing, sizes, or other information prior to driving out to look or purchase. Charity organizations such as RESTORE Habitat for Humanity, Salvation Army, Goodwill, or St. Vincent DePaul have stores chock full of pieces people have cast off and ready for updating. Search online under "thrift stores" for a local listing. These organizations rarely have an online inventory available, so going in person is often the only choice. Online sites like Facebook Marketplace or Craigslist have web presence in most metro areas and can be a fantastic and efficient way to search individual buyer offers, which occupy a similar niche to flea markets and garage sales. Communicate clearly in advance with the seller to ensure firm price and availability of a receipt for cash purchases. As with all individual transactions, be smart and be safe when arranging to meet someone face to face for a purchase of goods. Choose a well-lit and highly traveled public place, and be prepared to assess the quality of the item before handing over petty cash for your purchase.

The modern prop shopper has many more technological tools available as well. With most cell phones having a built-in camera, it's easy to snap a photo and email or text it off for confirmation. Many other instant social media platforms exist as well. It's best to lay out the preferred method of communication in advance with your team. This is especially helpful when fabric shopping, as a photo can show scale, texture, and design repeat/pattern. When furniture shopping, a photograph captures many choices for consideration from leg style and profile to detail molding or upholstery tufting. Taking an accompanying photo of the price tag, fabric content, or dimension sheet keeps all the information organized. If the designer is "online," the communication can be immediate. Otherwise it entails a return to the store for purchasing following affirmation to buy, but that is usually preferable to purchasing and then needing to return an item.

Given the responsibility of purchasing, it's important for the shopper to be organized with receipts and petty cash. Having a system to retain receipts safely is important; scanning in or taking a photo of the receipts allows a quick upload into the online shop bible. The shopper is accountable for the purchases made and for tracking the receipts to be entered in the budget in communication with the properties director. Some receipts will need to be split-coded to allow precise tracking, with expenses tracked to different shows or overhead/maintenance/other budgets. Making a habit of completing this daily keeps the accounting accurate. Trying to remember later what items were purchased for what show can be painfully inexact and stressful.

In the world of props, the adds and changes keep coming right up to opening. It's a rare build where some last-minute item is not needed and the shopper is challenged to get online, find something available, get it purchased, and have an overnight delivery arranged to facilitate the needs the of the show and the wishes of the director and designer. The shopping list is under constant revision as the many ways of solving the "build" evolve, and having a savvy "I know where I can find that" shopper is a life saver.

BUILD

Building props specific for the production are part of most show builds. Hopefully, the designers will give scaled drawings detailing the specific shape, finish, and construction for the prop. All too often designers communicate what they want by using a photo or set of photos demonstrating the desired look and the information about size or finish communicated by notation on the photos. And at other times, designers rely on the properties director to manage the building of props based on verbal descriptions of what the prop should look like, which may or may not be accompanied by a rough sketch or photocopy of research for confirmation. Knowing what to build can be a tricky balance of getting into the designer's head, doing research to inform the "design and build" process, and offering up as many solutions as possible, hoping one will hit pay dirt.

Each properties director develops a way of finessing the communication between the designer and the shop, and some are more likely to step into the designer's role of research and creation with only a confirmation of design choice coming from the scenic designer. Others strongly feel it is the designer's role to do that work and rely on the designer for all information . . . hopefully before the show goes into technical rehearsals. In worst case scenarios, props are left to the last. If getting information from the designer proves difficult, the properties director may be forced to take a more active role in determining how things look and "best-guessing" what the designer might have decided given the information on hand.

In many builds, the furniture pieces are the first items to conquer. Having looked through what is available in stock or possible to borrow from another organization and determined nothing will work, the consensus is often to build something specific for the design. Other times the design itself is so unique the furniture is conceived as part of the overall production aesthetic. Even when items have been pulled from stock for use, it is common to have the designer request alternations or a modified silhouette or, at the very least, a new upholstery job that allows it to fit the colors and look of the show design. This is all part of the build on a prop.

The properties director or prop shop supervisor assigns projects to the various artisans in the shop, and it is their responsibility to ask questions and carry the mission for completion of the prop to the satisfaction of the designer. The prop collective, from the

MAHARAM *INTRICATE* IN CRIMSON

MAHARAM *STRIPES BY PAUL SMITH* IN SYNCOPATED

MAHARAM *LETTERS* IN TAUPE

MAHARAM *WROUGHT* IN TORTOISE

Figure 7.13 Catalog Research. Preliminary information/research from a catalog to show basic structure, scale and upholstery options, allowing preliminary planning/budgeting to occur. It also allows the shopper to begin the search for the upholstery material desired. Takeshi Kata, scenic designer, *La Traviata*, Skylight Opera Theatre.

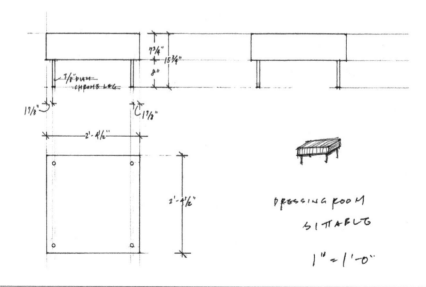

Figure 7.14 Designer Drawing. Evolving from the pictorial research, a prop drawing was generated by the designer for the 'sittables,' giving specific dimensions and general finish notes. This is what the artisan would use to draft a construction drawing specific to the step-by-step build process and would generate a buy list of materials.

Figure 7.15 Stage Shot. Full stage shot showing final pieces dressed in the scene. Takeshi Kata, scenic designer, *La Traviata*, Skylight Opera Theatre. Photo by Mark Frohna.

properties director to each individual artisan, discusses what processes to build with and what materials should be used, breaking the various steps of construction and finish down into a timeline of process. Depending on the size and setup of the shop, multiple artisans may be involved at various stages of any given prop on the shop floor. In the example given for the *La Traviata* sittables, in larger shops the shopper would be finding/purchasing the materials for construction (wood, steel, padding, upholstery fabric, etc.), the prop carpenter would build the frame, the soft goods artisan would do the upholstery and the crafts artisan would be painting/silver leafing the exposed metal legs. In smaller organizations, this would be done from shopping to final finish by a single artisan. Regardless of how many hands are in the process, each step must have consideration for the next step. The frame construction must have an understanding of how the padding and upholstery will be completed and the metal work finish of the legs must be done so the upholstery is not damaged. Good communication between all parties is essential as the project moves into and through the shop.

The priority of completion is set within the overall build of all items and may be moved about depending on the changes coming from rehearsal. Some props may be built to a certain level of function and sent into rehearsal to be used for a time before being returned to complete the final paint finish or upholstery to make it ready for load-in and technical rehearsals. This allows valuable response for specialty built items while time is still available to make alterations, as well as helping the actors understand how the final prop might differ from a rehearsal prop they had been using.

Many shows call for props to be altered or built to fulfill the requirements of the script. For example, in Tom Stoppard's *Arcadia*, letters must be made to support the specific action in the script—sealed and opened, read and referred to onstage, and finally burned. Choosing the right weight and size of paper for that specific character in that specific time and place, addressing and writing it appropriate to time period with necessary quoted passages, and making a way for it to be safely ignited and extinguished onstage are all points to be considered as the prop is made. And since they are a "consumable," enough will need to be made for technical rehearsals through the run of the show! Pulling old letters from stock might seem to be a quick rehearsal option, but this would probably need to be a "build from scratch" prop. In the same show, a stack of gardening diaries is referenced, opened and read from, and in one scene shows a sketch of a specific flower. While the books might start out as black blank books purchased from a stationary store, the prop shop would need to paint the covers not only to impart some interesting color but to give a sense of age and of being a "collection." By adding a period appropriate botanical print on the painted cover, the audience can identify the book as a garden diary. To match the script particulars and support what the actors must discover in the books, the pages are filled with writings, drawings, garden lists, planting plans, botanical sketches, etc. Building these types of props can seem time-consuming and tedious without an understanding of how important the proper completion of the prop is to the actor who handles and uses it to find character and support the action of the scene as well as helping advance the story for the audience.

Creating objects with a specific size or weight is a common request. Finding real objects may satisfy the visual look, but if the item is too heavy to be easily shifted or the stage space requires a low back or a different length to satisfy sightlines, then a build or modification may be necessary. Many built furniture pieces have additional bracing or even a metal reinforcing structure added to allow for the extra abuse prop furniture encounters. While one would never sit on the arm of a chair or stand on a sofa as a normal course of action, be prepared to get a rehearsal note making just that request! Having a tea set roll in on a cart would solve the difficulty of having the arrival of tea in a scene easily solved . . . but not if the set has a step down into the space. Sorting out how to build a lightweight, folding butler's stand able to be easily deployed while balancing a full tea tray and allowing the actor playing the butler to navigate the offending step while delivering his lines is a common and interesting challenge.

Sorting out how furniture pieces are shifted between scenes can be especially formidable, as the juggle of how something must look versus the need for it to have castors or ride on a small platform will impact the choices of how something can be built or altered. Using the wheelbarrow concept of adding wheels on one end of a piece of furniture to allow the opposite end to be the stabilizing end is a useful solution, but it has its limits, as do kick jacks, air casters, and other common scenic mobility solutions. Unfortunately, the silent tiny castor able to withstand heavy loads and roll over uneven floor surfaces is yet to be invented, and solving the shift challenges of moving pieces is a constant discussion as pieces are built.

Ephemera such as newspapers with specific headlines or family photographs using the actor's faces can require extra setup and build time. Using the computer has freed the manipulation of graphics from the old "cut and glue down" to a click of the mouse, making downloads of period documents, labels, and even whole newspapers possible. Adding in a photo of an actor or typing in a specific headline is possible using any of the various graphics programs and printing the paper out on a plotter or quality printer. Adobe Photoshop, Adobe Illustrator, and Microsoft Publisher are common programs used, and many shops now have a graphics work area in the shop with a scanner, wide format printer, and computer to generate these kinds of props.

Some items, such as handwritten letters, can also be produced on a computer, but the conformity of the machine makes them appear computer generated even when a "handwriting" script is used. If the letter might be seen by the audience, having calligraphy skills and knowing how to write in a period style allows the prop to have the appropriate randomness of handwriting "look" with dark ink splotches and all. In the case where *many* letters are required, it's sometimes possible to build an "original" and then make the required copies

Figure 7.16 Alley Theatre Graphics Area. The Alley Theatre prop shop has a conventional drafting table layout work area as well as a designated computer/scanner/copier for graphics creation and manipulation. Storage of multiple kinds of paper, standard and wide format printers, and paper cutters to create unique paper sizing allow period paper props to be easily built all in one crafts shop area. Karin Rabe Vance, properties director.

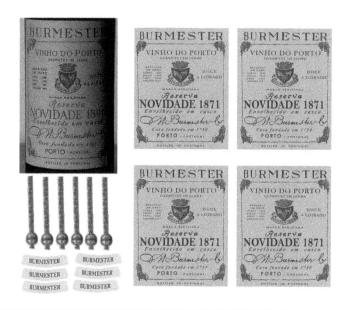

Figure 7.17 Reproduction of Graphics. Starting with original research taken from a bottle in stock, the label characteristics can be analyzed and recreated using computer graphic software and printed off to allow multiple copies and easy replacement during the run. Karin Rabe Vance, properties director.

using a photocopier to duplicate the document. Paper size can be modified after copying to make documents fit period appropriate paper sizes or colors. A wide variety of papers in various weights and colors as well as textures are available for use in photocopiers, allowing quick paper prop creations.

Building a prop also means making it look like it belongs in the world of the play. Understanding how to distress wood, fabric, metal, and other materials is necessary to instill props with a history. Once props are built, the final step is usually making it fit into the world of the other props by giving it the correct patina, polish, paint finish, or even wiping down with dirt or mud. Fabric might be bleached or toned with dyes, tattered or worn down with a rasp or sure-form, and trim pulled free and stretched. Upholstery is often layered to create a saggy cushion or flattened for a look of great age and use. Design Master floral sprays, which stick to almost all materials, are often used to tone and distress prop items. Design Master Glossy Wood tone is a personal favorite as it gives the perfect "dirt" tone to most materials. The Design Master "Tint it" series is a fast-drying dye and the Sepia color allows for subtle aging and distressing on many props. The Krylon product line used by many artists for acrylic and oil painting also offers multiple choices in prop use. Their clear flat sealer is an alternative treatment to take the edge of newness off of many surfaces.

Building a prop can be a time consuming, expensive, and laborious process, and accurately managing the fabricated items within the context of the whole build often determines the choice made between building or borrowing an item if it can be found in the community. On the other hand, building props enriches the prop stock as items are added to both furniture and hand props, expanding what will be available for productions in the future. More importantly, building is often the only way to create a specific prop that fits exactly what the designer envisioned, the story telling will most benefit from, and the show requires.

The prop list has been reviewed and every prop is notated with at least one way to solve the problem. The shopping list is made (at least for now). Stock has been reviewed and items pulled. Artisans are figuring out how to proceed with the individual projects assigned to them. Items to be borrowed are confirmed and pick-up times established. The build is on . . .

Negotiating the prop shop schedule and priorities at the onset of the build so often depends on the timeline for rehearsals, and what rehearsal needs may take priority. Moving real props into the rehearsal hall as soon as feasible is now more the norm than the exception. In ideal situations, the prop build commences a few weeks prior to stage management preparation week, but in many theatres, technical departments lack that luxurious cushion of lead time. Most LORT (**The League of Resident Theatres**) theatres tend to have a four- to six-week rehearsal period. This often corresponds to the shop "build" as well. As the run crew goes into technical rehearsals on a show, the prop shop artisans move to start the build on the next production, while simultaneously completing tech notes on the show moving to public performance. The properties director juggles back and forth between the two shows—one getting ready to open, one going into rehearsal—supervising the shop as well as attending technical rehearsals. According to a SPAM survey, the property director may work over sixty hours a week during the technical rehearsal week shift, attending nightly technical rehearsals and running the shop during the day. Hopefully the shop has been given enough information for completing the preliminary work on the next show to allow the shop artisans to move forward. Regional theatres also tend to have multiple performance spaces, with the prop shop juggling several "builds" at a time, so it might also be the case that an artisan or two get moved over to start on a different show even before the previous show is loaded in for technical rehearsals. Companies producing in several venues might utilize a large artisan staff supervised by prop masters for each particular show who report to the properties director, in order to have multiple builds happening at one time in the shop. On the other hand, small companies with only one person in the shop or perhaps with a single artisan rarely get the luxury of getting a jump start on a show and are often into significant overtime when opening multiple shows.

* * *

In a prop shop of any size, using the divisions of build, buy, borrow, and pull, a prop show build can be accomplished to bring an on-time, on-budget, to-the-satisfaction-of-the-designer conclusion. Working as part of the team in the shop, whether as artisan, shopper, or properties director, the ultimate goal is to manage the workload so all involved are equally engaged, to build high quality professional level props fulfilling the action needed while creating the designed "look," and to be ready to move into the theatre for the technical rehearsals when all parts of the production come together. The show moves out of the shop and onto the stage, into the hands of the run crew. The juggle of the build and final closure on the show build is ended at opening . . . then, on to the next build, the next magic melting pot of what to build, buy, borrow, and pull.

Working with Scenic Designers

An interview with Vicki Smith, Freelance Scenic Designer, Minneapolis, MN

How has the relationship between scenic designers and prop people changed over the years you've been working professionally?

Over the years, props people have generally become more professional. When I first started, some props people didn't really have any specific training; they just landed in props because they wanted to do theatre and that job was open. Now many of the people I work with are very skilled and very knowledgeable.

Vicki Smith
FREELANCE SCENIC DESIGNER
(VICKISMITHSETDESIGN.COM),
MINNEAPOLIS, MN

How do you now prepare preliminary design information and final design information to share with your prop director?

I have been doing the same thing for a long time: I start by putting all (or most) of the furniture and dressing in my models. I usually have done quite a bit of visual research at that point. Then I write out a detailed props list: first, I list all furniture scene by scene and describe as much as I know about the pieces; I can give a general size range based on what I have in the model. I then go through and list all the dressing scene by scene. For each listing where I have visual research, I make a note for the props people to see the accompanying photos. I then provide scans of my research in the same order as the list; often I provide several possible styles for an item. I used to do a hard-copy folder that I sent to props people; now the theatres almost always establish a Dropbox folder for each show so I put the lists and photos online. I don't list all the hand props unless there's something really specific or unusual that needs to be designed. I feel pretty strongly that if we are going to do a big props show, particularly one with a lot of set dressing, it needs to be substantially planned in advance. Trying to punt once we're in tech is a great way to make an already stressful time much worse.

What are your expectations of the prop shop:

- during your design process?
- when you've turned in your designs for feasibility costing & feedback?

During the design process, I usually contact the head of props if there's some particular item I think might be difficult or expensive to give them a heads-up, or perhaps to ask about what they might have in stock. Sometimes the props person has been in the initial meeting so we've already had initial discussions. If the props person thinks something will be available or very difficult to build or find, I might change my approach.

After I've turned in the design, I am obviously concerned to see if what I've asked for is affordable and, if not, I always want to hear suggestions for what else we might do. I'm always counting on working with people who have more specific knowledge than I do, either in building skills (wouldn't take much—I'm not a builder) or in where we might find an unusual piece.

What do you expect in the give-and-take between your design work and prop production constraints, and how do you shape your needs in line with available resources?

I expect a lot of back-and-forth. Usually after I give the prop shop my lists and photos, I start getting a lot of pictures from the props shopper. There is often a trade-off: if I opt for one pricey piece that I really like, then I might have to compromise on something less important. Also, I'm usually given maximum amounts I can spend for fabric and carpet. That virtually always means a lot of compromising; it's always lower than I wish it were. Also, there's the phase I call "we can't find it, let's build it," which means doing another working drawing.

What are you looking for in communication with the prop shop:

- during rehearsal before your residency begins?
- after your arrival during the final track to opening?
- What are your best or preferred practices in collaborating with the prop shop?

Besides ongoing photos from the shopper, I usually expect emails or phone calls dealing with any specific props notes that come up daily. Sometimes I email or call; sometimes the prop shop calls me. Then we discuss how we're going to approach an issue and whether I need to design something new to be built. If research is required, sometimes I do it; sometimes props does it; sometimes we both do it.

During tech, we always talk every day before rehearsal during work hours and after rehearsal during notes.

CHAPTER 8

The Rehearsal and Production Process

Properties production is the one area in technical production relying most highly on getting information directly from the day-to-day rehearsal process and coordinating that information with all the other production shops. During rehearsal, hand props not mentioned in the script get added, furniture is used in a specific way that impacts how it should be built or reinforced, a prop gets thrown and broken each night as part of the new staging, making it a consumable item, or an actor is allergic to wool and needs a cotton blanket for the bed covering. This information cannot come from the designer, the script, or research. It is directly learned from the rehearsal process, itself specific to this group of actors and this director. Information flow is critical as the play is staged when props are added or cut, use is changed, or stage action altered. An efficient conduit of information from rehearsal, open to discussion by all involved parties, allows the prop department to build the props in support of staging and cast-specific necessities. This requires a transparency about the requests based on what is happening in rehearsal and communicated in a daily rehearsal report.

WORKING WITH STAGE MANAGEMENT

Since prop people can't be everywhere, God made stage managers. They are the production area's eyes in the rehearsal and performance process with directors, actors, and run crews. A perceptive and nuanced stage management team can open the flow of communication, ideas, and collaboration between all parties.

Stage managers generate the rehearsal reports following each rehearsal and forward them to all involved parties. Most organizations utilize some method of email reporting, allowing for immediate communication following rehearsal and performance and facilitating a free interchange of information. Hopefully the folks involved with the production are reading their notes and copy responses to the necessary collaborators so all are kept on the same conversation path. Other organizations post the rehearsal report in a folder in the show online account instead of sending the report to individuals. This requires all parties to log in and read the report, which is less immediate and requires an extra step, making it somewhat problematic for those who aren't attuned to the need for immediacy of response. A compromise position to email reporting is to post all rehearsal reports in the online show account folder but also to email rehearsal reports out to the select group of decision-makers for review. Depending on the number of people who require reports and their level of interest and input, the latter method is often the best compromise. This allows upper administration to view reports as needed but gives the designers and production area heads the reports daily to their inbox. Working with stage management to insure prompt communication to the prop shop can be done in all of these scenarios.

Rehearsal reports contain the who, what, where, when, why, and how of what's happening with the entire rehearsal and staging process, including props and all other technical areas.

The rehearsal report should include:

- What part of the play was rehearsed
- Changes to calendar, rehearsal schedule, or actor "calls"
- Requests for upcoming rehearsal needs
- Notification of meetings scheduled
- Rehearsal notes listing by department:

  - Adds
  - Cuts
  - Changes in use
  - Maintenance issues
  - General information/questions

In the area of props, it is especially important stage managers communicate specific details having an impact on prop choices. This might include timing factors such as the length of a candle burn time, an actor's allergies or preferences for something eaten, any special needs for weapons or special effects in consideration of the staging, or anticipated difficulties for scene shifts due to actor availability, weight, size of items, or storage space backstage. Equally important, stage management should define the situation or problem and *not the solution* when giving notes. For example: "The actor needs to be able to sit on the stool with both feet on the floor and the stools used in rehearsal are too tall." NOT: "Please cut four inches off the stool legs."

THE HOT L BALTIMORE
Rehearsal #5

SM: Tyler Danhaus
ASM: Brooke Olson
PA: Eli Walker
Date: Monday, March 22nd, 2016

START TIME: 6:00   **END TIME:** 10:00

AGENDA: Staging pages 1-21
CALLED: K. Anton, W. Du Vernois, R. Graham, K. Robare, R. Simpson, M. O'Hara, A. Patrick
INJURY/ILLNESS: None.

PROPS:
1. Thank you for the Typewriter Table (F205).
2. Is there a house phone in addition to the switchboard? We need to have a "second line" somehow.
3. ADD: We would like to add a rag that Bill can use to clean up the hotel in Act One.
4. ADD: We would like to add a comic book for Jamie to look through in Act One.
5. Bill would like to confirm that we have a picture of the HOTEL BALTIMORE on the front of the Newspaper (1009).
6. CHANGE/ADD: We would like to possibly use the broom (D39) and possibly ADD a mop for Bill to use cleaning the space.
7. What kind of headset is on the switch board (phone or headset)?
8. ADD: We would like to add a deck of cards for April to play solitaire.

COSTUMES/HAIR:
No notes for today.

SCENERY:
1. We would like to confirm that performers are able to sit on both walls of the reception area and the front desk.

LIGHTS:
No notes for today.

SOUND:
1. The radio on the desk will be "turned on" and play music at top of Act I.

GENERAL
NOTES: No notes for today.&

SCHEDULING REMINDERS:
1. Our next rehearsal is Wednesday, March 23rd, in Mitchell Hall room 385 at 6:00pm.

| Tyler Danhaus | Rehearsal Report | Page 1 of 1 |

Figure 8.1 Rehearsal Report. Example of a rehearsal report for *Hot L Baltimore* showing the kind of detail and the importance of effective communication between the rehearsal space and the shops. Besides the specific notes directed to the prop shop, the arrow points out the impact other area notes might have on props as well. Note how the prop # is utilized for clarification of prop. Tyler Danhaus, stage manager, University of Wisconsin-Milwaukee.

THE HOT L BALTIMORE

Good Morning!
Prop Response to Rehearsal Report #5 follows:

2. Is there a house phone in addition to the switchboard?
   ADD: *Desk Phone (#D36)*

3. ADD: We would like to add a rag that Bill can use to clean up the hotel in Act One.
   ADD: *Clean Up Kit (#1004), will include rags in small bucket, spray bottle with water, risk broom and dust pan.*

4. ADD: We would like to add a comic book for Jamie to look through in Act One.
   ADD: *Comic Book (#1040)*

5. Bill would like to confirm that we have a picture of the HOTEL BALTIMORE on the front of the Newspaper (1009).
   Yes, there is along with a short article on the proposed destruction of the hotel.

6. CHANGE/ADD: We would like to possibly use the broom (D39) and possibly ADD a mop for Bill to use cleaning the space.
   ADD: *Broom (#1010)*
   ADD: *Rag Mop (#1011), damp for preset, stored in Bucket (#)*
   ADD: *Bucket (#D40), for damp Rag Mop to be preset in, kept in Janitor's Closet, not seen. No water stored in bucket.*

7. What kind of headset is on the switch board (phone or headset)?
   Handset phone with a long cord. Bracket for handset is on right face of the switchboard.

8. ADD: We would like to add a deck of cards for April to play solitaire.
   ADD: *Deck of Cards (#1026)*

Also per Sound note #1 : Radio on desk will be turned on and play music.
   Radio has two knobs- one for on/ volume and a second for "tuning". Radio will also "light up". Props will coordinate with sound for speaker placement and electrics to get power to the radio allowing it to light up. Radio speaker is NOT functional.

I am available from 3pm-5:30pm for you to pick up rehearsal deck of cards (1026), clean up kit (1004) and mop (1011) if you wanted to use them in rehearsal this evening.

Thank you,
Jennifer M. Higgins, Properties Master

Figure 8.2 Rehearsal Response. The prop master responds to each prop note from the rehearsal report, adding in new prop list numbers as needed. The sound notes are also addressed since they are influenced by the prop being used and, in this case, will eventually need coordination with both sound and electrics. This coordination is done in production meetings or individually with the shops. Jennifer Higgins, properties master, University of Wisconsin-Milwaukee.

Ideally, for clarity and continuity, the director should approve all rehearsal notes. Notes from actors must be cleared through both stage management and the director before they are put on the rehearsal report. Not only does this keep the director in the loop about any requests but it also guarantees the notes accurately reflect the directorial viewpoint. Some actors make requests the director would not want or need in the scene, and this "clearing" process keeps the communication free from any confusion.

Rehearsal notes are often emailed out following rehearsal to facilitate the best communication. The properties director reads the report and updates the prop list as necessary, sending on information or design concerns to the scenic designer. Requests should be discussed with the designer and the shop in a prompt manner and decisions made in collaborative discussion with the director and production areas. Some requests can be immediately answered by way of return email to the stage manager, copying any other departments impacted. The properties director prepares questions and feedback for the more complex cross-departmental/designer/director concerns, to be addressed either immediately via email or in the next production meeting. It might also prove useful to seek out information/assistance on a project by meeting separately with another department or colleague. Meanwhile in the prop shop, changes to projects in process will be discussed with the artisan in charge of the project, and work may be redirected until answers can be provided affecting the prop in question.

Responding to the rehearsal report with "adds" by assigning a number to new items allows the continuation of communication via the prop listing with the designer and rehearsal staff. Updating the prop list description as information comes in from rehearsal allows the shop to always be in tune with evolving demands. The prop list can be re-distributed as needed or, in the best case, made available on the online access feed so everyone can view it. It is helpful to protect the editing ability to a few people but have the *viewing* capability open to all. Setting the editing permission is usually done when inviting people to the link, under *preferences.*

PRODUCTION MEETINGS

The **production meeting** is the venue where all areas share information, clarify the needs of the department, establish deadlines, and create a schedule with consideration for each department's priorities. Generally led by the production manager, the basis of most of the discussions occurring in the weekly production meetings are formed of rehearsal notes and upcoming deadlines.

The properties director should attend all production meetings to keep everyone informed about the status of the properties build, to clarify any concerns from rehearsal, and to ask and answer questions about areas of production overlap necessitating collaboration. In props, overlap is common. Props are one of the most integral and interconnected departments in the theatre production area. Sharing the load of production by splitting the labor or dividing up the materials cost of a project uses the strengths of all departments and allows a better product through teamwork.

REHEARSAL PROPS

Rehearsal props stand in for the actual prop as the actor works out the stage action and movement in the rehearsal process. In many regional theatres, stage management has a stock storage closet of hand props and an assemblage of furniture pieces in the rehearsal hall for use during the rehearsal process. Many theatres use a cube system with standardized rehearsal cubes to represent the furniture. These may be complemented by an odd gathering of cast-off furniture pieces to set the rehearsal space. For specialty pieces not available in the stage management stock, the prop shop often works with the stage managers to assist in procuring something similar from prop storage.

Providing the actual furniture in rehearsal is the preferred level of practice since it most closely duplicates the actor's experience onstage, but at times it is simply unrealistic. Some organizations rehearse in shared or unsecured rehearsal sites, making utilization of the actual prop a hazardous choice. Others rehearse at an offsite location, making transportation a burden and adding the possibility of damage to the prop. In smaller organizations, the workload in the prop shop disallows the time and effort required to pull, prepare, and deliver the actual pieces to the rehearsal hall, especially if the pieces require re-upholstery, strengthening, painting, or other modification.

When the actual prop cannot be utilized, it is helpful for the furniture used in rehearsal to duplicate the qualities of the actual furniture piece. If a chair is to have arms or an especially high back, then the rehearsal piece should have some representation of those characteristics, even if it is only a piece of cardboard taped to the sides to represent arms or the back of the chair showing a similar height as the real prop chair. This allows the actors to understand the relationship of their movement in and around the chair to the actual prop chair itself, and it will be an easier adjustment once the rehearsal moves to the stage and uses the actual chair. If the staging requires specific action difficult to duplicate with a rehearsal prop, stage management may request the use of the actual furniture piece for several rehearsals to establish the action with the cast. Most prop shops try to accommodate such a request and work with stage managers to either provide the actual piece in the rehearsal room, a close duplicate, or may set up a session in the shop to try out the action. If the rehearsal hall is convenient and transportation can be accommodated within the build schedule, items can be sent to rehearsal before final finishing for actors to get comfortable with the real prop and then pulled for completion prior to load-in.

Encouraging stage managers to stop into the prop shop to see props helps them understand any specific qualities of the pulled pieces. When that is difficult due to schedules or transportation issues when the shop is away from the rehearsal site, utilizing a visual reference sheet for stage management, actors, directors, or any other interested parties to see furniture choices is especially helpful. The photos are best supplemented with sizing information as well as any notation about whether the pieces are being shop built, pulled from stock, or purchased. This information might also be provided online in the shared prop folder for the show, but this gives the rehearsal folks something to post for quick reference and understanding.

DESK

6' long, 2' 8: deep, 2' 8" high

DESK CHAIR

Alley Stock
2 '1" wide, 2' 6" deep, 3' 7" high

COFFEE TABLE

42" diameter, 20" high

SET OF 6 CHAIRS
(Actually ordered 8 for backups/additions)

38: high, 24" wide, 20: deep

TEA CART

25" wide, 17" deep, 26 ½" tall
33" tall at handle.

TELEVISION

3' wide, 1' 7" deep, 2' 6" high
Is being altered to be 5' wide.

REEL TO REEL CABINET

28" wide, 15" deep, 29" high

Figure 8.3 Furniture Reference Sheet. Having a quick reference sheet for set props allows a way to access information about 'look' and size, and if the piece is stock, being built, or being purchased. Note information about anticipated alterations as well as anticipated back-up purchasing. Karin Rabe Vance, properties director, Alley Theatre.

Stage managers should not expect the prop shop to provide a full complement of rehearsal props but should use what they can best create or pull from their rehearsal stock on their own to stand in for the actual item. An understanding of what the actual item looks like will allow the stage manager to communicate information to the actor and inform their choices in selecting a rehearsal substitute. A visit to the prop shop to see what is being selected, view pieces in process, or to talk with the artisan working on the prop about what things look like and how they function helps the rehearsal substitute choice. If an actor is blocked to carry a tray with six glasses, it is helpful to know the size of the tray and if the glasses are footed or flat, heavy-based style glasses. Often the prop shop will prioritize the completion of specialty props such as weapons or objects necessitating specific manipulation, allowing them to move to rehearsal and be used prior to technical rehearsals.

Once scripts are out of the actors' hands, it is helpful to have something to represent the hand props the cast will be working with to help them hook the action to the language. During this exploratory time, while actors are experimenting with how they are working a scene or playing around with ways to interact, using plastic or non-breakable items allows the actors to work the scenes without fear of breaking the props, or hurting themselves on a piece of broken glass or china. Having the actors move to either the actual prop or something duplicating the weight and feel of the actual prop is helpful once the staging is set and the action defined. This allows the actors to understand the interaction with the prop and affords opportunity to create a body sense memory aligning with line delivery

Figure 8.4 Rehearsal Props. Actors working in the rehearsal room using rehearsal furniture. The prop shop provided a rehearsal chaise to allow the actors to have a similar "sittable" in rehearsal while the other pieces are from the rehearsal furniture stock and selected to most closely match the actual furniture being used.

Figure 8.5 Staged Props. Actors playing the same scene, this time on the actual set with the prop furniture. Kurt Sharp, scenic designer, *Hay Fever*, University of Wisconsin-Milwaukee.

and blocking. Actors who have been working with a facsimile in rehearsal of significantly different size, weight, or function may have a more difficult time adjusting in technical rehearsals when so many other changes (lights, sound, spacing, etc.) are also occurring. This is particularly essential when dealing with weapons, where safety in staged combat is paramount.

STAGE WEAPONS

To enable best practices with regard to safety of humans and equipment, the discussion of weapons usage and staging ideas should start well in advance of the rehearsal process, and a back and forth conversation with director, fight choreographer, and prop director is mandatory to develop a cohesive approach. The fight director should be consulted about the design of the relevant physical elements of the production impacting safe weapons use across all departments—scenery, props, costumes, lighting, and special effects. The prop director and fight choreographer are responsible for ensuring only weapons specifically designed and engineered for stage combat are used—ornamental, antique, or costume reproduction prop weapons, while perfectly suitable as a costume accessory, are *not* acceptable for stage combat. This dialog affords the prop director/fight choreographer team the best opportunity to find the right weapons to fit each need from a visual/design/period standpoint as well as the practical handling aspect. Mandatory parameters can then be conveyed to the director and production

Figure 8.6 Weapons Lockup. Secure weapons lock-up with hanging racks for storing bladed weapons and a slotted wooden rack for long guns allows for quick inventory and safe management of the armory. Karin Rabe Vance, properties director, Alley Theatre.

stage manager in order to incorporate safe staging practices in advance of rehearsals. Following all of this preliminary communication and groundwork, the prop director can work with stage managers to schedule dedicated rehearsal times for safety demonstrations by the fight choreographer, bladed weapons and/or firearms hands-on training, blank firing tests, and combat staging rehearsals.

For liability reasons, weapons are the most tightly controlled of all objects under the prop director's purview. A general weapons protocol should include:

- All stage weapons should be locked in a secure limited access storage armory until they are assigned to a production. Additionally, storage and transportation of certain weapons such as replica firearms must meet the approval of the institutional policies and local police in some jurisdictions. Know your local laws and abide by them!

- Communicate with and *train* stage management so they can be partners in the chain of responsibility, observing all protective protocols as weapons are introduced to rehearsals. Chief among these concerns are security and safe handling practices.

- For each weapon transferred from the prop weapons storage to rehearsal, weapons sign-out tracking sheets should be completed, documenting both the individual weapon characteristics and the chain of responsibility.

- Weapons must be secured in a locked cabinet or case whenever they are not in use or under direct supervision, including all coffee and meal breaks.

- Weapons should only be used in rehearsal under appropriate supervision, with a stage manager, prop director, designated weapons master, or fight choreographer to oversee safe handling and use.

- Whenever possible, each actor should use the same weapon in rehearsals, technical rehearsals, fight calls, and performances.
- At no time should any weapon be accessible to other members of the cast who are *not* to be handling weapons or to members of the public.

As with furniture and other prop facsimiles, if it is not possible to use the real weapons, rehearsal weapons must be of comparable size, weight, and style in order for fight choreographers, directors, and cast members to fully embrace all possibilities and limitations of each chosen prop weapon. Best practices dictate the actual prop weapon should be introduced to the rehearsal process from the start, though in reality many theatres lack the resources to make this happen. The wear and tear on weapons used from day one in rehearsal, while still working out staging details, is also a weighty consideration for theatres with limited budgets for duplicate weapons. For these reasons, comparable facsimiles are commonly used until the cast has the piece on its feet in the rehearsal room. For organizations lacking secure storage or appropriate trained personnel to handle real weaponry in rehearsal, additional technical rehearsal time to safely integrate the real weapons on stage is imperative, along with training for all cast and stage operations crew.

STAGE FIREARMS

Firearms require special consideration in light of the ever-evolving rules about the carrying of guns by the public and the perception of others' safety when they see a gun. With the proliferation of actual firearms, it is even more critical to have a protocol in place for handling prop firearms onstage. Following the *general weapons protocol* above insures proper safety procedures, but stage firearm handling should also include:

- All replica firearms must be inspected for barrel or vent obstructions, cracks or defects, and security of grip.
- The properties director and fight choreographer should test fire all blank firing replicas to determine the *safe working distance*. A **paper test** determines the assured safe distance for powder and wadding exhaust.
  - Under no circumstances should staging allow the vent area of a stage firearm to be directed at anyone.
  - Safe lanes and directions should be maintained at all times during blocking.
  - Communicate these safe working distances to stage management, director and fight choreographer, weapons master, and cast.
- An **acoustic test** in the space determines acceptable volume level for blank loads. If using live blanks during a rehearsal run, all personnel in the vicinity must be warned and appropriate notices posted in shared public areas.

BLADED WEAPONRY

Bladed weapons come in all shapes, weights, and sizes. Determining what is best may take some time and exploration. In addition to the general weapons protocol, bladed weaponry use should consider:

- Examining the weapon prior to use in each rehearsal for nicks, burrs, sharp points, and edges, cracks or defects of any sort should be done by the stage manager or designated weapons master. A small kit of a flat file, oil, steel wool, and pliers should allow most rehearsal-related maintenance to be completed.

- Prior to use, engraving the date of purchase on the blade tang allows for accurate tracking of its age.

- As the fight rehearsals progress, the actor or the choreographer may request modifications to the weapon—a different hilt or wrap to allow for better grip, a change in blade length, or adding weight to alter the balance.

A detailed prop weapons safety protocol is a compulsory part of professional prop shop administration, along with the requisite safety training and knowledge of outside resources and support personnel. Additional aspects of stage weapons safety, security, and use during onstage tech and run are covered in Chapter 9 as well.

PRODUCTION COLLABORATION

The prop shop, perhaps due to its evolution into a separate department from other more specifically defined technical departments, overlaps into almost every other area in production. The scenic designer creates the largest overlap since that person determines the basis of most of the design decisions, beginning with the stage setting and completed with the prop detailing, but coordination with all the other areas (costumes, sound, lighting, projections, paint) is part of every build. Designers from other areas, especially lighting and costumes, will want to be part of the decision-making process to coordinate color, scale, usage, or movement. Working in collaboration with those areas is a critical component of every build and, ultimately, the success of the design rests on having strong communication and problem-solving between all areas.

SCENERY

The **scenery department** is closely coordinated with the properties shop and impacts teamwork from the very start of the design process. In any given design, the division of the elements as designed by the scenic designer must be divided up between props and scenery. This is often based on the size of the elements as well as the specific skills of the artisans in

Figure 8.7   Coordination of Scenery, Lighting, and Props. The prop built screen required a semi-translucent gathered panel to create the lighting effect desired. The chandelier hanging above was provided by the prop shop, rigged by scenery, and powered by the electrics department. Stage management assistance for accurate spiking around the feet on the screen guaranteed exact placement each performance to match the circle of light cast on the floor, backlighting the actors to create the desired effect. *Les Liaisons Dangereuses*, UW-Milwaukee Theatre. Photo by L. J. Fadden.

the different shops. Early on in the design process a production meeting is held to look at preliminary designs, and the division of who will do what starts even at this early stage. It is common for items to shift as the design evolves and the design gets either simplified or more complex. For example, the designer needs to create a downstage scenic element to establish an actor looking out a window and at first proposes a large flown header piece with a suspended window frame. Given size, method of installation (rigged), and need to visually echo the upstage architecture, it would make sense to have the unit built by scenery. But later the designer chooses to establish the window by simply rigging a drapery swag hanging above the stage where the window would be with a window bench placed on the floor. The drape and the furniture piece are obviously props and the rigging of the hanging drape would be coordinated with scenery.

Sometimes the lines are not so easily defined. Instances where props and scenery intersect often have to do with artisan skill sets and shop workloads. For example, determining responsibilities when large carved statuary is required, trees and other landscaping are needed, or when a large part of the stage space is completed with rugs or textured "landfill" are all frequently negotiable situations. It could go either way depending on budget, artisan availability and skill, and what else the shops are being asked to complete or build.

Figure 8.8 Scenic Collaboration with Props. Scenery built the welded metal superstructure while props provided the white silk panels covering the frames. Secured with magnets, panels were removed as part of the action to represent the descent into madness and chaos. The panels had to be constructed to fit the specific sizing of the scenic pieces, making the coordination between scenery and props essential. *The Tragedy of King Lear*, UW-Milwaukee.

Props and scenery, often with designer and stage management input, also need to coordinate the movement of scene changes. Talking through what has to move first and how props get safely on and off stage, as well as guaranteeing the security of actors and crew, is important for the entire production team to consider. Storage space backstage is often tight, requiring shop heads to be involved with stage operations personnel in how things track, where prop run tables can be placed, and how props can be pre-set or struck off during the show.

Props flying in or being rigged must be coordinated with the scene shop staff person responsible for rigging. The prop shop should be working with the technical director to build props with appropriate structure and points for either a single or multiple point fly, and that are properly weighted, neither too heavy or cumbersome to fly or so lightweight the prop cannot offset the rigging requirements. Size and spacing are often critical factors. Insuring the prop to be flown has proper clearance among the multitude of other things being flown or rigged must be coordinated between scenery, electrics, and the prop shop. A large three-dimensional chandelier may need to become a two-armed "flat" chandelier in order to have it fly between scenic pieces and electrical battens. All of these decisions are made in collaboration with the scenic designer and lighting designer as well.

Props should make any requests for special building considerations in order to accommodate set dressing in advance of scenic unit completion. For example, if the prop shop knows placement of pictures or wall sconces on set walls, the scene shop can install backings that allow extra support in those areas if given the necessary measurements and information to install them during the build. The prop shop also should coordinate the dressing of elements being flown or inaccessible from the floor with the scenery load-in. Hopefully the technical director is in communication with the properties director and production stage manager about any minor changes in things like sizes of windows or door openings, which may impact the building of props like curtains or props carried in and out through the door. Technical rehearsal is not the time to discover the door opening was shrunk three inches, making the entrance of a wheelbarrow loaded with suitcases impossible. The production meeting allows both departments to communicate any concerns or confirm changes impacting the other department's work or product.

The props department also needs to be in discussion about built-in items such as window seats, bookshelves, kitchen cabinets, or fireplaces to insure they will be able to support the dressing weight and function as needed to support the action of the play. Getting the sizes of the actual built objects and not relying on designer drawings is critical, as the scene shop must often adjust dimensions slightly for budget or ease of building purposes. If the prop shop needs to have bookshelves to support the weight of real books, the scene shop should be warned early in the process so appropriate bracing of the wall unit is planned and strong shelves can be built. Visits to each other's shops are also a great way to confirm vital information. For example, the prop shop should go to the scene shop and measure the window seat unit before it builds the pillow on the seat, to double check the size is correct. Or the scene shop could ask to see the wall sconces to be installed so appropriate bracing can be planned as the wall units are built. Coordination of the installation of "practical" elements is critical. This is especially true when re-creating something like a kitchen on stage and the running of water, electrical, and gas lines for a stove, sink, refrigerator, etc. must be coordinated between multiple areas of production.

SCENIC ART

The **scenic art** department is responsible for the painting and finishing of scenic items. Some prop departments have their own painters, but collaboration will still be necessary to visually coordinate the scenery with the props, and the scenic artists often share paint and processes with the prop shop artisans. The tone, texture, and finish of furniture should be compatible with the scenic items. Some shows require the elements to match, and in those cases the scenic artist will often paint both scenery and props. In situations where the scenic charge is also responsible for painting a prop, it is extremely important to discuss the surface preparation of the prop, how the prop will ultimately be used (use relates to wear and tear on the painted finish), dry time required that may impact readiness of the prop for rehearsal, and potential touch up and maintenance concerns.

Scenic artists often are the craftsmen filling the artistic space between the props and scenery shops when those large carving projects or landscape projects are required. Scenic artists also often come to the prop shop for collaboration on stencil production or pattern making requiring the finer tools or the computer graphic support found in the prop shop.

Figure 8.9 Scenic Art Collaboration. The prop shop, working from a front elevation and research provided by the scenic designer, drafts and builds the full-scale prop piece, coordinating the painting with the scenic art department. Van Santvoord, scenic designer, *Sunday in the Park with George*, Skylight Music Theatre.

COSTUMES

In many organizations, props will collaborate with the **costume shop** more than any other department. Both props and costumes provide the items that are closest to the actor and, hence, are most connected to character. Costume designers use props to help complete a costume ensemble and the items that the character carries or uses must be considered and chosen to fit within the definition of that designed look. Coordination of personal items is often a consideration between the costume designer and the properties director to determine style, color, size, and placement such as for a wallet, notebook, briefcase, or knife sheath. Working with the costume designer follows a similar research, option presentation, and response as with the scenic designer. The prop shop works to fulfill the look defining character as designed by the costume designer, just as they work to fulfill the setting requirements as designed by the scenic designer. Often these discussions are a full collaborative discussion and decision-making process with designers and both shops involved.

Is it a prop or a costume? Generally speaking, if you wear it, then it is a costume; if you carry it, it is a prop. Each theatre determines the answer, but most regional theatre costume shops have their own costume craft person who deals with these types of crossover requests in collaboration with the prop shop. For example: umbrellas (props) parasols (costumes), flower bouquets (props) boutonnieres (costumes), handbags (costume) suitcase (props), eyeglasses (costume) opera glasses (props).

Decisions about costume color palette and pattern might impact choices for props. Before shopping for upholstery, drapery, or other soft good fabrics, it is a good idea to know what the costumes look like. For pulled or borrowed costumes, the properties director can look at the items and perhaps take a photo to document the color and pattern to inform the fabric selection process. For items being built, small fabric swatches can be cut for prop shop use. Coordinating the look between the shops is important to prevent a clash of color, pattern, texture, or having it look too similar, which can be equally disastrous.

The costume shop often comes to the prop shop for assistance on casting and molding projects or when the need to use tools not usually found in the costume shop arises. Projects requiring prosthetics, missing limbs, extra tall extensions of legs, or peg legs are good examples of situations where the prop shop often collaborates to create fake body parts, build or find stilts to be built into a costume, or layout and turn a peg leg on the props lathe. Props crafts people may also work on costume crafts objects such as crowns or jewelry items when the costume shop lacks the skills, tools, or time to complete the job.

Figure 8.10 Puppets and Costuming. Wind spirit and Beast puppets created as a collaboration between costumes and props for *Zemire et Azor*, Skylight Music Theatre. James Ortiz, scenic and puppet designer; Shima Orans, costume and mask designer. Photo by Mark Frohna

Masks and puppetry productions usually involve a close collaboration between the prop and costume shops. For large puppets or units involving internal structuring, the costume shop often relies on the expertise of the prop shop for construction of the framework or armature, while they build the external costume. Many prop shops build the masks or collaborate with the crafts person in the costume shop at varying levels to complete the mask production. This may occur by dividing the process into definable processes with the casting of the actor faces done as a team project, the mask forms being built and painted in the prop shop, and the final decoration and fitting of the masks done by costumes.

Weaponry also presents an opportunity for costume/prop collaboration. The weapon is always a prop, but finding a way for the weapon to be carried or worn by the actor requires a close collaboration between the shops. Belts often fall to the costume shop and a baldric or sword carrier is usually produced in the costume crafts shop so it will look and hang appropriate to the costume. Communication of weapon size and weight is important for items pulled from pockets, concealed in bodices, or hidden up a sleeve. Holsters must fit specific guns and are usually a prop but must be coordinated with the belt from costumes. Undercover holsters and the appropriate gun should be provided early on to allow the costume to be fit wearing the weapon. In the case of military or police officers, the belts holding all the officer equipment require the close collaboration of shops to provide the correct tactical belt for the uniform with all the accompanying and appropriate handcuffs, holsters, flashlights, keys, radios, ammunition pouch, etc.

When an actor is staged to perform a magic trick requiring items to be concealed in the costume, the prop shop, which usually provides the magic items, must coordinate the trick requirements with the costume department to insure the effect will succeed. Having both the costume and the magic tricks early in the rehearsal process allows the actor to have more time to make the effect appear smooth and natural.

Props also relies on the costume shop to provide items for stage dressing or hand props such as clothes to pack in a suitcase or hang on a clothesline, hats and coats to dress out a coat rack in an entry hall onstage, or jewelry items handled but never worn. The "look" of those items is coordinated with both the set and costume designers.

ELECTRICS

The **electrics department** collaborates with the prop shop for all items needing electricity to operate, including table lamps, chandlers, sconces, lanterns, appliances, radios, clocks, "live" outlets, street lights, smoke effects, electrically controlled special effects—anything requiring an electrical hookup so it can be function or be turned on/off. Special effects such as radio controlled and wireless DMX controlled props usually are a cross-departmental collaboration allowing both areas to explore the technology to achieve remote effects as well as sharing the expense.

In the world of props, many items are dressed onstage to give the appearance of real items but not requiring the actual need to work. However, some items *do* need to actually function. These props are called **practicals**. Practicals are any device giving the appearance of functioning as they would in real life—lighting up, emitting sound, smoking, vibrating, turning a turntable, etc. These practical props do work to some degree but are often only the illusion of reality. Many are controlled from offstage to work on cue from the soundboard operator with the sound emitting from speakers hidden inside or disguised in a nearby location and the light bulb illuminating when activated as part of a lighting cue from the light board. It might look like the actor is turning on the lights as he enters the room, flipping on the wall switch, and causing the sconces on the wall and the chandelier hanging in the room to light up, but it's controlled offstage and not by the actor.

Electrics will need to understand where the props requiring electricity will be located on the set to coordinate the installation of electrical power with the scenery department at load-in. Working with stage management, the prop shop can provide a close approximation of where items will be placed on a ground plan of the stage setting. Electrics personnel also need to know what voltage is required and how the prop is to be controlled. Some props may be controlled onstage by the actor (rarely), while others need to be controlled from the booth to allow the actor to appear to turn on a lamp but also allow the lamp to be faded out with the stage lights at the end of the scene into blackout. Other props may require control from backstage by the run crew taken from a "visual" of the actors on stage. A **visual** is a cue

Figure 8.11 Practicals Onstage. Practical props on the set of *Hot L Baltimore* needing support from both sound and electrics include the wall sconces, the light on the switchboard, the desk light, the calculator on the front desk, the coffee pot behind the pillar, the front desk phone, the radio on the back desk, and switchboard phone. The wall switches only give the appearance of controlling the lights. Sandra J. Strawn, scenic designer. Photo by L. J. Fadden.

coordinated with a specific action viewed onstage, often dependent on a piece of action that may be inconsistent in each performance, requiring timing to be taken from what is happening onstage at that particular moment. Determination of where a cue is controlled from may not be settled on until technical rehearsals, but props and electrics must work to provide the best options available.

Props with electrical hookups may require special wiring or a special plug installed to allow it to be used and controlled with the light board. Departments and theatres have varying policies about who does what, and these projects should be negotiated based on who has the time and who has the skill. If the theatre is a union house, it may be covered in the union contract. While the prop shop provides the actual unit such as a chandelier, wall sconce, or radio needing to light up, if the unit needs to be wired the responsibility may fall into either shop's jurisdiction. In most cases, once the prop is built in the prop shop, the electrics department takes the prop for final wiring and, in the case of flown props such as the chandelier, coordination with the scenic department for rigging of both the unit and the cable for electricity.

Props installed on the set as part of dressing, such as wall sconces, fireplace logs with a "flame," a wall clock, or shelf radio, are coordinated for electrical run to be completed during set dress. The prop shop will often drill the hole for the props electrical wire to pass through to the back of the set where it is connected to the appropriate electrical run provided by the electrics department. Props set onstage near a wall in the scenery such as a floor lamp or a television can use a standard wall socket installed in the set wall. Props placed on a thrust or out away from the walls where a wall socket is unavailable might require a floor plug built into the stage floor at scenery load in. Procurement and installation of the necessary plugs and sockets and getting the electricity run to make them active is coordinated between props, electrics, and scenery.

Electrics is often asked to wire **special effects** coordinated with the prop shop. Just as with chandeliers or traditional set dress items, the prop shop provides the item, electrics provides the power, and the installation is coordinated with scenery. This is especially important when working with anything that might give off smoke, flame, or heat, as all items near the special effect unit must be flame proofed or otherwise safeguarded. Costumes should also be alerted to flameproof costumes as necessary and scenery may need to treat the adjacent walls and floor.

Battery-operated props require a special level of coordination. Batteries can be bulky and heavy, requiring the prop shop to build an item larger or to remove unnecessary internal parts to allow space for the batteries. Installation of lamp units in a prop has often been problematic in the past given the size of sockets, bulbs, and batteries. The growing use of wireless technology to control practicals has allowed greater flexibility in placement and use than in the past. Incorporating these control units into props requires a higher level of coordination between the electrics and props shops.

LED light sources allow for much smaller sources and are more conservative in battery usage, allowing props and electrics to place effects in props more easily. Investment in rechargeable batteries and a battery charger keeps battery cost down, is more environmentally friendly, and helps guarantee a fully charged battery for each performance. Battery purchase is negotiated between the shops depending on budget and other uses. Switches are often installed to allow easy operation by the actor and to prevent accidental discharge draining the batteries. In some props, a switch is installed that automatically turns on the light or begins operation of the device when the prop is opened or in some specific way manipulated. For example, the director may wish to have a trunk of gold and jewels glow after it has been carried in and then opened. Since it is not a pre-set item but must move, it cannot be plugged into the wall for an electrical source, so the effect must be battery operated. It should operate only when the lid is opened so the batteries don't run down. A switch must be installed in the trunk that activates upon opening, pulling power from batteries secured under the trunk dressing, operating tiny lights concealed in the jewels and gold coins dressing the interior and creating illumination on the trunk lid, actor's face, and the interior trunk dressing. For the effect to work successfully, all parts must have been coordinated and thought through by both shops. Additionally, stage management and the run crew must understand the workings of the prop so batteries can be recharged and installed as needed without damaging the prop or affecting the dressing. If the effect is triggered wirelessly, the coordination of all parts is critical to the success of the moment.

A Christmas Carol   Dallas Theatre Center
                                            Rich Gilles, Props Master
Practical List

Location	Practical	Quantity	Power	Source		
Back Wall	Oil lamps	14	AC	light bulb		
	Single Candles	3	AC		flicker candle	
	Triple Candle	3	AC		flicker candle	
Street	Brazier	1	AC	light bulb		
	Lanterns on Poles	2	battery		flicker candle	
Office	Oil Lamps	2	AC	light bulb		
	Cratchit Candle	1	battery		flicker candle	
	Scrooge Lamp	1	battery	light bulb		
Bedroom	Oil Lamp	1	AC	light bulb		
	Scrooge hand held candle	1	battery		flicker candle	
	Past's Hand	1	battery	LED		
Fezziwig	Chandeliers	54 to 66	AC		flicker candle	
	Table Candelabras	0	battery		flicker candle	
Cratchit Table	Candle in Chimney	1	battery		flicker candle	
	Totals:	**85 to 97**			**20**	**65 to 77**

Flicker Candles: Have 53 good quality, 7 that are poor

Figure 8.12 Practicals List. List of prop practicals for *A Christmas Carol*, Dallas Theatre Center, used for coordination of use with stage management and the electrics department. Rich Gilles, properties master.

SOUND

Similar to electrics, the **sound department** ("sound") collaborates with props to bring the props to life with audio support. Radios, record players, televisions, telephones, doorbells—anything with a speaker—requires the coordination of installation with the sound department. While props provide the actual physical source for the sound, such as a radio, the sound department is responsible for making the sound emit from the source. Other times the sound department is asked to provide sound support for special effects like an explosion coming from a smoke effect or for a prop needing to look like it is making sound, such as a piano played by an actor who cannot play the piano but is simply moving his hands about on the keys. This coordination of sound and props is best worked out early in the production process.

Many sound departments will prefer to simply replace the existing speaker in the prop for a different, more powerful speaker or will conceal a separate speaker near the location where the prop is used. For example, a radio might be dressed on a desk and is required to play a song at a certain point in the play. The radio's own speaker is far too small to fill the theatre, so the sound department may conceal a separate speaker on the underside of the desk, or it might need to be disguised in a stack of books on the desk or perhaps other dressing sitting on the floor beside the desk. The props department will be asked to dress out the area to blend the speaker in with the stage environment. This is coordinated with the stage designer. Location of the speaker, whether inside the prop or hidden nearby in other dressing, must be coordinated with scenery as well so audio lines can be run either up through the stage floor or installed as the scenery is being placed.

Some sound departments utilize wireless speakers, allowing props to emit recorded sound when running a wire isn't possible or when the prop is picked up and moved about the stage. This is especially helpful when a unit cannot be actor operated. In actor operated situations, a small tape recorder, MP3 player, or similar audio device can be concealed inside many props. These units make the cue dependent on the actor flipping the switch at the correct moment. A wireless speaker gives the freedom to broadcast a variety of cues or change volume from the soundboard run by the sound operator, not the onstage actor. These systems are battery operated and require the same considerations for battery space as well as the speaker and audio receiver. Getting the wireless unit to the prop shop and working with the sound department from an early stage in the show build allows the prop to do everything needed to support the action required by the play. Security of the unit and battery maintenance by the run crew should be considered as the prop is built and the speaker unit installed.

Live sound effects previously were the province of the prop department. Today, sound effects are coordinated between both props and sound departments, sometimes including the music department as well in opera and music theatre houses. Offstage sound may be done as a simple live effect or utilize microphone amplification to reinforce the sound of a live effect, or it may be recorded. For example, a doorbell rings offstage to signal the arrival of a guest. Traditionally, the prop department would simply pull a hand-operated doorbell from stock and the run crew would ring it on cue. This can still work in small theatres where the sound of the doorbell is easily heard. In many theatres, however, the sound department controls the doorbell as a recorded cue, manipulating volume, length of ring, pitch, etc. They may ask to use a doorbell from prop stock for the initial recording, but as sound effects and sound libraries expand and the digital ability to create and manipulate sound changes rapidly, the use of a live effect is becoming obsolete at the professional level.

Sound departments often underscore live effects onstage with recorded sound made with the same instruments used by the actors to more effectively fill the space. The prop shop may be approached about providing instruments for those recording sessions; most prop shops have a large collection of musical instruments to access as needed. As new instruments are requested, the purchases can be coordinated with the sound and music departments. For those theatres doing musicals or opera performances, the professional musicians who play the orchestration provide their own instruments. In some cases, the prop shop may be asked to provide an instrument not in the usual repertoire for a sound effect from the orchestra or for a performer to use on stage. The props department also may arrange for piano tuning or other support.

Collaboration between electrics, sound, and props is necessary when the prop must emit sound but also light up such as a TV set. Plays using television often face them away from the audience as they tend to draw focus away from the actors, but the action of turning on the TV usually requires both sound and some minimal light effect to occur. If the TV also has to have a picture, then the image feed is coordinated with all departments as well.

Modern computer-based projection has grown as a scenic choice, and larger theatres may have a separate department devoted just to this area that requires props to coordinate effects and practicals with that department as well.

* * *

Working on a show with the other specialty artists found in the various shops around the the-atre is where the collaborative nature of theatre-making sets the theatre world apart from other trades utilizing similar skill sets. As the artists share in the process of solving the problems by offering solutions, using their ideas and skills, and working together to build the world of the play, the enormous creative support provided behind the scenes adds a dimension to the production unimaginable to the average theatre viewer.

CHAPTER 8.5

Working with Stage Management

An interview with Daniel J. Hanson, Production Stage
Manager—Skylight Music Theatre, Milwaukee, WI

What do you expect from your prop director:

- prior to rehearsal preparation
- during the rehearsal process
- during tech
- throughout the production run?

Daniel J. Hanson
PRODUCTION STAGE MANAGER—SKYLIGHT
MUSIC THEATRE, MILWAUKEE, WI

I think it is imperative to have a good working relationship with your props person. Out of all the other design aspects, props is usually one of the first elements the actors actually get to work with. That being said, it is also probably the design element that is tweaked the most throughout the process of putting a show together. As a stage manager, one of my responsibilities is to be the eyes and ears of the designers in the rehearsal room. For props this is really important because the way an actor uses a prop can change every minute in the rehearsal room. And a good props person recognizes this fact and expects it to happen. An idea that comes out of a production meeting will likely change three or more times before it is actually at its final stage.

Prior to rehearsal, I expect the prop director to have communicated with the director and scenic designer enough so that a props list has been generated. I also expect the props director to have gathered/assembled rehearsal props to be used by the first day of rehearsal. Obviously some of these will clearly be rehearsal props and may not even be close to what the final prop ends up being but something for the actor to work with is extremely helpful. Besides, the only way to get notes on a prop during rehearsal is for the actor to play with the prop in a scene with the director watching. I also expect the props director to communicate with the stage manager prior to rehearsal about what props, if any, stage management wants to have in the rehearsal hall. I also expect to have a clear understanding of what prop is in which scene.

During rehearsal, I expect the props director to be in constant communication with stage management regarding any changes to props. During rehearsals decisions can be made fairly quickly based on staging choices by the director and if stage management has background info on all of the props (for instance, this prop is rented and can't be altered or this one is my first choice) it will help immensely. It amazes me how much influence stage management actually has over which prop is chosen by the director. I have countless stories about a props director asking me to get the director to choose this prop over another one for various reasons.

During tech, I expect the props director to be present and really paying attention to the props onstage. Once we are in tech and adding so many new elements, some directors won't even see the props (especially if we've had them in the rehearsal room). Also during tech is when the props director will begin to interact with the assistant stage manager a lot more regarding props. The stage manager will really only be giving blatantly obvious notes to props—I rely much more heavily on the assistant stage manager to really take those detailed notes about props that are or aren't working.

Throughout the production run, I expect the props director to check in at least weekly to see how props are doing. On an extremely prop heavy show the props director may even check in more often. The props director should be available to problem-solve any issues that we might have with a prop. An example would be the need to change out a prop because an actor is having an issue with it. So as the stage manager, I would look to the props director to pick out some other options that stay within the context of the show.

What do you feel you give best TO your prop director during those same segments of our collaborative process?

As a stage manager, during the collaborative process I feel the best things I give to the props director are communication, problem-solving, and being creative. Funny how the things I expect from the props director are also the things I feel I best give to the props director.

What do you expect as best practices in the communication give-and-take between the two departments?

Open communication is the most important thing between stage management and the props director. How it is achieved is also important. Manners matter! Stage management should never really make outright demands for prop changes or prop adds unless of course it is a safety issue (at which point hopefully the props director would be making the same request). It is important for stage management to know the process of each prop shop so if the stage director is requesting to add a prop super late in the rehearsal process you are able to anticipate if this is even an option. Essentially the stage manager is a part of the props team since a lot of decisions are made during rehearsal. In that regard, stage management should strive to not create a lot of extra busy work for the prop shop. Remember, we are all working toward one goal—the best production possible.

Has the relationship between stage managers and prop people changed over the years you've been working professionally?

Over the years, I have worked with many different types of props people. I've had props people that are really good at communicating, problem-solving, and (being) creative. I've also had the opposite. Those three characteristics don't necessarily make or break the show but they definitely make things much smoother if done well.

The Production/ Tech Process

During the weeks of the build, the prop shop is in full production mode finalizing the set props, pulling and finding dressing pieces, and building hand props. Stage management and actors are invited to drop in and see the props they will be using on stage. Whenever possible, completed props are shunted into the rehearsal process. The designer is often "in house" and available for all the last-minute tweaking and decision-making. The final coordination between the other shops is completed and the production calendar breaks down into more task-oriented goals specific to each area.

Every theatre has a "technical rehearsal to opening" sequence, but within that time frame many of the same goals must be accomplished. These may include: set load-in, set dress, light and sound load-in, light focus, sound level set, prop check-in, spacing rehearsal, weapons rehearsal, technical rehearsal, dress rehearsal, preview, opening, run, and strike. It is a logical additive process layering each level of production on the show, working toward opening night, anticipating the run, and the eventual strike of the show.

Load-in and **tech** week are the time when all the elements must come together and hence can be fraught with differing goals from the various production areas. Time on stage becomes an intersection of many interests with sometimes competing priorities. Scenery is installing walls and platforms and finishing out trim. Electrics need time to hang and focus. The scenic artist needs to do touch-up work on the scenery or paint the floor after final scenic installation. The prop shop wants time to set the furniture with stage management and dress out the set, preferably when the stage has light enough to see, but occasionally under illumination by headlamp or task lighting. Light and sound levels need to get set. The actors want to move from the rehearsal hall onto the stage to become accustomed to the space. Access on stage becomes a precious commodity. Some areas require another area's completion before progressing and if (or when) things fall behind, the stress of deadlines loom large.

Pre-planning and establishing priorities allows this schedule to build logically and give time for everyone. This is often worked out in the weekly production meeting far in advance of the actual load-in weeks and is monitored and managed by the production manager. When the schedule needs to change, the production manager must juggle the priorities to insure the needs are met and each department still retains at least some time on stage to perform their work.

Collaboration, space sharing, and cooperation are paramount to achieve successful completion of all technical department goals. Being an advocate for the prop department and understanding sometimes things just can't be planned for and the path forward goes awry, the properties director must plan for an efficient and prioritized set dress in order to protect the time needed on stage and to use the time allotted in the best way possible. That takes forethought and preparation—the heart of each successful load-in and technical rehearsal process.

LOAD-IN

All set dressing, hand props, and furniture should be onstage for the first technical rehearsal. How and when that happens will often be determined by the individual show needs. While the three areas can be checked in all at once, often they are done separately given the time constraints of stage availability and of the stage management or stage operations team. Specific props might be checked in early to accommodate a specific request or need from another area. Selected props may see a later check in if they are actively in use in a separate rehearsal space. Each show tends to have different requirements; remaining flexible about "check-in" supports the needs of each particular technical load-in.

Prop check-in should be scheduled to accommodate a chance to go over all the props with the backstage run crew, to show how the props work, and to discuss any special needs or instructions on use, storage, cleaning, or other maintenance. Those organizations with a union contract and run crew will need to accommodate the strictures of time and availability for the union prop crew. Different contracts have different limitations about who can handle props once they have been checked in and who does onstage installation of dressing or shifting of furniture pieces. It's essential to know the agreed upon rules to avoid conflict and/or fines. For non-union houses, given the load the prop shop faces to get ready for technical rehearsals and coordinate with the other areas for installation and stage dress, it may be helpful to consider over-hiring some folks to assist. Tech week commonly necessitates longer work hours with work calls beginning early in the morning and rehearsals running late into the evening. Shifting work schedules to best utilize the time or adding in some over-hire labor to supplement should be considered since overtime earned by the full-time staff quickly adds up. Balance the cost of hiring in some additional folks to assist (when available) versus overtime added to regular staff to make the best use of resources, and avoid the hazards of abuse and burnout.

Checking in the furniture pieces and doing set dress can happen before hand prop check in. **Furniture load-in** often comes first, starting as soon as scenery and the paint department have the architecture of the setting in place with a finished floor, and followed by or at the same time as set dress, when further installation or paint touchup won't jeopardize the props. Consideration must also be given to the effect of dressing on the lighting and sound departments, and load-in of crucial prop pieces interfacing with other departments may need discussion and prioritization.

Furniture props are set on stage in collaboration with stage management. As pieces are checked in, each piece's needs should be noted. Some pieces may have known weaknesses the crew should be alerted to check each night to prevent breakage or damage. Stage managers who are particularly detail oriented and collaborative will add these notes to the run crew paperwork, often in the form of pre- or post-show checklists. This is especially important in a show where the furniture is abused or used in a way that causes extraordinary strain on the furniture joints, legs, arms, or upholstery. Minor adjustments to the staging area during the rehearsal process often invalidate the designer's original floor plan specifying furniture placement, and taking measurements in the rehearsal hall to transfer the same relationships to the stage is helpful. Following preliminary prop placement, it is common for the director and designer to alter where things were set in rehearsal to allow for sight lines or better spacing flow now that they inhabit the actual stage environment. In the best of all circumstances, most of the props will have already been in rehearsal or a close facsimile used, allowing stage management, the director, and the actors to have an easy transition to the stage with minimal furniture placement adjustments.

Stage managers often tape markings on the floor to create a way to track where the furniture is placed, utilizing different colors for different scenes. This process is called **spiking**. Once the furniture arrangement is finalized, and prior to opening, the tape is trimmed to smaller tabs or even painted so it becomes less visible to the audience yet still present enough for the shift crew and cast to follow. Furniture is spiked even in shows where the furniture is not shifted, allowing the floor to be swept, mopped, and furniture replaced accurately. Spiking the furniture guarantees the accurate positioning for crucial lighting cues as well as guaranteeing the spatial relationships between all props, stage edge, steps, walls, entrances, or exits remain the same for the stage action.

In shows with multiple scenes and with furniture shifting along with scenery, setting the offstage pre-set is as equally important as positioning the pieces in the onstage location. Some designers actually plan this as part of the overall design, but it is often left to the production staff to sort it out between the various areas, taking into account how the elements move, fly, roll, light up, or are elevated through the floor. The coordination of how props travel and where they are pre-set must be done in collaboration with the stage operations personnel to sort out the safest location of those items offstage until they move onstage as the larger pieces move between scenes. Sometimes props move in on scenic pieces or rolling platforms, and sorting out the shift process must be a coordination with stage management, scenery, the designer, and the prop shop. Having a preliminary strategy on paper is a useful exercise. Often, though, the reality of how something rolls or the visual coordination of how the various units move within the scene change will alter the scheme worked out before adjusting to the space and embracing the reality of multiple components moving in space and time.

Figure 9.1 SM Load-in. Stage manager Brandon Campbell checks measurements from rehearsal for placement of furniture with the prop shop during set dress. University of Wisconsin-Milwaukee.

Set dress is the process of adding all the additional props *not* handled by the actors but which help set time and place in setting the stage environment. Ingredients such as draperies, hanging chandeliers, photos on walls, magazines or newspapers on a table, or clothing hanging in a backing closet assist in cohesive storytelling. Set dressing is often coordinated with the scenic designer for the final placement and dressing decisions. While some things can be completed at the same time as a light level set or while scenery is working on backing flats or securing trim, adequate time should be allowed for the dressing of the stage with sufficient lighting and obstacle-free working conditions. This keeps the process moving safely and quickly forward. Scheduling a set dress time, especially on a realistic set with time-consuming picture placement, curtain hanging and draping, bookcases to be filled, rugs stapled down, and furniture placed and dressed out, is just as important a part of the pre-tech load-in as hanging the lighting instruments or putting in the scenery. Reasonable time must also be allowed for a certain level of reworking and arrangement, as the designer works with the prop shop to make the final tweaks and touches to this last prop layer of the creative vision.

In order to use the time most efficiently, the prop shop staff can utilize several strategies to be prepared to make the set dress easier. Certain elements can be **pre-dressed** in the shop to establish the desired style and photographed for reference, and can then be organized into labeled boxes. Once the piece is on stage it can be quickly dressed out from the box and photos, specific to location.

Figure 9.2 Pre-dress for Load-in. The table is pre-dressed in the prop shop to confirm spacing and layout of the tableware. A photo of the dressing is taken and given to the run crew, allowing them to duplicate the staging each performance. Napkin folding lessons are part of the 'check-in' and laundry duty for maintaining the linens is coordinated with costumes.

Having collections of "like" items such as books, kitchen utensils, "tchotchke" décor, photographs in frames, etc., available to be placed as needed also speeds up the dressing process. Pictures should be framed and all the necessary hardware attached for all wall décor to facilitate hanging. When filling out an exterior scene, having bags of mulch or moss and small plants pre-set in plaster for easy placement fills in gaps quickly, completing the look. Many shops use a portable tool cart with an organized hardware kit including a variety of screws, hangers, nails, floral putty, felt guards, wire, and tools to solve any installation or dressing needs.

It is a smart practice to do the hem on curtains once the set has been installed or, at the very least, once the actual window is built and accurate measurements can be taken to guarantee the final length from rod to floor. Drawings from the designer are often altered slightly by the scene shop and a difference of a few inches is disastrous when determining the finished length of drapery. Having a stock of safety pins or hem clips to pin up the curtains to their desired size for the first stage rehearsals is necessary unless requisite time is available to complete the sewing prior to first tech.

In some situations, set dress is completed before **lighting focus**, since stage dressing may impact specials. As the crew focuses the lights, props such as foliage dressed outside a door, drapery over a window, or a hanging chandelier can limit the area to be lit or impact on the angle or location of the instrument supplying the light. Having the dressing complete before the focus happens prevents a need for re-focus, or the request to drastically adjust dressing. At the very least, inform the master electrician of anticipated dressing conflicts. More importantly, it is helpful for all props, including furniture, to be onstage for **light level set**. The colors, textures, and shadows created by the props can dramatically change the appearance of the stage space once the stage lights are illuminated.

When producing large musicals or shows with multiple scene settings, some organizations have a **shift rehearsal** allowing the run crew personnel to practice pre-sets, set and prop cues for onstage internal/act changes, and fly cues. Practicing these types of shifts works best when *all* the crew is available. In some cases, however, actors assist in scene changes by either carrying off props or bringing on props. In those instances, the shifts must be rehearsed during the technical rehearsal time when everyone is available, or by finding someone to stand in for the actor during the shift rehearsal.

Hand prop check-in usually occurs in the prop shop with representatives from stage management and the props run crew or stage operations folk as needed. Going down the prop list or utilizing a prop pre-set list from stage management, each prop is loaded into the appropriate rolling prop run cabinet or into carts to be moved to the stage and placed on secure run tables. For those theatre companies with the production studio located in another building or even across town, props must be boxed up, loaded into rolling cabinets, or in some way safely transported to the theatre. Prop check-in is then conducted at the theatre as the props are unloaded and unpacked.

Prop check-in is where the prop list and numbering system proves especially helpful. As each number is called out, each prop is explained and any concerns about maintenance or handling addressed. If, for example, the prop is a diary the actor reads from and also writes in nightly, the prop crew may utilize different colored bookmarks to assist the actor in finding the specific written passages or may cut corners off from the page to make those specific pages easier to find. The pages getting written on each night may be only temporarily affixed and require additional pages to be added each night. Showing this to the run crew and explaining the use guarantees consistency and understanding of how the prop is to be used as well as required nightly maintenance to keep the diary consistent for each performance. It might also be something as simple as proper storage of an item so it is more easily maintained, such as rolling a flag or banner so it doesn't have fold lines, eliminating nightly pressing or steaming.

As the props are checked in, it is common to sort them by pre-set or storage location with accompanying paperwork for documenting tracking. This is easily done using the item name or number. Hand props are checked in to the run crew for placement in secure cabinets until it is time to set them out on the run tables for the technical rehearsal. A **run**

table is the location where hand props are set prior to the start of the show for actors to pick up or drop off items used in their particular scenes and are usually set up and maintained by stage management or the props run crew. Prop run tables are set up in the wings or offstage areas of the stage, allowing actors to easily find a prop adjacent to the entrance being utilized. Some organizations have **prop run cabinets** doubling as the prop lock-up for storage between shows. Having a plug strip for powering electrical items or charging batteries built into the cabinet as well as interior lighting makes a self-contained and safe prop run cabinet.

Whether using run tables or running props out of a storage cabinet, the prop lay-out areas are usually labeled with the individual prop name and maybe even the scene used. This practice allows for quick, consistent, and efficient prop set up and makes it easy for the actor to find the prop in the same place each performance. It is equally important for an area to be set aside for any prop to be dropped off by the actors as they exit the stage. On occasion, a prop must travel from where it is dropped off on one prop table to be pre-set again on a different

Figure 9.3 Prop Run Cabinet. Shelves are marked for each prop and labeled so pre-set is easily viewed and actors can quickly find their props in the same place for each show.

prop table for in a following scene, or a prop may get struck from where it is left onstage to return as a hand-off later in the show. Under these circumstances the prop run crew must know where and when the prop moves and designate a person to do it.

Once all the hand props are checked in, set dress completed, and furniture placed and spiked, the prop shop is ready for technical rehearsals and for the actors to inhabit the space.

TECHNICAL AND DRESS REHEARSALS

Technical rehearsals are the times scheduled to layer all the elements of production onto the rehearsed performance. Actors are in the stage space defined by the designer, using the props, and eventually wearing costumes and enveloped in the lighting and sound effects. Technical rehearsals are when all aspects come together, and while often a time of some anxiety and stress, can also be immensely rewarding when the elements start to really work and the play comes to life.

The first rehearsal where the real props are used onstage will often generate many notes, and it's essential the properties director be in attendance to assist with any adjustments or offer advice on prop use. When there is time, this first prop rehearsal is often done in what is called a **spacing rehearsal** without lights or sound but on the completed stage setting. The spacing rehearsal allows the director to make adjustments in the blocking and staging, giving the actors an opportunity to experience the stage space in full work light. This helps them understand how to safely move in the space both onstage and off. During the spacing rehearsal, all furniture must be in place onstage, allowing the actors to begin to set their movement and understand the adjacency to the audience and offstage areas. The prop run tables should be set up offstage with all hand props available so the actors begin to know where to pick up and drop off their props. The stage has at least the minimal dressing impacting the actor's entrances, exits, movement on the stage, or action. Hopefully the stage masking is in position and any light stands, speakers, or other technical support elements are set, which allows the actors to see travel paths backstage and know where it is safe to move and stand prior to entrance on the stage.

Prop department input in the collaborative problem-solving process with the director and designer is critical during this process of staging. Offering options to make an action easier or suggesting alternatives available when a prop is not working as hoped goes a long way to making the technical rehearsal process support the overall goal of creating a complete production. The intent is to be helpful, and each design/director team has a different dynamic. Some teams work in an open process, accepting ideas from the technical staff, while others prefer to keep the discussion within the design team. The properties director probably has a notion of how to best present advice based on prior interactions with the director and designers during the build process of the prior weeks. The properties director must always step in when a situation endangers the safety of people on stage or the integrity of a prop. While the director may desire a specific action or visual, the properties director should suggest ways to handle or move props to insure the prop is not broken or damaged. If that is not possible, then the risk (and expense) of breakage should be discussed and evaluated in the context of budget, personnel, and time needed to repair or replace the prop if it should be damaged. Many stage directors are able to effect compromise to an action allowing for safe handling of the props on stage.

At the first *full* **technical rehearsal**, when the elements of light, sound, and scene shifts are added, the spacing rehearsals value becomes evident, as many of the prop notes have already been solved. Those theatres lacking the time to have a spacing rehearsal will need to deal with prop notes during the technical rehearsal, layered with the challenges from all the other areas.

At the first full technical rehearsal, notes from the designer for additional toning or aging of props are common, as the exposure of light makes evident the need for adjustment to color or distressing. A low light level or the length of scene change music complicates scene shifts previously working in full light without music. Actors suddenly have difficulty with a prop they handled successfully in the previous day's rehearsal. This is all normal and usual as the elements of technical storytelling layer onto the rehearsal process. Keeping a supportive and pleasant attitude to resolve the challenges helps make the time more useful and less stressful for all involved.

The properties director also assists in the fine-tuning of the **scene change choreography** to help insure the safety of the props and to suggest ways to assist in an efficient prop run. This might include providing a special padded box to strike stemmed glassware, placing small tabs on a circular tablecloth to allow the scene shift person to feel where to place it on the table in the darkness of the shift, or showing a crew person how to pick up a chair from the seat and *not* the arms. This process should always be worked out with the stage management or stage operations person responsible for leading the run crew.

Beyond working with the scene shift crew, the prop shop might be asked to work with an actor who has to handle a specific prop to help solve a particular problem or to show the actor the easiest way to manipulate the prop. If weapons are called for, the properties director should attend the first fight run-through in the space to work in the safe coordination of the weaponry with the director and/or fight choreographer in relation to the audience and stage setting. Most weaponry would have been tried out in rehearsal, so the adjustment is primarily to accommodate the specific use of the weapons now that the actors are in the theatre. All too often, action staged in the rehearsal hall requires adjustments to choreography on stage. The properties director should advocate for the appropriate use of the prop as well as any concerns about audience proximity or safety.

As the technical rehearsal progresses, the properties director makes notes of articles to be altered as well as requested adds or cuts. By closely watching the play and how the props are utilized, often the properties director is able to make suggestions for simplifying or adapting a prop in support of the full show experience. It may be something as simple as folding a letter smaller to allow the actor to access it from a costume pocket more easily or lining a tray with a non-slip surface to keep glasses from sliding around as the actor carries the tray. It might also be toning props down into the scenic palette or adding additional color or trim to a prop to connect it to a specific character or costume.

The designer may give notes as observed throughout the technical rehearsal or hand them all off at the end of the rehearsal. Many production teams utilize various online note sharing software to send notes *during* the rehearsal. All requests should be clarified and discussed with concerned parties along with any notes the properties director has made or received from the director, stage management, or actors. It isn't unusual for an actor to take the properties director aside to ask for a change to a prop without going through the standard protocol for such requests. These requests should be passed on to stage management and all modifications approved by the director or the designer before changing anything once the prop has been checked in and used on stage. Other production areas may make requests to the prop shop as well, and those should be coordinated in the production meeting held at the end of the rehearsal.

Costumes are often added later in the technical rehearsal process, after light and sound cues have been roughed in and actors have been on stage for a few rehearsals. Those rehearsals are called **dress rehearsals** since the actors are now in full costume, makeup, and designed hair style. Actors often experience additional difficulties with handling props when the layers of wigs, make-up, and restrictive clothing are added. Adjustments to hand props are common to accommodate a too small pocket or to allow a movement the costume requires. Even when a prop has worked previously, until all elements of the production process have been added, it's best to keep an open eye to the props and a generosity of spirit as to what might be added, changed, or cut.

Generally, a mini production meeting follows each tech rehearsal, attended by the director, production management, stage management, department heads, and designers. The purpose of this meeting is to communicate or clarify the notes, collaborate with other departments, confirm the following day's schedule and space usage, and prioritize use of the stage or tasks to be taken care of before the next rehearsal. Problem-solving as a group with all of the pro-duction and design team available allows maximum collaboration to identify solutions for any challenges occurring in the rehearsal. This process will continue at least through the first preview and, in some cases, all the way through opening. Stage management may publish production notes from these meetings and distribute them via email to be sure everyone is aware of changes, adds, priorities, and scheduling requests.

The prop artisans complete the requested changes or prop notes during the standard work call the following day. Letting stage management know when a prop has been removed from the storage cabinets for any reason is important. Many companies use a check-in/check-out system to notate a prop's status on the door of the prop run cabinet. Notification may be also done via email with appropriate follow-up on the status of the piece. If the note requires painting or re-building, sufficient drying and/or repair time should be planned for, and an alternate rehearsal prop provided if the actual prop cannot be returned in time for the next technical rehearsal. Any new props added must be checked-in to the run crew with stage management and appropriate notation on prop lists, storage cabinets, run tables, and tracking sheets completed. In a union house, check the contract to see who is allowed to do prop notes. It may require an additional call for the union prop person to work on items once they have been checked into the show.

By opening night everything must work smoothly, and the technical rehearsal process is the time to join forces and sort out what has to get done, by whom, on what priority, and how. It is the best of times where all production areas rally together and create the world where the actors perform.

OPENING NIGHT/RUN

Opening night signals the point where the show leaves the "shop and build" process and is fully in the hands of stage management and the run crew. The **run crew** is responsible for maintaining the props and doing small repairs as necessary. Once the props are backstage, it is the responsibility of stage management and the props run crew to safely manage and maintain the props during the technical rehearsals, opening, and run of the show.

In the event something critical is broken or a repair is beyond the skill of the run crew, the prop is generally returned to the prop shop. Even in a union house, major repairs are often done by the prop shop staff, though in some venues the union run person may have additional maintenance hours available to do some repairs and may assist when a major repair is needed. It is critically important for any significant problem to be immediately communicated to the properties director, allowing adequate time to implement a solution before the next performance call. Using the check-out and check-in system keeps everyone in the loop when props are removed from pre-set for any reason. Any prop removed should be returned with plenty of time for proper check-in and placement by the run crew. If an item is damaged beyond immediate repair or is lost, the prop shop will need to provide a comparable substitute to allow the performance to run unhindered . . . hence the importance of a detailed and timely performance report to all areas.

Running props during a show is an important part of the entire mechanism. Props must be consistently placed in the same location for each performance, oriented in the same way every time, ready to complete the action required. Working with stage management as the show progresses throughout the rehearsal and tech process, pre-set and tracking sheets are developed indicating top of the show positions for all props, either onstage or on an offstage prop run table or cabinet. The **tracking sheets** follow each prop during the play and show all exits or entrances of the prop as well as any required location transfers between scenes or acts, and a final track point where it can be found at the end of the performance.

As the scene shifts are choreographed, the tracking of the prop is incorporated in the shift, changes are notated on the tracking/run sheets, and spaces are delineated on prop tables to accommodate necessary placements or drop-offs. Stage dressing for the top of the show and any movement of props done at intermission may require a deeper level of documentation to be sure everything is placed identically each performance.

The Spitfire Grill Show Run Sheet   Updated

6/14/08 MKH

PRESHOW DUTIES

WHO	WHAT	NOTES
ANDREW	Unlock stage areas and dressing rooms, check crew sign-in, sweep/mop stage, help set needed furniture, unlock headsets, rail check, check in with PSM	
NIKKI	Check & set onstage & SR props	
ALEXIS/MAGGIE	Pick up artists, check & set SL props	
MICHELE	Set water stations & green room/coffee, check all presets, DND phone, report to PSM	
KOREN	Conduct dimmer check, report to PSM	
GARY	Check & set cast wireless mics, check any headset problems, report to PSM	
JUSTIN	Wardrobe presets, assist actors	
JANINE	Turn on spotlight, check in with crew chief	
TIM	Turn on spotlight, check in with crew chief	

TOP OF SHOW PRESET INFORMATION ******Italicized items are used in Act II only******

ONSTAGE		STAGE LEFT	STAGE RIGHT
Suitcase – Top Level	Butcher Block with: (DIAGRAM)	Lantern	Act II Tub #1 with:
Percy's Green Scarf – Costumes	*Top Shelf:*	Potato Bowl w. Peeler	Spice Rack
Percy's Blue Pea Coat – Costumes	Metal Oatmeal Pot w. Lid	Percy's Green Apron	Act II Salt Shaker
Bus Ticket in right pocket	2 Cast Iron Skillets	Egg Bowl	2 New Potholders
Picture of Gilead in left pocket	Act I Salt Shaker	Colander	2 New Kitchen Towels
Percy's Grey Sweatshirt inside Coat	*1ˢᵗ Shelf:*	Sack of Onions	Shelby Stack of Essays
Pack of Cigarettes in right pocket	Metal Baking Pan	Metal Lunch Box	Percy Stack of Essays
Stump – Down Right	*Bottom Shelf:*	White Phone	Hannah Stack of Essays
Axe – on the floor, right of stump	Secured Cutting Board	Cream/Brown Oatmeal Pot w. Lid	2 Blue Tin Cups
Rocking Chair	Oatmeal Canister w. Lid	Ketchup Refill Bottlw & Rag	Jug
Wood Box full of wood	Stack of Small Bowls	Order Pad & Pencil	
Hannah's Book w. Eyeglasses	Stack of Small Plates	Rolling Pin	Act II Tub #2 with:
Shelby's Brown Apron	Pyrex Glass Measuring Cup	Flour Canister	Act II Coffee Pot
Counter with: (DIAGRAM)	Stack of Big Plates	Corn Husk Broom	3 Jars of Flowers
Top Shelf:	Stack of Big Bowls	Hannah's Crutches	2 Small Menus
Cash Register	Trick Oatmeal Bowl – 2ⁿᵈ from top	Hannah's Cane	Cash Box w. Money
Eraser	1 loose bowl on top of trick bowl	Gardening Hoe	Candy Dish
Act I Chalkboard	*Stage Right Side:*	Chains	2 Wrapped Aprons – Shelby on top
Order Keeper	2 Loose Act I Dish Towels – Blue	Ice Testing Rod	Shelby Stack of Letters – 17 Letters
Jar of Pencils & Chalk	*Stage Left Side:*	Effy's Whistle	Shelby Final Essay
Sugar Shaker	2 Act I Potholders	Recipe Card	Percy Essay #1 (Green Folder)
Creamer	Tray w. Utensils:	Effy Letter #1 – Philly w. Check	Percy Final Essay
Order Pad & Pencil	Large Wooden Spoon	Effy Stack of Letters #2 – 8 Letters	Effy Essays #2 & #3/Final
Blank Order Pad	Spatula	- 8ᵗʰ w. $100 Bill	Joe's Final Essay
1ˢᵗ Shelf:	2 Wire Whisks	Effy Stack of Letters #3 – 11 Letters	Hannah's Ad Newspaper w. Keys
Act I Coffee Pot	Blue Metal Spoon	Percy Stack of Letters – 12 Letters*	Percy's Prison File
3 Bread with 3 Folded Towels	Fork on Top	2 Newspapers w. Spitfire Ads	Joe's Coffee Cup
3 Cups w. Saucers	Tobasco Sauce	Xeroxed Newspaper Articles &	Joe's Rolled Deed w. Red Ribbon
1 Cup w. No Saucer		Whisky Bottle	Eli's Feather
Stack of Silverware:	*Stage Left Table w. 2 Chairs:*	3 Letters for Joe	Eli's Bird
2 Knives, 2 Spoons, 2 Forks	2 Forks	Accordion Stack of Letters w. Effy	Joe's 2 Newspapers– Gilead Reporter
Record Ledger	2 Knives	Essay #1	Cash for Joe's Tip
2ⁿᵈ Shelf:	2 Spoons	Joe Essays #1 & #2	Hannah's Ribbed Kitchen Towel
Plastic Water Pitcher, on its side	2 Cups w. Saucers-cups upside	Hannah Essay	Caleb's Phone
Rag & Spray Bottle	down	Shelby Essay	Axe Head, Sharpening Stone, Rag
Caleb's List of Supplies	2 Salt/Pepper Shakers	Act II New Chalkboard	Caleb's Large Ratchet
Dustpan & Whisk Broom	Ketchup Bottle	White Blanket	Road Salter
Water Glass	Napkin Dispenser - Full	Breakable Plate	Hannah's Blanket
Bottom Shelf:		1 New Kitchen Towel	Metal Bar for Top of Show
2 Grey Bus Tubs – Empty	*Stage Right Table w. 2 Chairs:*	2 Rolls of Silverware	Pitch Pipe
	(SL Chair is throwable)	$1 Bill for Effy's Tip	Box of Toothpicks
	2 Forks	3 Tablecloths – Ironed & Folded	Effy's Shovel
Wire Wood Crate	2 Knives	2 Pieces of Chalk	Effy's Push Broom
2 Stools	2 Spoons	Tissues for Effy	Black Fishing Pole
	2 Cups w. Saucers-cups upside	4 Bags of Letters in Wheelbarrow	Empty Black Bin
	down	- Strings should be pulled tight	
	2 Salt/Pepper Shakers	2 Sconces	
	Ketchup Bottle		
	Napkin Dispenser		
	Creamer		
RAIL:	**ORCHESTRA PIT:**		
Moon OUT	Sound FX Ratchet on Maestro Stand		

Figure 9.4 Pre-set Sheet. *Spitfire Grill* run sheets from Skylight Opera production showing pre-show duties for run crew and prop pre-set. Katie Kragiel, stage manager; Lisa Schlenker, properties director.

ACT I DIAGRAMS:

The Spitfire Grill Show Run Sheet

COUNTER - BACK VIEW

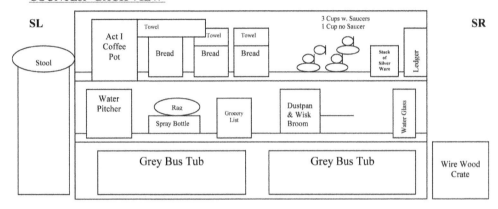

NOTES:
- The Chalkboard is leaning against the Cash Register, with the Eraser between them.
- The stack of silverware should be able to all be grabbed in one hand
- Two of the coffee cups on saucers should be placed upside down. The third one on a saucer should be placed right side up.
- The towel on the SR loaf of bread is folded 2X. The middle and SL bread towels are folded 3X.
- The water pitcher should be placed sideways, with the handle pointed upstage, so it can be easily grabbed.

NOTE: Italicized Handoffs/Receives are where actors have a little bit of time to prep before their next entrance. These are not immediate.

ACT ONE – 1:05:00

WHEN	WHO	WHAT	NOTES
"Places"	ANDREW	SL	
	NIKKI	SR – Places for Orchestra, then RECEIVE: Pitch Pipe from PERCY SR	
	ALEXIS/MAGGIE	SL – ACTOR PLACES: HANNAH	
	MICHELE	SR – ACTOR PLACES: PERCY, JOE. ALSO: Preshow Speech Announcer	
	KOREN	Booth	
	GARY	Sound Booth `	
	JUSTIN	Stage Right	
	JANINE	Spot #2	
	TIM	Spot #1	
SCENE 1 – *A Ring Around the Moon*			
00:00	MICHELE	SR3 - Bars	Q from PSM
	ANDREW	RAIL: Moon IN	Q from PSM
	NIKKI	SR2 – *HANDOFF: Coffee Cup & Percy File to JOE*	
	ANDREW	SL1 – HANDOFF: Lantern to HANNAH	
5:00	NIKKI	SR2 - RECEIVE: Coffee Cup & Percy File from JOE	
8:10	MICHELE	SR2 – HANDOFF: 2 Newspapers to JOE, RECEIVE: Lantern from HANNAH, TRACK Lantern to SL,	
	JUSTIN	**SR2 – RECEIVE: Blue Plaid Overshirt from HANNAH**	
9:15	ANDREW	SL1 – HANDOFF: Percy's Apron & Potato Bowl w. Peeler to HANNAH	
9:45	ALEXIS/MAGGIE	SL2 – RECEIVE: Coat, Scarf, Suitcase from PERCY	Warning from PSM
	NIKKI	SR Side Stage – STRIKE Bread & Towel, Remove axe from stump and set on the floor SR of stump	Warning from PSM
	ANDREW	RAIL – Moon (Line set #???) OUT	Q from PSM
SCENE 2 – *Something's Cooking*			
12:00	ANDREW	SL1 – HANDOFF: Egg Bowl to PERCY, RECEIVE: Cigarettes, Have Water Ready for PERCY	
13:05	ANDREW	SL1 – HANDOFF: Onion Sack to PERCY	
	ALEXIS/MAGGIE	*SL3 – HANDOFF: Lunchbox to SHELBY*	
16:00	ANDREW	SL1 – RECEIVE: Onion Sack from HANNAH	

Figure 9.5 Run Sheet. Run crew sheet showing stage dressing placement and listing prop run handoffs and moves during the show for *Spitfire Grill*. Katie Kragiel, stage manager; Lisa Schlenker, properties director.

Figure 9.6 Dressing Documentation. Taking a photo to document pre-set allows for a quick identification of all the props relative to placement and insures consistency for each performance from the specific ordering of the bottles or glasses placement to the orientation of the handles on the pitchers. As pre-sets change during tech, an updated photo allows quick revision for the run crew. Mike Gerlach, properties master, *Ruined*, UW-Milwaukee theatre.

For those props set on stage, a diagram may be created that shows placement and notes any specific details. Digital photographs are an especially handy way of documenting as they can be easily updated during technical rehearsals when dressing evolves.

WEAPONS

Prop weapons check-in, run, safe storage, and maintenance require special consideration. The prop director, with stage management, should apprise Security and Building Operations as well as House Management of the use of any weapons onstage. In the case of gunfire, identifying an approximate time and duration of the effect keeps everyone advised, and alerting management to post lobby signage informing the audience of firearms or other loud effects. If the performance space is adjacent to other occupied spaces, it's also best to notify neighbors of any anticipated noise issues.

A designated **firearms master** should be selected from the stage operations crew. They will be responsible for issuing, collecting, loading, cleaning, maintaining, storing, and inventorying all weapons and ammunition for the production's run. Weapons should be checked in separately from other props, allowing them to be placed directly into the backstage secured lockup area. Access to the backstage lockup should be limited to only those critical technical personnel dealing with the weapons, and should never be left unsecured and open. Transportation of weapons between spaces and locations should be done in secure containers. No weapon should be carried in plain view or moved in the passenger compartment of a motor vehicle. As noted in Chapter 8, know your local laws regarding transportation and handling of weapons and scrupulously abide by them.

During technical rehearsals and the production run, weapons should *never* be placed on prop run tables, but stored in the locked weapons cabinet and handed off only as the actor prepares to go onstage. This prevents any accidental mishandling of the weapon, especially in the case of a blank loaded firearm. Guns loaded with stage blanks should follow a special high-security protocol to guarantee every precaution has been taken to insure the gun will fire as rehearsed and required. The actor using the gun, as well as anyone onstage when the gun is fired, has the assurance that all established safety protocols have been followed to keep everyone out of harm's way. Actors have the right to witness the loading of the weapon or to request inspection of the weapon following loading. Based on acoustic tests previously conducted in order to support the rehearsal process (Chapter 8), performers and crew who request hearing protection should be accommodated, working with costumes and the actors to find ways to disguise the earplugs or by altering blocking for adjacency

Assassins
Gun Plot

Quadracci Powerhouse
2012-2013 Season

#	Gun	Who	Exhaust	Notes	# Shots	Totals (Live/Dry)	Reh/Perf
102	.32 Iver-Johnson REVOLVER	Czolgosz	Front	Will have to dry fire and live fire without being reloaded; Max. possibility: 3 dry & 2 live (or we have to duplicate gun)	Sc.1 (0), Sc.7 (3d), R on stage, Sc.8 (1), E, Sc.15 (Empty), R, Sc.18 (1)	2/3d	-#4
107	.22 Rohm RG-14 REVOLVER	Hinkley	Front		Sc.1 (0), Sc.10 (5?), E, Sc.15 (Empty), R, Sc.18 (1)	6?	-#4
109	.442 Webley British Bulldog REVOLVER	Guiteau	Front		Sc.1 (0), Sc.11 (1), E, Sc.15 (Empty), R, Sc.18 (1)	2	-#4
700	Duplicate Bulldog REVOLVER	Guiteau	N/A		Sc.7 (1d)	2d	!#"0
111	.32 Pistol?	Zangara	Front		Sc.1 (0), Sc.4 (1), E, Sc.15 (Empty), R, Sc.18 (1)	2	-#4
114	.22?	Byck	Front		Sc.1 (0), Sc.15 (Empty), R, Sc.18 (1)	1	-#4
116	REVOLVER	Fromme	Front		Sc.1 (0), Sc.6 (5), R, Sc.13 (1d), E, Sc.15 (Empty), R, Sc.18 (1)	6/1d	Reh
119	.38 Smith & Wesson REVOLVER	Moore	Front		Sc.1 (0), Sc.6 (6), R, Sc.7 (1), R, Sc.11 (5), E, Sc.15 (Empty), R, Sc.18 (1)	.5	Reh
1301	Trick REVOLVER	Moore	N/A	The chamber lock will be loosened, but not disengaged	Sc.13 (5b)	5 blanks fall out	-#4
128	.44 Derringer single shot	Booth	Front	Hammer must be cocked in order to shoot; Will have duplicate if needed to dry fire	Sc.1 (1), R, Sc.7 (3d), E, Sc.15 (Empty), R, Sc.18 (1)	2/3d	!#"0
211	.44 Colt 1851 Navy REVOLVER	Booth	N/A	Hammer must be cocked in order to shoot; Will be dropped	Sc.2 (0)	0	-#4
221	.44 Colt 1851 Navy REVOLVER	Davey	N/A		Sc.2 (0)	0	-#4
1604	.38 Smith & Wesson REVOLVER	Oswald	N/A	Will be cast replica and not have the ability to fire at all	Sc.16 (0)	0	-#4
.676	6.5mm Mannlicher-Carcano RIFLE	Oswald	Front	Will enter with safety on; Must disengage safety before firing	Sc.16 (1), R, Sc.18 (1)	2	-#4

Prepared by: MFR   1 of 1   12.32.3

Figure 9.7 *Assassins* Gun Plot. Milwaukee Repertory Theater's *Assassins* gun plot, noting each weapon's description, use, handling, loading, and firing information for the safety and security of the actors and run crew. Jim Guy, properties director.

or placement to minimize the effect of loud gunfire. Preparing for the event of a weapon or ammunition failure with alternate dialogue, a change in blocking, an offstage sound effect, backup weaponry, or other action is critical to allow the play's story to move forward if the unexpected happens.

Protocol between stage management, the firearms master loading the gun, the hand-off to the actor prior to entering the stage, and the exact physical spacing for all gunfire effects should be practiced as part of the technical rehearsal or during a designated weapons call. The hand-off of the weapon as the actor exits the stage and the safe securing of the weapon back into the weapons lock up must also be coordinated between the actor, stage management, and the run crew. Firearms should be unloaded at the first available opportunity. Under no circumstances should a weapon be stored in the dressing room with costumes, as too many people have access, leaving the weapon unsecured. Weapons must be cleaned and inspected following every performance.

At strike, the weapons should be checked thoroughly by the prop crew and a final cleaning and oiling or appropriate maintenance completed before locking items back into the prop storage armory. Any tape or markings should be removed and the weapons inventory updated as needed to reflect the condition and status of each weapon.

CONSUMABLES

Consumables (also called **perishables**) are the items used up, eaten, destroyed, broken, manipulated, or handled in such a way that they are only good for one performance. These items must be replaced every performance and a sufficient supply provided to the run crew for the full run of the show.

Consumable hand props can run the gamut from simple letters getting opened each night to pieces of pottery being thrown and smashed. Flower bouquets may need to be arranged with fresh flowers or candles replaced in lanterns after burning down each night. Checking cigarette lighters for fuel, accounting for discharged blank loads for practical firearms, ensuring the seltzer water dispenser is charged, making tea sandwiches and tea: these all live on a consumable list. For consumables, it is usual during tech to check in only what is most convenient to store safely. In the case of a torn-up letter, often an entire run's worth of letters can be checked in with the multiple copies in a clear plastic bag for safekeeping, labeled with the prop number. Larger items may require only a few pieces checked in and the run crew given the rest on an as-needed basis from the prop shop over the run.

Perishables such as food or fresh flowers are usually not checked in until late in the rehearsal chronology. Policies vary as to when food is introduced into the technical rehearsal process unless it is critical to the action of the scene or for timing with lights and

PROP DIRECTOR, JIM GUY

MILWAUKEE REPERTORY THEATRE
CYRANO CONSUMABLES LIST

#	Prop	Qty./Show	Who	Notes
P1103a	Wicks	3	Theatre Employees	For lighter snuffers, each snuffer will have a wick, only 3 will be used each show. Replace as necessary.
C1109	Oranges	1 to 3	Orange Girl (Ms. Silhelmer)/Crowd/ Pickpocket (Mr. Knight)	1 Tossed into air, replace as necessary.
C1118	Macaroons	TBA	Orange Girl (Ms. Silhelmer)/Crowd/ Cyrano (Mr. Ernst)	Broken in half and eaten by Mr. Ernst, Sold to crowd
C1120	Grapes	3 bunches	Orange Girl (Ms. Silhelmer)/Crowd/ Cyrano (Mr. Ernst)	One grape is eaten by Mr. Ernst, sold to crowd
P1236	Pie	1	Cyrano (Mr. Ernst), Musketeer (Mr. Neugent)	Mr. Neugent's face is smashed into a pie by Mr. Ernst, meringue
C1226c	Small Cakes	21-28	Poets	Consumed on stage
P1304	Candles (5)	10/run	Ms. Apalategui, Ms. Brennan, Ms. Beyer, Ms. Seilhelmer, Ms. Germany	Replace as necessary
P2505	Thread	1 spool/Run	Roxane (Ms. Partin)	Cut on stage. Rethread Needle (2505a) as necessary.
	Paper Props			
P1207	Brown Paper	1/show	Ragueneau (Mr. Hanson), Cyrano (Mr. Ernst)	Blank, at least one piece used per show
P1222	Paper cones (6)	12/wk	Lise (Ms. Apalategui), Ragueneau (Mr. Hanson) Poets	Begin flattened, will hold Pastries (#1202a). Replace as necessary.
P1222a	Recipe (1)	3-4/wk	Ragueneau (Mr. Hanson)	Folded into cone, unfolded on stage. Replace as necessary.
P1222b	Paper cones (2)	6-8/wk	Cyrano (Mr. Ernst), Duenna (Ms. Pickering)	One will hold 6 Cream puffs (#1212); one will hold 1 Jelly roll (#1209); will begin open. Replace as necessary.
1222c	Paper cone- openable (1)	2/wk	Cyrano (Mr. Ernst), Duenna (Ms. Pickering)	Opened on stage by Cyrano (Mr. Ernst), Replace as needed.
1136	Folded note	2/wk	Duenna (Ms. Pickering)	Replace as necessary
1137	Crumpled scrap of paper	2/wk	Ligniere (Mr. Silbert)	Replace as necessary
P1226a	Loose Paper	1/show	Cyrano (Mr. Ernst)	Same stationary as Letter (#2404) and (#2508)
1302	Letter	2/wk	Ligniere (Mr. Silbert), Roxane (Ms. Partin)	Replace as necessary
2404	Letter	8/wk	Cyrano (Mr. Ernst), Christian (Mr. Martin)	Tri-folded and passed on stage, replace as necessary.
2508	Letter	2/wk	Roxane (Ms. Partin), Cyrano (Mr. Ernst)	Folded and placed in silk bag. Will be removed from bag on stage. Replace as necessary.

Figure 9.8 Consumables List. Listing of all consumable props to assist the run crew in monitoring use/maintenance issues for Milwaukee Repertory Theater's production of *Cyrano*. Jim Guy, properties director.

sound. Using food onstage during technical rehearsals can be problematic. The length of the rehearsal scenes is often not an accurate reflection of the actual action, causing food to sit longer in pre-set or under the lights onstage as various technical problems are worked out, making it unsafe to eat. For this reason, food is often introduced when the technical rehearsals are able to move at a "run" pace and prudent practices for safe food handling can be put in place. Food pre-set backstage should be appropriately stored, shielded from tampering by others, and maintained with any required refrigeration/heat. If food must be cooked or otherwise handled, a protected food handling area must be provided to guarantee the food is kept at a safe temperature and free from contamination during the preparation time.

Food and drink props should be addressed early in the rehearsal process far before the actors step foot on stage. Coordination with costumes, scenic art, and scenery for colorants and other substances used to prepare stage food needs to occur allowing input into clean up processes, stain remediation, or alternatives. Anticipating any difficulties, stage management should determine special requests or allergy restrictions when actors must consume food or liquid on stage. For example, some people will not eat meat, and if their part requires them to consume a meat sandwich then a substitution must be found. Many performers also prefer to only consume easily chewed and swallowed food. Pears are a common solution since they can be conveniently colored with food safe coloring, store readily, are relatively inexpensive, available year-round, and can be cut and shaped to look like a wide variety of food items. It would be rare to use peanut butter, which makes it difficult for the actor to speak, or crumbly dry crackers, which make a mess onstage. Many performers also prefer low fat or diet foods, and liquids without caffeine and sugar. It is typical to substitute plain water tinted with caramel coloring or other food coloring for wine, soda, or alcoholic beverages. Special thought should be given to what and how much an actor will eat on stage. Many scenes requiring practical food can be supported by a minimal quantity of actual food consumption.

For example, scenes set in Victorian times often have tea served, and while an entire tea service may be presented, the sandwiches and other items may all be fake with only a single plate of cookies being edible. This gives the necessary visual appearance required by the script but limits the action to easily consumed and easily managed food. Other plays, such as *The Art of Dining*, set in a restaurant kitchen where actors must prepare and cook full meals which are then served in the restaurant's dining room to other actors acting as patrons of the restaurant, requires an entirely different approach. The provision for that level of consumables is enormous and requires considerable forethought and an appropriate level of funding to comply with safe food handling rules and regulations. Appropriate rehearsal and training of the actors preparing the food, and of the run crew in pre-set and post-show handling of the food and cleaning of the stage kitchen area are also enormous factors to account for in budgeting personnel hours.

Often prop food is entirely faked. Styrofoam and plaster can be crafted to create beautiful pastries. Rubber bands painted and toned make realistic noodles. Fish and poultry can be carved from foam and painted to look like a completed dinner entree. If the show has a short run, often times the food can be real food, refrigerated at the end of each performance, and disposed of at the end of the run. The expense of buying real food and using it over and over, when *not* consumed, is often a more cost-effective option than the time and expense of manufacturing exquisitely realistic fake food. It is of critical importance however that everyone, including the crew, understands the food is only a prop and not to be consumed, since the food might not be safe after being pre-set under stage light for several performances.

When edibles are consumed onstage they must be kept at safe storage temperature, and any food handled should be dealt with in ways guaranteeing the welfare and good health of those who may eat the prop. Many regional theatres provide a prop run room including a kitchen with refrigerator, stove, microwave, and sink allowing for the appropriate storage, preparation, and run of prop food. When a prop run kitchen is not available, a separate clean "kitchen" show run space should be set up.

Having a list of all the consumable/perishable items needing to be replaced, fixed, checked, or "made/cooked" helps the run crew keep an accurate calculation and insure they have sufficient supplies on hand and can quickly communicate any needs to the prop shop when stock runs low.

PERSONALS

Some items are considered **personal** props; those props *are* often checked in to the actor or the costume run crew at the start of the technical rehearsal process and may be stored in the dressing room with the costume. Examples of these kinds of personal props would include an eyeglasses case, contents of purses or wallets, a cane, a cigarette lighter or case, or a holster for a gun. If kept in the dressing room, they should become part of the costume run crew check list and are the shared responsibility of the costume run crew. These items are checked back into the prop shop at strike.

If no costume run crew is available or if the dressing rooms are crowded and the security of the prop might be compromised, it is wise to have these items tracked by stage management or the prop run crew during the run of the show, with the understanding the prop is pre-set in the dressing room each performance and then checked back into prop storage, rather than left in the dressing room. This is the preferred method, as often these props tend to be the ones that go missing if simply left unchecked and unaccounted for by a crew member.

RUN STORAGE

Safe and secure storage of props between show performances is a critical part of prop run crew responsibilities. Many organizations have a designated room or space to temporarily store the hand props and stage dressing struck from the set following the performance. Some dressing can be left in place, but any prop critical to the action of the play should be struck for safekeeping to either a lockable prop run cabinet or to a secure prop run room. Any cleaning of props should be completed immediately following the performance, including weapon maintenance, washing of glassware or dishes, laundry of towels or other soiled soft goods, and wiping down of tables and countertops. This is especially important when special effects such as blood are used. Stage blood is difficult to remove when dry and will stain fabric or painted surfaces if not cleaned up immediately following the performance. At the end of each performance, all furniture should be covered with muslin dust covers to discourage anyone from sitting on or moving the pieces, as well as to keep the items clean.

PERFORMANCE REPORTS

At the end of each performance, stage management completes a performance report (similar to a rehearsal report) distributed to all area heads, administration, and anyone else who needs to be informed of the status of the show. This report usually includes the following information:

- Name of show

- Date and curtain time

- Act timings/run time

- Performance notes about anything occurring during the play such as incorrect pre-sets, accidents, slow pacing, missed cues, etc.

- Actor notes such as missed entrances, dropped lines, or "off" delivery

- Production notes such as broken props, headset difficulties, maintenance issues, costumes needing repair or adjustment, and any technical difficulties encountered by the run crew.

The production notes section is where the properties director can expect details regarding anything dealing with props, and can determine if the run crew will be able to fix or adjust the prop or whether the prop shop should take over repair. It is also where stage management alerts the prop shop when food or other consumables are running low and need to be replenished. In the case of disaster striking, a phone call to the properties director immediately following the performance can assist in more prompt action, rather than waiting until the following day when the performance report is read at the start of the work day.

STRIKE

Strike is the reverse of load-in, when all elements for a production are removed from the theatre in order for the next production to begin the move from rehearsal room to stage. At many theatres, strike begins immediately following the final performance. Some organizations prefer to schedule strike the following day, and in that case, the props should be stored in their normal and usual show run storage position unless other arrangements have been made with the prop department.

Strike is logically done in reverse order from load-in. In order to remove the scenic elements, all props and set dressing must be removed from the stage space beforehand to guarantee the safety of the props. Usually the prop crew is the first on stage to clear their items as the other areas re-configure backstage areas and prepare for the load-out. In order to facilitate all areas and allow the strike to progress without delay, dressing and furniture items are often temporarily transferred to an adjacent area backstage where they can be later packed in boxes or placed onto a cart for return to the prop shop for cleaning and final storage or disposal. Union contracts vary as to who can actively be onstage during strike, moving furniture and removing dressing, so when operating in an IATSE house, know the rules and expectations in advance that govern who handles what and where the union juris-diction and control ends.

Once all stage props have been cleared, the scenery and electrics strike can continue more efficiently and without fear of damaging the props or competing for workspace on stage. This is the best practice to assure the safety and security of the crew as well as the props. Hand prop cabinets are rolled back to the prop shop or the props are loaded into boxes for return to storage. Personal props pre-set with the costumes are collected from the dressing rooms or costume shop. Flown props such as chandeliers or dressing on flown scenic units are removed as the pieces become available during the strike in coordination with the corresponding areas. The electrics crew often removes any additional wiring apparatus or rigging prior to returning items to the prop shop following strike.

A written **strike plan** aids in completing an organized and efficient strike, giving each artisan a list of specific responsibilities during the strike by priority of what needs to happen in coordination with the other production areas.

White Christmas Prop Department Strike Plan

Immediately post show, On Stage and in wings:
With Prop Run Crew:
  Move all furniture pieces from stage & wings to loading dock area of scene shop, and check them
  in on master storage list
  Check all hand props and Inn desk dressing back into prop boxes for transport to storage
  Collect, wash & dry dirty dishes, check in to prop box
  Gather soiled linens, take upstairs to prop shop for laundering
With Stage Management:
  Clear personal props from dressing rooms to prop boxes
With Scene shop strike crew:
  Roll Train Wagon into Scene Shop space for later disassembly
  Roll WWII unit into Scene shop space for later disassembly
  Fly in Inn wall, remove dressing, drapery, and fixtures; check in and bag or box appropriately
  Fly in Inn Chandelier, disconnect from rigging and unplug power supply,
    Transfer to rolling storage rack for loading onto truck

First Priority off deck:
Lisa and Jen: Unbolt and remove train benches from wagon unit
  Remove curtains and valences from train flat and bag for storage
With Electrics staff:
  Disconnect power to Train unit sconces and Army drop lighting
  Remove wall sconces and box for storage
Brian, Ana & Meghan: Bag army Xmas tree, Inn Xmas tree, Chorus Xmas all six Finale Xmas trees
  Begin dismantling the army drop unit for storage

Second Priority:
Lisa: With Sound Crew:
  Disconnect and remove speakers and wireless equipment from both prop piano units
Brian: pull box truck into loading dock; load furniture

Third Priority:
All Prop Personnel: transport all White Christmas from scene shop to warehouse.
Meghan: Do White Christmas prop laundry and shelve run crew supplies back in to prop shop stock.

Figure 9.9 Strike Plan. Strike plan for Skylight Opera's production of *White Christmas* showing the specific duties of each artisan and the priorities for prop removal and coordination with other production areas. Lisa Schlenker, properties director.

Following strike, all prop rentals and borrowed items need to be returned. All props returning to prop stock should be cleaned or laundered. This is especially critical for items having been in contact with food, contaminated during the action of the play, or which may have utilized floral putty or other substances to secure set dressing. Soft goods should be laundered, china and dishes washed, furniture wiped down or vacuumed as needed, and weapons cleaned and oiled. All props should be returned to their proper storage location, and if a prop inventory is maintained, it should be updated to reflect the most recent adds, alterations, or cuts. Items borrowed from costumes for dressing should be laundered as needed and returned to the costume shop.

In the case where the show is moving on to another theatre (a co-production), the props are loaded into labeled packing cases to provide for their safe travel to the next location, with all appropriate paperwork and documentation of run, maintenance, or usage included. Co-productions and rentals are covered in Chapter 10 of this book.

Some shows are stored for package rental, or for re-mounting on an annual basis (*Christmas Carol, Dracula, A Christmas Story,* etc.) and the show will need to be stored and documented in an appropriate way. If items are boxed, label the box with the name of the show, include an inventory on both the inside and the outside of the box, and mark which side is UP. For larger items such as furniture or dressing items, it is handy to sew lightweight muslin covers stenciled with the show name to be tied over the piece to repel dust. All pieces to be loaded into a truck or moved should be well padded and secured to protect the integrity of the prop. Props returning for re-mount may be stored in a separate storage area, often with the show scenery and other show-specific elements rather than mixed in with the usual prop stock. Ensuring the props are safely stored and covered to keep clean and secure from accidental damage is important.

Following opening, the properties director should complete the show bible with the pre-set and run lists, perishable checklist, photos of the show and set dressing, and all final notes and responses. This allows maintenance of an accurate record about the show, and information can be easily accessed in the case of a remount, co-production or transfer, or when questions about research, sources, or processes arise. Following strike, the show bible is closed with a final accounting of the budget and rentals. Retention of show bibles or keeping a show file on the shop computer enables easy access to the production history and is a valuable resource.

CHAPTER 10

Co-Productions and Rentals

Recognizing the all too real phenomenon of shrinking resources available to produce large-scale productions, as well as the increasing interest in networking among major artistic leaders (including playwrights, composers, and producers intent on developing new works), many professional companies increasingly rely on shared production resources, in the form of **rentals** or **co-productions**. While this has been common in the grand opera world for decades, LORT theatres are now creating production partnerships and seeking out rental packages for their seasons. While the savings on the production side is debatable and rarely realized in the prop area, a savings of staff time, scenery budgets, rehearsal expenses, and artist housing expenses may in some instances be enough to move such arrangements forward.

PROP RENTALS

Rentals differ from a co-production arrangement. A rental package typically involves the theatre company of origin producing a show to market to other companies following the close of the original run, normally as a straight fee for an existing package deal involving no creative control or negotiation on the part of the renting company. Much like renting a car—it is what it is, a package product available for a fee to anyone wishing to use the entire unit for stipulated rental terms. Rental packages vary widely in quality and price, sharing commonality with co-productions in reducing or eliminating the number of production staff required to get a particular project on stage. Production management, truck unloading, and set up on stage requires stagehand calls, but not necessarily skilled fabrication artists or shop spaces in which to build, representing significant labor and materials savings to management.

Complete prop packages as rental inventory are increasingly popular. When planning a large build of a frequently produced show such as *Sweeney Todd*, *Little Shop of Horrors*, or *The Seagull*, a larger budget allocation may be justified in anticipation of potential rental income. Some productions requiring highly specialized or difficult props might offer an opportunity to rent a reduced package including only those specialty items, often called "hero" objects. This can offer a valuable income source for prop departments and the theatre's bottom line in general.

In most cases, when preparing production packages for a life of rentals, several considerations must be kept in mind.

- Engineer each prop for a longer life of abuse. The prop will need to withstand not just one production run, but many, and at the hands of a wide variety of skill levels. Rentals commonly go out to other professional colleagues in a national network, as well as local community theatres, colleges and high schools, and a host of commercial filming and events clients.

- Keep props lightweight and unbreakable whenever possible, making certain breakable items have a consistent source of available and cost-effective replacements. On large package rentals, be sure to send along "where to purchase" information and/or back-ups if possible, keeping a detailed source materials and documentation bible for each potential renter as well as for prop shop records to more efficiently maintain the package between rental clients.

- The rental packages are only as good as the last client's treatment, so factoring in labor and materials costs for repairs in between rental periods is mandatory. Photo-document each return for general wear and tear or damage over and above expected use.

- Consider crating and packaging costs to protect the rental asset during transportation and storage.

- Anticipate staff/administrative time—fielding email inquiries and arranging contracts, scheduling, invoicing, checking rental items back in, assessing for damage or wear and tear, sprucing up the rental prop and repacking before it goes out on the next engagement.

- Budget for storage space and costs.

- Plan for disposal of the asset when obsolescence is reached. Occasionally, when the prop director assesses a rental item is near the end of its lifespan, arrangements can be made to simply sell the item to the last prospective rental client. When this is allowable by management and not in violation of any other rights or credits clauses, a sale neatly takes care of the disposal concerns.

As an originating company, management may consider the investment in extra budget lines well advised if they foresee potential for annual income across multiple seasons. In some cases, companies may even be able to secure financial backing or grants to support the build of large or extravagant props in exchange for naming rights or program credits. These credits can be for only the originating company production or can reach outward to every subsequent use of the rental, depending on the terms of the grant awarded to the producing prop shop.

Using Audrey II

<u>Audrey II #4</u>
Eating Mushnik

<u>REQUIREMENTS</u>: To eat anyone, the lower jaw MUST be resting on the rootbed. The size of the actor to be eaten is limited by the space between the puppeteers legs while they are spread.

1. The front stage left root on the rootbed is stuffed with hard foam for stepping on while getting into the plant. There is also one tooth missing on that side to provide space for entering the pod.

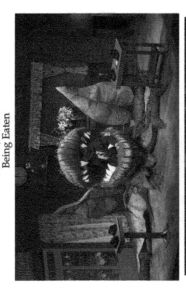

2. Kneeling and bending forward will allow the pod to close. Once inside you can exit out the back head first, on your front, or turn over on your back. Exiting feet first can be done but is more difficult. Rubber soles will grip to the mouth fabric, and should be avoided if possible.

These are also the general instructions for eating both Audrey and Seymour. In both those cases entering where the tooth is missing is suggested.

Using Audrey II

<u>Audrey II #4</u>
Being Eaten

Mushnik and Audrey being eaten during the Skylight Opera production of *Little Shop of Horrors*.

Figure 10.1 Audrey #4 Rental Plant. Instruction manual pages documenting an Audrey rental plant prop, indicating safe use of Audrey #4 for rental client use, to complete the scripted business of eating various characters.

Skylight
music theatre

RENTAL CONTRACT

Equipment Rental Agreement
This Agreement is made between the parties at Skylight Music Theatre ("LESSOR"), 158 N. Broadway, Milwaukee, WI 53202, and ("LESSEE) XXXXXXXX, Theater Department, 1234 ABC Drive, Anywhere, USA C/O Theater Director

➤ **Equipment to be rented:**
   A. **Basic Plant Package**

Equipment Value $75,000.00

➤ **Rental Period**
The equipment shall be **picked up by LESSEE** on or after **Monday April 4, 2016**

The equipment shall be **returned to LESSOR** no later than **Monday April 25, 2016**

➤ **Notice of Defects**
Unless Lessee gives Lessor written notice of a defect to an item of equipment within four hours after receipt thereof, it shall be conclusively presumed, as between Lessee and Lessor, that the item was delivered in good repair and that Lessee accepts it as an item of equipment described in this Agreement.

➤ **Terms**
A. The billing period shall commence on the day the Lessor ships the equipment or the equipment is picked up by the Lessee or the Lessee's agent and terminates on the day that the equipment is returned to the office of the Lessor.
B. All rentals must be paid in full prior to shipping. Any subsequent charges shall be at Net 15 days. Overdue accounts (excess of 15 days) will be charged an interest fee of 1 ½% per month on the unpaid balance.
C. Rentals shall be F.O.B. the Lessor's warehouse facility.
D. All freight charges incurred by Lessor on behalf of Lessee shall be billed to Lessee at the terms listed in (4B).
E. Lessee accepts responsibility for any delays due to import/export customs and agrees to pay rental fees for all days that the equipment is not at Lessor.
F. Lessor is not responsible for the use or misuse of the equipment by the Lessee.

5. Use
Lessee shall use the equipment in a careful manner and shall comply with all laws relating to its possession, use or maintenance.

All equipment should be assumed not to be waterproof and should not be used near water.

Lessee shall endeavor to keep equipment free from dust, dirt and materials that could be destructive to the equipment or its operation.

☐ **Alterations**
Lessee shall not make any alterations, additions or improvements to the equipment.

☐ **Loss and Damage**
Lessee shall bear the entire risk of loss, theft, damage and destruction of the equipment for any cause whatsoever, and no loss, theft, damage or destruction of the equipment shall relieve Lessee of the obligation to pay rent, repair or replace the subject equipment.

The equipment consists of delicate materials and hardware and as such must be handled with care by trained technicians. Damage can occur due to dropping, pulling, twisting, and getting wet and excessive force.

All equipment must be returned in clean, working condition. Lessor reserves the right to apply cleaning fees as necessary.

(A) Pursuant to paragraph (2) herein, it shall be presumed, unless notice is received in a timely manner, that Lessee received the subject equipment in working order. The parties hereto conclusively agree that Lessor shall have sole discretion in determining whether the leased equipment has been returned in working order or whether same is in need of repairs.

(1) Any damage done to the subject equipment shall be repaired by Lessor and billed to Lessee at two times the repair cost to compensate Lessor for lost rental use. Payment terms shall be the same as (4B) regardless of Lessee's insurance coverage, if any.

(B) In the event of loss or complete destruction of the subject equipment, Lessee shall be responsible for the full cost of said equipment. Equipment value is stated in (1A)

➤ **Indemnity**
Lessee shall be solely responsible for and shall indemnify, defend and hold harmless Lessor from and against any and all claims, suits, damages or losses, specifically including loss of use of property, and all other liabilities whatsoever, including injuries to or death of any person, including but not limited to the property of Lessee, Lessor or Lessee, in any way sustained, directly or indirectly, by reason of or in connection with:

A. The performance of the work by Lessee, its employees, agents or sub lessees or their employees, including but not limited to the use of any equipment or material furnished by Lessor.

B. The presence of Lessee, its employees, agents or sub lessees or their employees on the premises of Lessor.

Lessee shall procure and maintain, with respect to the work, such insurance with such companies as shall be satisfactory to Lessor evidenced by Certificates of Insurance to be delivered to Lessor prior to commencement of the rental, stating limits under Lessee's Comprehensive General Liability Insurance of at least:

Single Limit Bodily Injury	$1,000,000.00
Single Limit Property Damage	$1,000,000.00
Equipment Value	$75,000.00

➤ **Insurance**
Additional Insurance Documents: As required by Lessor. Lessee shall make Lessor an additional named insured under Lessee's Comprehensive General Liability Insurance Policy applicable to the work by means of an endorsement to the policy signed by the insurer, a signed duplicate of which shall be furnished to Lessor with the required certificates of insurance.

Terms and Conditions Agreed to:

Dated: _____

Lessee: _____

By: (Print) _____

By: (Sign) _____

Address: _____

Address: _____

City: _____

State: _____

Postal Code: _____

Phone #: _____

➤ **Credits**
Whenever the equipment is used in production, the following credits shall apply and are **required in each program:**

"Man-eating plants created by Skylight Music Theatre with generous support from Rockwell Automation."

➤ **Rental Rate for: 4-4-16 through 4-25-16**

$1200.00 for Basic Plant set

Total Rental fee: $1200.00

➤ **Security Deposit**
Lessee shall pay a Security Deposit to Lessor prior to shipping of equipment. Lessor shall return such security deposit to Lessee when and if all rental items are returned to Lessor and Lessor is satisfied that said equipment is in good condition in accordance with (6). If Lessor is not satisfied that the equipment is in good condition, Lessor will retain from the security deposit the amount necessary to repair or replace the items. Lessee shall be invoiced for all damaged or missing items according to terms stated in (4B).

Security Deposit: $600.00

Contract Grand Total: $1800.00

Payment due prior to 4-4-16

Insurance certificate due prior to 3-4-16

Dated: _____

Lessor: Skylight Music Theatre

By: (Print) _____

By: (Sign) _____

Figure 10.2 Audrey Plant Rental Contract. Stipulation of program credits for Rockwell Automation from *Little Shop of Horrors* rental contract, Skylight Music Theatre.

Companies considering a rental should investigate:

- Artistic integrity, stylistic and dimensional harmony between rental items and the receiving organization's own designed scenery or other props

- Condition/age of the rental item

- Technical support available in the event of problems during rehearsal and run

- Span of potential rental days—availability of the rental prop for all or part of the rehearsal period and the affordability of extra time

- Stipulations for certain types of use or other contractual restrictions

- Available space to store any shipping crates or support paraphernalia

- Shipping charges—round trip cost to get and return the package

- What is included? Sometimes rental packages come with both scenery and major or large props, leaving the assorted perishable letter or added hand prop to be dealt with by in-house prop staff, or stage management if no prop personnel exist. Stage directors hired in on such projects have little say in this matter, and are left to play the hand dealt by the package secured.

- Impact on staffing. Executive level management may choose to lay off some or all salaried staff in hopes of saving a few bucks through use of a show rental package. In some cases, a shop may elect to rent a hero item to help keep labor and materials budgets within constraints or when the prop is beyond the skill set available in the shop. The man-eating plants for *Little Shop of Horrors*, the *Avenue Q* puppets, or the barber chair and blood effects razors and bibs for *Sweeney Todd* are examples of props extremely labor intensive to fabricate, but readily available on the prop rental market.

CO-PRODUCTIONS

Generally, a **co-production** is a single project embarked upon by two or more companies sharing the same creative team and vision for the production. Different companies may prioritize in vastly different ways, including defined job responsibilities, scope and skill of production staff, differing show models for navigating the journey from inception to product, and numerous other convoluted dynamics. The co-production contracting process should work to codify all of these variables.

The collaborating parties draw up a legal agreement stipulating the contributions expected and required of each participating organization, including but not limited to:

- Percentage of financial responsibility or "buy-in" from each producer as well as the profit sharing or royalties divvy from revenues gained

- Amount of design input into the creative process

- What parts of the production travel to each partner, if not the show in its entirety

- Key personnel involved in addition to the primary creative team members (specific casting, conductor or music staff, assistants to the designers, director, choreographer, who may travel to subsequent venues to put in the production with cast changes. etc.)
- The order and schedule by which the production travels from theatre to theatre
- Joint marketing or advertising
- Shared producing credits
- Storage both between venues and after the last co-producer has completed their run
- Disposition of the package in the event it is not deemed feasible to store for future engagements.

There are as many versions of co-production contracts as there are stars in the sky—each one has unique, different, and interesting fingerprints, making generalities on this subject a challenge. In many cases an originating producer is identified early on, sometimes based on season planning and scheduling, and sometimes based on shop availability within the producing partner organizations. If no partners have in-house technical departments available or able to build the production, then outsourcing the build to a commercial shop is common. The financial terms of who pays for what are dependent upon the resources of each partner theatre and on the business and legal savvy of the negotiators from each company.

After all partners are in agreement and the creative team is ready to proceed with designs, each venue's technical parameters must be incorporated into the design plans, sometimes requiring scenery designed in modular ways. Larger venues may need additional scenic pieces and sometimes also additional props for expanded scenic locations and more square footage of dressing, or extra hand props such as champagne glasses for additional chorus members. If the production and design teams are communicating well, fit should not be an issue and will be tailored to each theatre's constraints well in advance of the build. If designs are last minute, partners are added *after* construction begins or communication is poor, the resulting insertion into each unique theatre space is in jeopardy. Solutions for these pinch points often fall on the house technical staff at the venue encountering issues.

The co-pro contract should also delineate expectations of the design staff to ensure artistic integrity between venues and head off unpleasant surprises or scenery/props not working well from venue to venue. Occasionally the contract will require the scenic designer or an assistant to travel to each producing venue to iron out any unexpected concerns. When this is not written into the agreement, the production director, technical director, and other technical department heads become involved in problem-solving and must work together to meet the expectations of the director or artistic director in their own space. The latitude for visual changes given to each co-pro partner is typically spelled out in the contract before all parties sign on, though when a co-pro is developing a new work, changes are endemic throughout the entire process. Each theatre stop will add or subtract based on how the new work is changing or morphing, guided by a typically very hands-on director and design team.

The best co-production agreements see a planning process starting significantly in advance of a normal in-house show. Transparency, while definitely a best practice in these agreements, is often elusive due to the nature of upper level management negotiations. At first whiff of a potential co-production arrangement, prop directors are well advised to bend the ear of the production and artistic directors with a bucket list of considerations to keep in mind as agreements are forged across company boundaries.

The many factors deserving specificity include:

- Schedule and budget
  - Technical staff must help define the resources necessary
  - Codify which prop shop pays for what beforehand
  - Establish a timeline for all involved parties
  - Examine increased labor and materials budget implications for all involved.

- Communication
  - Chain of command (a chain of detailed responsibilities)
  - Who does what from which organization
  - Advance planning—the more information decided and communicated in advance, the better the process will be, the better the product will look, and the better the budget will be adhered to
  - Networking up and down the command chain and across partner organizations

- Infrastructure
  - Accounting for the demands of widely differing rehearsal and performance spaces
  - Anticipating provisions for staging changes from venue to venue having potentially large prop impact
  - Identifying prop stock use.

- First-hand knowledge
  - Subsequent prop directors viewing originating production in person
  - Networking with house personnel and observing set up and run needs and practices
  - Budgeting for on-site time and travel expense.

- Documentation
  - Comprehensive bible from originating organization
  - Subsequent prop directors add updates as details change and information develops
  - Talking with all colleagues!

- Storage
  - Intelligently packed and designed system of crates and road boxes working for all partners from both *space* and *logistics* viewpoints

- Prioritize required storage between stops and at the end of the line
- Foresee disposal of the entire package.

Establishing a **timeline** is critical to the success of the project. The single constant in all co-pros is there is *no typical timeline*. Sometimes organizations begin the planning process years out, some a matter of months, some companies join mere weeks before opening—literally just before tech. There are advantages and disadvantages to all. More time can often blur lines of communication, with few or no prop folks available to the process years out. Generally, less time means less organized transfer of information and less smooth process between partners. No lead-time may equate to no prop resources allocated, severely impacting companies with scant prop talent available in-house. Shorter lead time may be an advantage in terms of paying for less storage time/expense/hassle, but the flip side is less time allowed for potential new cast members to acclimate to the props, diminished problem-solving capabilities for the in-house staff when encountering difficulties of any sort, be it a lost or broken prop, something expected but not actually shipped, fit and finish concerns, etc.

In an *ideal* world, the best-case timeline would follow these general parameters:

- 3 years out:
  - Workshops for discovering the bugs in a new work
- 2 years out:
  - Share partners known
  - Contracts signed
  - Libretto/translation/script finalized

- 1 year out:
  - Preliminary designs adjusted for idiosyncrasies of each venue
- 6 months out:
  - Final designs approved
  - Prop directors can analyze share impact on schedule and stock

- 10 weeks out:

  - Build begins
  - Production resources then unfold as normal, but with a far wider communications net encompassing all co-pro technical staff from each partner theatre.

Concerns of the prop director for the **originating company** may include the need for a larger initial labor and materials budget. Greater resources are often required to supply all show props out of whole cloth. *A co-pro is not like a normal one-off show*. Be doubly aware of all contingencies. Prop directors should assiduously review the contract details with production management to determine if all items will end up back at the home base when the co-pro run is complete. The temptation is to make life easy and pull many appropriate props from stock if they fit the design and staging specifications. This, unfortunately, can have significant impact on prop stock if these items are destined not to return to the originating company. Wiser to budget for as many original props as possible, particularly weapons or fragile items. Props should be made or acquired specifically for the shared production. Labor and materials to buy and/or build all necessary packing crates and road boxes must have a separate line item in the prop budget. Estimating labor to strike and pack up the show at the originating company for safe travel to the next venue takes advance administrative time, as well as extra hands to implement the packing strategy and insure all props arrive at the next location intact and undamaged.

Throughout the co-pro build process, normal **documentation** of prop paperwork will need augmentation and greater detail in order to fully prepare the subsequent producing partners. In the process of tech and the push to opening, the prop director should anticipate the needs of the other organizations and document accordingly. A broader, more thorough prop bible is ideal. Generally, prop directors will use the existing in-house systems they have in place for prop tracking of a co-pro prop list, including any numerical tracing system preferred.

The ideal co-pro prop bible will include:

- Final up to date prop inventory checklist
- All stage management run paperwork (pre-sets, run sheets, etc.)
- An accurate list of all sources for purchased goods and raw materials, photos of each prop from several angles
- Wiring diagrams for any electronic components
- Paint and finish product notes, and recipes
- Step lists to aid in potential touch up notes
- Photos of prop run tables showing layout and site-specific backstage details necessary to clinch a smooth show run
- An archival video (within Equity/AGMA or other union guidelines) to document any special prop effects, general flow of action and scenes, scene changes, and crew requirements
- Packing lists for each box and crate used to transport the prop package
- Photos of the pack if not self-explanatory through the written word
- Contact information for the liaison who can answer any further prop questions for the receiving team.

Getting detailed rehearsal and performance notes from the originating production—either in real time via stage management routing or an archive of notes in the bible—gives the subsequent prop directors valued insight into how a given prop evolved to the final form and may flag ongoing maintenance concerns, or clarify prop–performer interface concerns cropping up with cast changes between venues.

houston grand opera presents

THE LITTLE PRINCE
MEMORANDUM

Houston Grand Opera

THE LITTLE PRINCE
Critical child replacement blocking   July 16, 2003 (eds)

TAKE NOTE OF PLANE/FLIGHT PROP?

TO: Stage Managers of *The Little Prince*
RE: Production Specifics you might want to know
DATE: 7/16/03

Hello to Stage Management: The following is a listing of things involved in Francesca Zambello's production of *The Little Prince* that might be helpful to know before you get started.

TECH/SET:

We used the deck (dunes) in the rehearsal room.   We couldn't have the large plane in rehearsal because it wasn't finished being built so we used long benches as the DS wing and short benches as the body of the plane.   As it turned out, I'm glad we didn't have the plane in rehearsal.   I don't know how we would have done Act II in the rehearsal rooms since we don't have crew until we go onstage.   It turned out to not really be a problem since there was minimal staging ON TOP OF the plane and it seemed to be easily transferred to the stage during technical rehearsals.   Ms. Zambello was not happy about not having the plane but I think she would have been less happy if it had been stuck there for all of the rehearsals.

We used a set of rolling steps to represent the curved portal.   They were a bit deceptive because they weren't curved in the same way as the real portal so on rehearsal sometimes items were blocked that could really be seen onstage.   We rolled the steps off of spike slightly in rehearsal and used a ½ apple box as the bottom step.   We also had 2 level scaffolding units each side that we put people into as the portal windows.   We kept these in the offstage positions and didn't roll them along with the step units (just too much to do).

The Businessman and Geographer rehearsed on music stands on floor level (between the rolling step units and the scaffolding).   It just didn't work with all their business between the bars of the scaffolding.   We used an extra scaffolding floor piece on an angle for the lamplighter – he needs to get used to singing while lying on his stomach – not exactly a piece of cake.

We had 5 carpenters in performance.   The cue that contained most carpenters was the first flying sequence.   Portal closed, then hookup and fly prince, then King's Throne on as Prince flying off.   2 carps on the rail and one of those came off to run the rise of the flying sequence.

PROPS:

We used all real props as soon as they were built.   Make sure to pin the cranes back up after each session so they don't wilt.   We put the kids names in tape on the back of each bird – that way, they would know which bird was theirs since they were arranged by height AND if you could see your name then you knew your bird was facing away from you and toward the audience.   Not all children had birds but we tried to give the kids who didn't have birds in Act I a bird for Act II.

The lanterns are difficult to store in the rehearsal room and not vital in my opinion – we used sticks for a very long time until they were finished and there was no harm done.

ACT ONE:
First Entrance:

1) **Teddy bear** should go to Anna if Meredith missing
2) Stephanie should be with Lucas if John Preston performing
3) Do not worry about hot water bottle
4) Lisa should have **small plane** if Rebecca missing, Jeffrey assist
5) Evan and John should handle **double sided picture** if Gabi missing
6) Alison should handle **breast picture** if English missing
7) John should stash **double sided picture** in portal steps if Lisa missing
8) Lizzy permanent cover for "**three small stars**" (as per Karen).   For John Preston performance, etc.
9) **final check for envelopes** left of stage Lisa should do if Rebecca missing
10) **children should help** each other out, for plane passing…as they have when John missing
11) **Plane hand off** SL – Anna is back up if Kathleen missing

BIRD FLIGHT #1 (King)
1) if anyone missing, do not make position changes.   If Anne is missing, and John NOT performing, he should be point person
2) V formation …if Rebecca missing, Alison should move onto Dune and NOT hand off bird
3) if Alison missing, Rebecca should have her bird

BIRD FLIGHT #2 (Vain Man)
1) Anne missing from DR, stage management should just make sure Lucas starts DR

BIRD FLIGHT #3 (Drunk)
1) if anyone missing from US cross over, do not replace

BIRD FLIGHT #4 (Businessman)
1) if Anne missing from DR, stage management should just make sure Lucas starts out DR

BIRD FLIGHT #5 (Lamplighter)
Should be OK

BIRD FLIGHT #6 (Geographer)
1) if anyone missing from US cross over, do not replace

ACT ONE FINALE:
1) circle of 9 gifts: if anyone missing, do not replace.   Tell girls to keep moving
2) if Lucas missing , Rebecca should start lamp lighting at pg. 206

ACT TWO:
Preset: if any children who carry birds in this flight are missing, then give birds to Meredith or Gabi, but do not adjust spacing

ROSEBUDS:
Adjust spacing if any missing (because there aren't any other costumes)

CHILDREN IN WINDOWS:
1) Lizzy in for John Preston when he performs
2) Any one else missing --check with Karen for vocal concerns.

DURING WELL:
All should adjust spacing along the dune
ACT TWO FINALE:
Do not adjust spacing

Figure 10.3   Co-production Bible Pages. Excerpts from Houston Grand Opera's co-production prop bible for *The Little Prince*, including items not often found in one-off show prop documentation, such as rehearsal notes regarding props, and cast substitutions involving prop tracking during the performance run. Megan Freemantle, HGO properties design director.

RED ARK
(PERFORMANCE LTD. LONDON)
ARTISTS & DESIGNERS

DIRECTOR: GORDON ALDRED

MANAGEMENT: CHIMERA ARTS LTD, 41 ROSEBANK, HOLYPORT RD, LONDON , SW6 6LQ, UK
PH: (44) 207 385 5724. E-H: [illegible]
C: SADIA

GORDON ALDRED, STUDIO ONE, LAUNDRY MEWS, 16A HERSCHELL ROAD, LONDON, SE23
RD. UK
PH: (44) 07931 544 382. Fax: (44) 0208 699 9508.
E-M: [illegible] or [illegible]

FIRE CERTIFICATE

PRODUCTION: *Little Prince*

THEATRE / PRODUCTION COMPANY: Houston Grand Opera Texas USA

ITEM: The Letter Drop (including envelopes)

BASE MATERIAL: Twingmth fireproof cotton (Woven H.UK)

APPLIED MATERIALS: Von Poir water dyes

APPLIQUE BONDING: N/a

APPLIED MATERIALS SOURCE: N/a

FIREPROOFING PRODUCT: FLAMEBAR PF6

BRITISH STANDARD: BS. 9SE

NUMBER OF COATS: 2

MAINTENANCE: 1 Fresh application every 2 years.

SCENERY/PROPS

Date of Load-in:	**Monday, May 19th, 2003**
Scenery constructed by:	**Ravenswood Studio, Inc. Chicago, IL**
Drops Constructed by:	**Ken Creasey, Ltd., London, UK**
Drops Painted by:	**Gordon Aldred, London, UK**
Number of trucks and length for cartage:	**3 @ 53' X 110"**
Technical Director:	**Greg Weber**
Master Carpenter:	**Eddie Creasy**

Special Props provided by:	**Mark A. Jircik Exhibits Fabricators, Inc. Houston**
Prop Master:	**John Gorey**

Number of Prop crew: Load-in   Running crew

	Load-in	Running crew
Crew heads:	2	1
Crew members:	4	4

Prop items not included with show package: **Batteries, Dollies and Glitter**

If I do not hear from you today, I will ring you after discussing with Megan on Wednesday morning.

greg

-----Original Message-----
From: Christopher Sprague <
Sent: Mar 7, 2004 11:26 PM
To:
Subject: Little Prince Praticals

Greg,
  The question has come up and I want to punt it back to you. The handheld lanterns were a maintence headache in Houston and continue to be one here in Milwaukee. The prop shop here is considering re-wiring them to make them more friendly to work with. Kurt wanted to know if HGO would consider spilltting the cost with Skylight since it would work
out to our advantage as well? i told him that I would pass the question
on to you. If you want to give me a call, my cell will be on after 9:00
Monday morning. Otherwise, I will check my email after rehearsal Monday
night.

Thanks.

Hope all is well in London.

From:	Megan Freemantle
Sent:	Wednesday, March 10, 2004 9:39 AM
To:	Christopher Sprague
Cc:	Greg Weber
Subject:	Re: Little Prince Praticals

Dear Chris, After speaking with Greg briefly , You can do what needs be as long as the look { battery packs not in the lantern head}, swing { freedom of the movement of lantern to pole} not change so that the original blocking with the prop can remain the same. The wires should be taped with black duct tape to the hooks in three spots. We're aware that batteries are needed to be replaced and this takes resoldering. There's no interest at this time in sharing costs to accomplish the changes Lisa wants to make. The wire on the hooks should goes along the bottom edge underneath to the eyescrew. Sorry I'm not able to be of more help. Any further concerns or questions please call Greg or I. Megan

>>> Christopher Sprague 03/09/04 11:55PM >>>
Greg,
  Give me a call on Wednesday when you can. But here's what Lisa, the prop person, woudl like to do. There are two weak points in the electrical rig. One is the 24 gauge wires that break very easily as they go over the hook that holds the lantern. The other is that the batteries are soldered together and can't be removed from the tube without ruining the entire wiring harness.
  Lisa woudl like to re-wire them with a higher gauge wire in some sort of protective sleeve that will lessen the amount of breakage there. The also want to try and figure out some way to make the battery pack easier to change out and get to.
  None of these changes should affect the visual aspect of the prop, but hopefully will lower the daily maintenance that is required. I know our guys had to re-wire 2 or three every day during the run. The SKylight staff would like to not have to go through this and wanted to explore the idea of sharing the cost of re-working the electrical side of the props.

Let me know what you think.

Figure 10.4 Co-production Bible Pages (Cont.). Excerpts from Houston Grand Opera's co-production prop bible for *The Little Prince*, with items not often found in one-off show prop documentation. Included here are contacts for the commercial production shop of origin, prop letter flame proofing certificate with two-year reminder to reapply, and an assortment of personal correspondence regarding alterations of props by the receiving company. Megan Freemantle, HGO properties design director.

The value of the archival video cannot be overstated as it so often reveals concerns and information that paperwork alone is insufficient to communicate. For example, in a production of *Two Women*, action takes place in WWII Italy. Staging and performance reports indicate a bomb effect on stage, which destroys an entire storefront. The video shows a fully dressed out period store interior and shelves, packed with products, tipping over in a domino effect, props and dressing strewn over the stage in wild disarray.

If paperwork is scant or communication stifled, receiving prop directors are left with the task of recreating through forensic science what should be on stage. When prop directors are already in close communication on co-pro projects, information traveling through the chain is complete and clear, and timing of the bible hand-off can be orchestrated at the convenience of each. Having the documentation before any additional rehearsals or techs in the next venue in line begin can be an enormous benefit to the receiving prop director's sanity and preparedness. When the next producing partner in the chain has no prop staff, or has a prop staff arriving around the same time as the show package ships, an analog prop bible will be sent along with the rest of the props with a digital version also available. With the advent of file sharing websites and cloud-based computing, all this information can be shared electronically as well as physically, and electronic backups will save resources on many tight turnarounds.

PACKING AND SHIPPING

When addressing how best to prepare a prop package for shipping to other partner theatres, some foreknowledge of available receiving staff, facilities such as loading dock and road box storage areas, and size of any choke points for transport within the other theatre spaces are all essential pieces of the puzzle. For example, if a prop director builds large scale road cases meant to fit through a large roll door into a semi-trailer or shipping container, but the next company has to move everything through a door three feet wide and seven feet tall, the resulting road block will be extremely unfortunate on the receiving end, and could potentially result in a lot of extra labor and maybe even damage to the road boxes if they must be left out in the elements for lack of proper sizing.

Once the specs of all loading and backstage areas for all venues are determined, and assuming props and scenery together will travel via freight transport (truck, train, or ship), then planning for road cases or other shipping boxes can proceed. Road boxes to house all fragile furniture pieces must be purchased or designed and built, hampers, or gondolas for odd sized foliage arrangements or large-scale prop soft goods laid out to nest with other packing crates, and boxed hand props either packed in larger reinforced containers or strapped securely to pallets for ease of moving. Ideally, hand props can be packed in sturdy flip-top plastic totes and the totes loaded in rolling road boxes built to accommodate them securely. If the prop package is known to ship in a container, use of carts or **cages on wheels (COWS)** will be extremely handy to protect furniture while in container transit, saving labor and effort on the receiving end with smoothly rolling units rather than unpacking and schlepping individual furniture items. On some occasions when a prop design includes extremely sturdy and open plan furniture such as large steel rolling tables, other smaller props such as crates, single steps and boxes of hand props can be padded and stored within the larger furniture items, saving valuable truck and storage space. Each box, crate, or other container has a photo-documented list posted on the outside and included inside the pack as well. These correspond to the same documents in the prop bible handed off to the next prop director.

In many cases, some road boxes can also double as the backstage run prop boxes; hampers with hard lids may turn into prop tables, helping to defray costs of providing those run areas for venues devoid of such infrastructure. Though offering sturdy structural shipping carts and mobile storage boxes is a boon for safe prop storage, transport, and efficient handoff between companies, it's also a significant labor and materials expense to be accounted for in the preliminary budgeting phase for all producing partners. Unfortunately, when turnarounds between the producing company and the next partner are tight, issues such as lack of time, staff, or other resources to complete the planning and packing job can derail even the best plan.

In the unfortunate event of damage or loss of props either during transport or between the various partner companies, repairs and replacements are on a case-by-case basis, depending

Figure 10.5 Co-pro Road Box. Stage left prop road case for Skylight's co-production of *The Spitfire Grill*, traveling to co-pro partner American Folklore Theater, showing labels and documentation on the exterior of the sturdy travel box.

Figure 10.6   Road Box as Run. When open, this road case doubles as the back stage left prop run cabinet, with pre-labeled storage positions for all necessary stage left hand props.

greatly on the available resources of the theatre confronting the lost or broken prop. Again, close contact between prop directors goes miles to address these situations in a collaborative and collegial way, sharing information, advice, and strategies. Two heads are many times better than one! In less ideal circumstances, breakage may be relegated to slap dash repairs by underpaid interns who lack the experience or focus to achieve stellar results. The end repair product passes on to the next partner down the line, or back to the theatre of origin for rehabilitation or release into the great prop heaven beyond. In rare and truly unfortunate circumstances, the shipment will return home with missing or grossly broken and unsalvageable props, justifying pursuit of reimbursement or compensation for loss, and labor and materials to replace damaged items. This awful scenario requires prop directors to work hand-in-hand with their production management team for redress.

RECEIVING COMPANY

On the **receiving company**'s end of the process, the prop director has a tangential but sometimes slightly different list of questions and concerns. Of high priority is ensuring management realizes secondary partners will certainly incur costs along the way, including:

- Perishables
- Repairs

- Costs for props not included from the originating company
- Supplements to the original show prop requirements
- Crew time for packing/unpacking labor
- Labor to set up for any pickup rehearsals needing props
- Administrative paperwork/documentation time.

Ongoing expenses should be budgeted for those items not gracefully weathering the vagaries of transportation and multiple different crews unpacking and packing. Obtaining a clear and accurate perishables list by opening of first run from the originator is essential to predict budget implications. Written paper trails in most cases are highly useful to document all production details, including budget overages or other deviations to the proscribed plans.

It never hurts for the receiving prop director to be a proactive and competent detective— early offers to lend a hand through commingling of prop resources may benefit everyone, will help propel the communication and prop acquisition process, and can be quite well received. Make certain any stock sharing is clearly spelled out and documented!

A word here about communication and networking: the importance of making friends and contacts throughout the production hierarchy cannot be overemphasized. Not just prop director to prop director relationship building, but also making friends with assistant directors, assistant designers, choreographers, and key performers will open additional floodgates of valuable insight.

Ideally all prop directors in the partnership will glean some observations from the originating rehearsal process, either by contact and updates from the first prop director in the chain, or by inclusion in the stage management rehearsal and performance reports distribution list. This is crucial to understand changes happening to props throughout the process of rehearsal and production and to anticipate challenges ahead. Without such insight, it becomes difficult/ impossible to predict budgets for labor, perishables, or fill in props that may not be sent with the original package. To inform the estimating process for receiving prop directors, this strong communication network with the originating company and creative team is paramount. Assistant directors or choreographers may have private photos or notes on blocking particulars or may travel with that sacred archival video. An assistant scene designer may be the person who originated the prop design package and can aid in comparing the original information with the final documentation bible. Verbal conversations from prop director to prop director might include pointing out anomalies, breakage reports, substitutions, stock items not included, and other problems best not discussed on paper. Without the central keystone of a deep and strong communication network, a number of challenging strategies may come into play.

In some cases, theatre managements may view co-productions as a place to save staff salaries by closing down the prop shop or layoffs for a portion of the staff. Ethically, advance planning is crucial in order to keep employees informed, but still leaves individuals with an unfortunate gap in income. Additionally, when a director or actor arrives at a secondary theatre and doesn't like things previously built, there isn't time or money to change them without in-house staff to do that work. Quite often the shows are a direct transfer, so a truck arrives, scenery and props are loaded in, and tech begins, leaving little time for needed maintenance or alterations. If rehearsals begin at secondary stops with alternate casts *before* the show package arrives, the prop director must try to find out what is needed for rehearsal and supply props as close to the real thing as possible—another factor in labor and materials management.

In an effort to preserve sanity and high standards of production quality, convey to the production director the importance of sending a prop representative to the originating theatre. Seeing the show in person and meeting the crew to find out what worked and what changes may be necessary is the best and first line strategy. There is no substitute for "boots on the ground" to gain critical situational awareness. This offers a pivotal opportunity to determine specific prop use, condition of all materials, implications of fragile or perishable props, stock items the theatre of origin does not intend to include, and a host of unforeseen factors affecting budget and planning. Being able to inspect the backstage setup at pre-show, intermission, and post-show, as well as meet and talk with the prop run crew and stage management while getting a first-hand look at all the show props provides all important particulars informing the prop director's next steps and planning processes. It is so much better to communicate face to face, affording a great opportunity to build relationships and deliver consistency to the process.

Sometimes theatres send only a technical director (TD) to handle outreach and advance work. If this is the unfortunate case, generate a highly detailed and specific list of prop-related questions to send along. Expecting the technical director or other representative to get the information or watch a show with specific prop concerns in mind *must* be clarified beforehand. Most TDs will have their own list of pressing scenic concerns to field, including scenic construction breakdown and handling methods, safe transport and truck pack arrangements, breakdown and transfer of any motion control motorized and/or rigged effects. TDs and other tech department heads, while well intentioned, often lack the in-depth prop training necessary to keep their spidey senses attuned to a prop director's viewpoint, missing important factors—be it weapons-specific staging, rough handling of fragile props, backstage storage, run issues particular to each space, or any of a multitude of other prop-related details.

BUDGET/PLANNING AFTER ORIGINAL RUN

Although it is tempting on the part of theatre management teams to assume the show will run exactly the same way at each subsequent theatre stop, the prop directors down the line would be well advised to petition for the resources to address adds and changes specific to either their particular venue, loss or damage en route, cast changes affecting actor-specific props, or a neat idea the next artistic staff feels strongly about inserting into their production. The list of factors is endless. The solution is simple—have a contingency budget in place, backed up by your production director's support. Clarify at management level what the latest and greatest version of the production entails, have all parties sign off on the version, update the prop documentation and paperwork and budget accordingly.

As an example, a flower cart in a co-pro of *La Boheme* at the originating company may not have been completed with the time and resources necessary to be impactful. At the next stop the director and designer wish to address this note—prop staff and materials must be accounted for. If the next stop in the chain lacks the necessary staff to change or the time to rework, hopes are dashed and relationships can be sorely tested.

Common factors impacting budgets and planning for partner prop directors are cut props, perishables, and weapons. Props eliminated at subsequent co-pro venues are rarely shipped back to the originator, but rather left dead at the later stop. Perishables are always an issue from partner to partner, and must be budgeted specific to each venue. Weapons are of significant importance. Make *no* assumption weapons will be transferred as a part of the co-pro prop package. Security concerns and restrictions involving the shipment of stage firearms and bladed weapons across state borders or internationally are prohibitive. Again, the formal contract from management may not be thorough enough to include this seemingly minor detail. Factor in that weapons will probably *not* come along for the ride. This can have dramatic budgetary implications, depending on the number of swords or firearms needed, if they are used for extensive live combat, the period and style of the weapons package, and the style of combat. The prop director must confirm details with all co-pro partners and discuss weapons early on with production management, either relying on theatre stock or, more likely, developing a budget for rental of a weapons package to fill the staging needs.

Show maintenance of props will be an on-going necessity. In an ideal world, a show will get a spruce-up after the initial run before loading on to the truck for the next stop. At that time, the prop director in-house can put together a list of general maintenance and condition notes for the next prop director in the co-pro chain. The best experiences allow a section in the prop bible for each theatre to add their notes as the co-pro moves through different companies. Maintenance of co-pro prop packages is rarely spelled out in the contract, and mostly defaults to relying on trust in partners and availability of resources—time and money. But of course, the theatre world is not ideal at all. Shows may transfer without the benefit of any prop oversight or accompanying paperwork documentation, in which case the receiving prop director is best served to shoe horn in a couple of days to unpack and assess. Tight turnaround times necessitate immediate evaluation and maintenance of all items before sending props on to rehearsal or tech. If the theatre does not have an in-house prop staff or has unwisely furloughed those folks, potential prop director overtime or over-hire costs can add up quickly. If not originally budgeted for, this ah-ha discovery requires immediate response and support from the production director.

Storage specifics should be delineated in the co-production contract or agreement. Storage costs are formidable in most major cities, and only somewhat less so in more remote locales. If the co-production ends up dead-ending in a state or country far from the originator, management may include a clause indicating how the cost of storage or disposal will split between the various companies. While prop directors have little or no control over these contractual details, they are often left to deal with the ramifications, sometimes without much notice and no allocation of resources.

In some cases, shows may get delivered at the end of a company's production run and have to be stored by the next partner in line. The advantage in this scenario is prop availability for earlier sorting out, assessment/spruce-up and check in, and possible rehearsal use. Disadvantages include storage room, usually at a premium, sometimes adds costs. If there is no receiving resident tech staff, it can be overwhelming for whoever is left to receive the package. Picture a stage manager, a bunch of college kids or volunteers faced with unpacking and safeguarding an unfamiliar show!

Customarily, the originating company will store and ship when the next company in line is ready to receive. Sometimes the originating company will ship at strike and the next partner in line will store. It all depends on the negotiated agreement—each situation is unique. Partner companies having significant timeline changes or who default completely are subject to financial implications/loss and potential lawsuit. How does that affect props personnel? Packages end up in limbo, not returned to the originating company, abandoned, or sold off, and the prop department has little to no control over the outcome.

Disposition of goods at the end of a co-pro run after all partner companies have completed the work is governed by the terms in the negotiated contract. Factors include the cost of materials and the cost of labor to salvage the props versus the cost of outright disposal to a landfill.

Commonly one of several courses will unfold:

- The last partner in the chain will store the package until further decisions are made
- The contract may stipulate the return of all or part of the package to the originating producer
- The entire package may be disposed of, the end theatre salvaging or recycling as many useable items as possible to conserve resources and minimize waste
- The package may be sold, when all partners are in agreement, in whole or in part to other interested parties.

* * *

Teamwork, collaboration, and strong relationships between all home-based technical department heads are, as always, crucial in crafting a sane experience in each co-pro situation, as well as in sending out large prop packages for rent to other organizations. Building a strong professional network of national and even international relationships is an enormous help as well. A prop director with such contacts can pick up the phone or dash off a series of emails to trusted colleagues and clarify many murky aspects of joint ventures. So often, those "up the food chain" who arrange co-pro agreements rarely have all the detailed facts pertinent to prop directors, even with proper groundwork and excellent communication. Prop directors who talk to one another directly will be able to better share information and resources, making a smooth rewarding transition between companies.

Working in Children's Theatre

An interview with Elizabeth Friedrich (Fried), Properties Shop Manager—Seattle Children's Theatre, Seattle, WA

What originally brought you to a life in professional prop direction?

I stumbled into managing a prop shop a few years after starting to build props. I didn't go to school for theatre; my degree is a BFA in furniture design. While I was in school I worked in offices and by the time I graduated I was comfortable working in offices as well as in shops. Without a formal theatre education, my transition into managing a prop shop was a bit rocky

Elizabeth Friedrich (Fried)
PROPERTIES SHOP MANGER—SEATTLE
CHILDREN'S THEATRE, SEATTLE, WA

but studying and learning on the job have helped me settle into the work comfortably. During my twenty years working in prop shops I have bounced back and forth between building and managing, and I have built in nine different shops. This variety of experience, I think, has helped me develop a broad understanding of what it takes to produce good props and maintain a supportive and safe shop environment. My background in building is helpful to me as a manager because I have an idea of the challenges that my employees face and I can be part of brainstorming solutions to some for our trickier challenges. My education in design helps me understand my designers' artistic motivations so when they ask for the moon I really want to give it to them! When I help open a show that realizes the artistic vision of my designer and director, comes in on budget, and has given my builders an opportunity to produce props they're proud of, I find professional satisfaction in a profound way.

Can you compare your experiences running a LORT prop shop with the current children's theatre prop shop you run presently? Is it all the same work, or is there a marked difference in children's theatre props production? Is it more joyful? Less? More technical? Less?

My work as a manager is very different here than it was at La Jolla Playhouse or at Intiman Theatre. Here, I spend a lot more time sourcing unique materials or parts and facilitating communication between departments.

Here, we spend more time building peculiar props than we spend on set dressing, so I would say that it is more technical than what I've done at other theatres. We rarely have a fully dressed set of, say, an apartment or a store. We do, however, build complicated moving contraptions like the *Chitty-Chitty Bang-Bang* breakfast-making machine, or that have significant interactive factors like the ball that the Cat in the Hat stands on (on one leg) for several minutes while balancing a load of props on his arms and the other leg. There's a higher percentage of creative problem-solving for our prop builds than there was at my other theatres: less reupholstering, more whiz-banging. I also buy more moving parts than I have elsewhere. We build a lot more props here that pivot, light up, or spring open than I've seen in any other prop shop I've worked in. I also shop for our puppet designer/builder, which provides me intense searches for unique parts. We use lots more foam, plastics, and moving hardware than I experienced in producing theatre for adult audiences.

Because we use less set dressing my prop storage is considerably smaller than it is at most theatres. I don't have multiple sofas, piles of radios, stacks of carpets, etc. Many of our shows have props that will only work for that show (*Cat in the Hat, Elephant & Piggie, Go, Dog, Go*), so those props don't go into storage but might get auctioned off at our Gala, put on display in our shop, or recycled for materials. I have yet for any other play, for example, to call for Harold's purple crayon (or, more accurately, any of Harold's many trick purple crayons).

I have more props here that interact with pieces from other departments; lots of practical electrics, and deep coordination with costumes, for example. We wire most of our own electrics unless it's something that our ME (Master Electrician) wants to do for some particular reason.

The work is considerably more joyful. It's hard to stay grumpy when you're building *Goodnight Moon.* Also, the work is mission-driven; it's about helping kids develop into well-rounded adults, and that sentiment permeates the organization. Sitting in a house full of 9-year olds who are completely engaged in the work on stage is a thoroughly satisfying experience.

How does being a prop director differ from your supplementary work as an IA (International Alliance of Theatrical Stage Employees) rigger?

Ooo—that's a great question. At SCT (Seattle Children's Theatre), my position is not part of the IATSE unit so I don't build props. My background is in building and I enjoy hands-on work, so rigging on the side gives me an opportunity to put on my Carhartts and get my hands dirty. I like working at height and with big hardware, so what could be more fun? That being said, I don't find rigging as interesting on a day-after-day basis so it's not as good an option for me as a full-time profession. Rigging pays a lot better than prop work, though, so it's a nice way to supplement my income with an activity that I enjoy.

What advice would you give to the next generation entering our discipline?

- Learn, learn, learn. Build your skill set because the broader your knowledge the easier everything is to do.

- Definitely run some shows so you understand what is needed backstage; it's a lot more rough-and-tumble during a show than you might think.

- Work on your people skills. If you don't understand something, don't be afraid to ask for clarification. This is a collaborative art form and keeping lines of communication open is the best way to succeed.

- Approach your coworkers in other departments as your allies, not as adversaries. Before rolling your eyes at a request, consider why it might be important.

- Take care of yourself. The people who give 24/7 are the ones who burn out early or fall into poor health. During tech watch your diet and get some exercise. No, really: I mean it. It's easy to treat every play like it's the most important thing in the world, but you have to take a break sometimes.

- Work on your writing skills; being able to express yourself clearly via email is essential. Also, the ability to write notes clearly for your artisans may mean that you get a couple of extra hours of sleep each night during tech. If you can write notes that are easy to understand you don't need to be there for them to start working in the morning.

- Build trusting and collaborative relationships with your peers.

Having a Career in Props

Having a career in props opens a wide variety of job opportunities both inside and outside of the theatre world. For those committed to working in the performing arts, the United States supports theatre in every state of the Union and in cities and towns of all sizes. Some are year-round operations and others only a few weeks in the summer. Putting together a career out of the various levels of theatre and moving from one organization or location to another for employment is common as people begin their careers. A tremendous diversity of theatre is available to shape those choices. In the United States, over 350 professional theatre companies and over 2600 community theatre companies produce live theatre. **LORT (The League of Resident Theatres)** has seventy-two members in twenty-nine states and the District of Columbia. Eighty-six companies/festivals produce Shakespeare and over two hundred companies/festivals deliver opera on their stages in America. Finding the right company, one matching the interests and skills of any one individual, can take persistence and patience, but opportunities open each season. Prop skills also adapt to multiple kinds of jobs outside of theatre, including work in museums, web page creation, film, commercials, entertainment support, or design in all vocations.

Cost of living comparison sites are available online, allowing two cities to be evaluated on quality-of-life factors such as economics, security, housing stock, population, education, ethnicity, education, climate, crime, etc. Looking for work and accepting a new position needs to also be a step forward on the professional career path, and balancing the potential of a new city with present known factors can inform the decision-making process. The salary and benefits offered in one part of the country might seem paltry in different, more urban areas with higher costs of renting an apartment, buying food, paying for parking, etc. Having an understanding of individual areas' cost of living will save a lot of heartache and regret and can provide a productive outcome in the negotiation of a contract.

FINDING WORK

Like much of the arts, finding a properties position is commonly done by word of mouth, with people seeking out others they know and advertising openings through email distributions and websites. Most large organizations utilize publications such as Artsearch or online job listing services like offstagejobs.com. Theatres also advertise openings on their own web pages under a Staff or Employment Opportunities header.

To find a listing of professional theatres, do an online search using keywords such as "professional theatre companies, US" or by state or region like "Kentucky theatre companies." Some people need to stay in a region of the United States or desire to work only in a large urban city. By exploring the theatres online first using specific keywords, the search can be significantly narrowed. Using the theatre companies listed in the keyword search, it is easy to discover webpages for the individual companies and find out information about seasons, production history, designers, staff listings, recent news items, and awards, as well as potential openings or opportunities.

While a wide range of theatre sizes and specialties can be found in every region, it is worth noting some regional characteristics. On the East Coast, a densely populated area rich in diversity, art, culture, and theatre experiences spanning the gamut of style, there

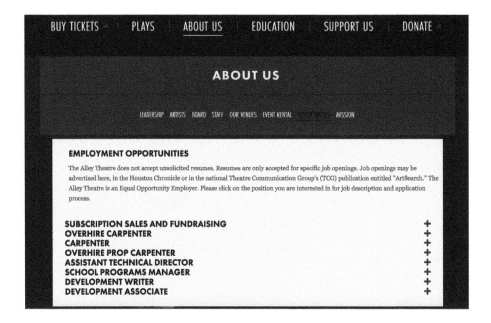

Figure 11.1 Career Listing Online. An example of how to find employment opportunities on a theatre's website. This one was under *About Us* with the subheading of *Opportunities*. It gives information on open positions as well as the hiring process.

Figure 11.2 Keyword Search. By putting in "Summer theatre companies" as a keyword search, a long list of organizations pops up for review. Clicking on the sites allows a review of possible job opportunities specific to summer theatre as opposed to general or full-time work.

is hardly a theatrical experience or company one cannot find, from Broadway enterprises to experimental street theatre and everything in between. The East Coast epicenter in the greater NYC area offers large well-established companies and many small independent theatre freelance opportunities to the energized and ambitious, as well as a gumbo-like scene rich with contacts and opportunities in film, TV, commercial shops, IATSE work, and positions in academic institutions. The network of mass transit through the region allows for easy and fast access to other major entertainment hubs, including DC, Philadelphia, and Boston. The West Coast, particularly the LA area, is famed for opportunities in "the movies," with a heavy film and commercial studio presence, a large concentration of special effects and animation businesses, and a reputation for fast-paced, high-tech work situations, all in addition to the more mainstream cross section of theatre and performing arts thriving in abundance up and down the coast. The Southern US presents an interesting combination of strong regional repertory theatre companies, a large up and coming film scene in bustling Atlanta, plus the Disney machine. Generally, a more conservative theatrical environment indicative of the regional culture and values, there are extremely exciting opportunities for growth and for establishing professional roots. Similarly, the Midwest/Heartland, the largest land area in the US, features a very sizeable number of repertory companies spread out among the widely spaced medium-sized cities, whose populations have come to value "big city" amenities in less high priced and congested locales. The Midwest is led by anchor regional companies such as the Goodman, Lyric Opera, and Steppenwolf in Chicago, and the Guthrie, Minnesota Opera, and Minneapolis Children's Theatre in the twin cities of Minneapolis/St. Paul as standard bearers of theatrical opportunity for the region. These larger city population centers and the dense array of theatre found therein also allow for prop freelance work as a viable career choice for the nimble and adventuresome prop artist to find openings that expand one's comfort zone and scratch the itch for constantly changing and challenging work.

Networking to find potential openings or to discover any upcoming staff expansions is always helpful. Putting the call out to friends and acquaintances in theatre or related businesses may connect to a job opening yet to be advertised. It's also a good way to find out relevant information about job descriptions, salaries, benefits, organizational structure, and culture. The world of props is small and the players are known to each other by professional connections as well as being active in national theatre organizations such as **USITT** (**United States Institute for Theatre Technology**) or **SPAM** (**Society of Properties Artisans/ Managers**). Whether just starting out or as a seasoned professional, word of mouth and a recommendation by a credible theatre maker opens many doors, and, given the turnover in staff at many regional theatres, jobs open up with some regularity as people advance in their careers.

CONTRACTS AND SALARIES

Contract length and salaries of prop staff have evolved along with the definition of job titles. Salary is determined by many factors, including size of the organization, length and complexity of the season, historical precedent, geographical location, and health of the organization. If the theatre has a contract with IATSE, those union salaries are determined by negotiation, and non-union employees not covered in those negotiations will probably be impacted by those pay scales. Contract length is determined with many of the same factors in mind as well as reflecting specific show builds when labor requirements can vary. Mid-season furloughs, when the season is lighter and fewer staff members are required to produce or run the shows, are a common tool by management to decrease expenses but with a drastic impact on the yearly salary for employees.

Depending on the internal accountability structure, many properties directors are making a comparable wage with the technical director and other departmental heads. The properties director is an "administrative" or "artistic" position and is not usually a part of an IATSE contract. Due to its salaried nature, **overtime** is not usually granted, so during tech and load-in weeks, while the hours spent at the theatre may double, the salary remains the same.

Those shops with IATSE contracts who have staff earning overtime may soon see the staff earning more than the properties director during crunch times when the hours in the shop increase.

In the 2016 survey of eighty-six prop shops across the United States by SPAM (Society of Properties Artisans/Managers), the national organization for prop directors in the United States, the *average* salary for a properties director was $47,300 a year. Top tier theatres (LORT A/ B) with full year contracts pay an average of over $53,600 a year and provide full benefit packages, including retirement, vacation days, and health care coverage. Smaller theatres or companies in smaller markets pay far less and employ the properties staff for less than full year contracts or hire in prop people on a show by show basis. Yearly incomes for prop directors at those organizations range as low as $28,800 a year. At the opposite end of the spectrum, an IA prop head working a 32-week run on Broadway plus off-season work reported a yearly salary of over $100,000.

Properties artisans are in the same range for salaries and contract lengths as a scenic carpenter or costume artisan, since those are lateral colleagues in the accountability structure. Artisan salaries for *beginning level* positions start around $18,200–$19,800 for a 32–36-week contract. The *average* yearly salary is $32,270 with an average contract length of forty-two weeks. Many artisans employed at top tier theatres (LORT A/B) in major urban centers make over $45,000 a year and receive full benefit packages. The hourly rate for *non-salaried* staff reports quite a wide range from $12 to $20 an hour with the *average* being just over $16 an hour. IATSE prop artisans generally make a higher hourly rate, averaging around $26 an hour, but may have a shorter contract length or have lay-off periods through the season, making their yearly rate similar to a non-union artisan. Most theatre organizations offer health insurance, some kind of retirement plan, overtime pay, and vacation/sick days to artisans employed on seasonal contracts (2017 survey—SPAM).

For most production employees, many theatres offer some form of overtime pay or **compensatory (comp) time** off for hours worked beyond the forty-hour week. State and federal labor guidelines define what qualifies as overtime for specific classifications of employees. The rules are constantly changing and hotly debated between various governmental agencies. Finding current information relevant to a specific position can be difficult but is essential to knowing one's rights. The Department of Labor is a good first start.

If comp time is allowed, the trick is finding time off within the contracted season to make up those comp hours without impacting the next show build. All too often overtime hours worked are never compensated equally to the time earned. Some organizations may even have a "No Comp Time" clause written into company personnel policy. Asking to review a copy of a theatre's written staff handbook may reveal an answer to this question, as well as provide many other insights into the company's operational culture. If they don't have a written staff handbook or are unwilling to share it as part of the interview negotiation process, that also reveals something significant about the company.

Those shops operating under an IATSE contract negotiate pay with the local representatives; the rate varies from theatre to theatre but generally is within a close range within a city. Union rates vary widely depending on the city and availability of work. Union workers are paid an hourly wage and are paid overtime for work over the standard forty-hour workweek. Some contracts may set the workweek differently.

Larger LORT (League of Resident Theatres) companies pay better in acknowledgement of the additional administrative responsibilities and the size of the season. Smaller theatres with shorter seasons and many summer theatres pay far less than the average, making it a challenge to survive financially. Many who find themselves in this "underemployed" situation must resort to doing side work for other theatres, having a second job outside of theatre in retail or other better paying occupation, or finding ways to supplement income as an independent artist, designer, or craftsperson using the same theatre skills in a different way.

Benefits are available to many full-time and contracted seasonal staff, including health and dental coverage, disability insurance, some form of a retirement plan or investment savings plan such as a 401K, and vacation/sick days. Some companies provide other benefits, such as a free parking space, use of the shop for personal project work, complimentary tickets to productions, and reimbursement for personal use of your car.

Whether being hired on as full-time staff or as an intern, having a letter of agreement or contract is essential. A **letter of agreement** is an arrangement between two or more parties about their rights and responsibilities. A **contract** is a specific type of agreement with legally binding elements that is enforceable by law. As long as the essential elements of a contract are met (both parties are providing something of value and mutual assent to the terms, meaning both parties sign the agreement), a letter of agreement is just as legally enforceable as a traditional contract.

It is fairly common to have letters of agreement offered in theatre hiring arrangements. Since most of those letters have elements of a contract, they are commonly considered a contract but, as in all things legal, it's best to have a lawyer look it over if anticipating any difficulties.

Most agreements include the following information:

- Concerned parties (name of organization and name of person being hired)
- Job title (properties artisan, properties master, intern, etc.)
- Compensation (weekly/monthly or fee, pay timeline)
- Job duties
- Rights and responsibilities—provision of tools, overtime considerations, expected weekly reporting hours, etc.
- Starting/ending dates of agreement, including any furlough dates or other possible suspensions in weekly employment

- Termination/notice terms
- Organizational signature
- Offer date
- Acceptance signature
- Acceptance date

With a letter of agreement, both parties know the expectations for work and have an understanding of the critical details for employment. If during an interview or in negotiation for a job, verbal assurances are offered, request they be put in writing and attached as part of the letter of agreement. It helps keep "honest people honest" and offers a fallback when or if those conditions are not met.

The caveat to contracts and letters of agreement is the rising commonality of the **at-will workplace.** In some instances, an employer will stipulate up front during the interview process the company has an at-will workplace policy. In other cases, an applicant or newly hired employee may discover this when reading the letter of agreement from management, or when perusing the company personnel policies after being hired. The simplistic gist of an at-will employment situation equates to this: an employee can be let go at any time for any reason, or even no reason at all. If this happens, an employee in this situation has few legal rights on which to rely. In fact, in many cases, unless a contract, letter of agreement, company personnel policy document, or other verifiable verbal or written communication specifically delineates a probationary period after which the employee cannot be fired without due cause, the law may assume that the business policy is at-will. The flip side of such arrangements is an employee can also leave at any time for any or no reason without suffering legal consequences. What's good for the goose could be good for the gander. For clarity's sake, make sure to ask detailed questions about the terms of employment should the hiring organization leave it vague. If, during contract negotiations, an employer asks for a signature on a legal document that is difficult to understand, appears to limit employee rights, or seems otherwise sketchy, put on the brakes and do some homework before signing. To learn more about employee rights in general and rights specific to at-will agreements or right to work state laws governing and limiting collective bargaining agreements between employers and unions, it's best to consult a legal professional.

FREELANCE WORK

For those folks in the **under-employed** category who are balancing a contract of thirty-six weeks of full-time employment and hoping to pick up a summer contract, it may seem easier to have a side gig that supplements the full-time jobs. Given the range of skills many artisans possess, having a side job such as making and selling things online, picking up freelance design/painting work, assisting a designer with model making or drafting, restoring "found" pieces of furniture for resale, or crafting objects for historical reenactment groups or cosplay activities and conventions may be a way to capitalize on the skill-set used in the full-time job but for a little extra money on the side. For some, it can turn into a profitable and fairly steady income. It's wise to check with the full-time employer before taking on any job which might impact work schedules or conflict with work at the theatre, but many employers approve of and support those who are pursuing alternate jobs outside the workplace. It shows initiative and drive as well as creativity. Some organizations even allow use of the shops for outside work as long as it's cleared prior to any work starting and doesn't interfere with what has to happen for the show. The trick is finding the balance to have enough mental and physical drive to do both . . . and find time to sleep, have friends, do the laundry, and have a life!

The IRS is also going to want to know, so keeping careful records is important. Save invoices and receipts, since full-time employers will not be reporting this extra income and the responsibility for self-employment taxes falls to the individual, including estimated taxes each quarter if more than $1,000 is owed at tax time.

For more insight into working as a freelance prop maker, please see the interview with Deb Morgan following this chapter.

APPRENTICESHIPS AND INTERNSHIPS

An entry level position in some organizations is the **properties apprenticeship**. An apprenticeship is usually for a recent college theatre graduate whose training has been primarily in the educational environment, lacking any experience working in props at the summer theatre or professional shop level. The pay is often minimal in acknowledgement of the experience and skill level of the applicant and a mutual understanding of the value offered by being exposed to the prop shop work environment and getting on-the-job training by working with trained artisan colleagues at the professional level. The best apprenticeships are a two-way street: the expectation of a certain amount of "grunt work" tasks assigned, balanced with projects that stretch and grow a skill set. In ideal cases, the shop head and staff take time to review apprentice work on each project, share thoughts and solutions, and fill in the knowledge and skills gaps an emerging prop artist may have, offering master class style learning opportunities during slow periods within a season. Portfolio building is also an extremely valuable component of a quality apprentice opportunity, with portfolio and resume reviews to help launch a more advanced job search toward the end of an apprentice's contract period. Apprenticeships can be a good way to get a toe hold into a full-time position with a professional company, as well as to gain contacts, connections, and introductions from the prop director and staff to open doors into other professional organizations.

Another pathway for an on the job training level position is via a **properties internship**. An internship in the prop shop of a regional theatre is one of the best ways to make the move from theatre training at a university to the professional theatre world. Many educational institutions offer classes for credit in the final year of the training curriculum that support an internship for either a full or partial semester. This allows the student to get the professional exposure needed to transition to work while still being under the mentorship of a faculty member for guidance in the sometimes-overwhelming challenge of working in a professional shop.

Professional theatre companies offer these entry level positions knowing they are preparing the next level of crafts persons to be hired into the profession. In a SPAM (Society of Properties Artisans/Managers) survey of both regional and summer theatres, thirty-eight regional theatres offered some form of an internship, with many offering a small stipend or other financial support. Of the twenty-three summer theatres responding to the survey, most offered a small stipend as well as housing. The title of apprenticeship and internship can be used somewhat interchangeably so exploring both keywords in a job search is helpful.

An apprenticeship or internship exposes the student to professional work processes and products, building on whatever level of training was offered in the university. By engaging with craftspeople, designers, and directors in the professional environment, the beginning prop person learns professional work standards and develops the professional contacts necessary for a successful career within the theatre industry.

Most apprentices are expected to work the same hours as paid staff and, depending on the skills of the individual, may be assigned as an assistant to a full-time staff member or even given individual projects to complete. Internships may be arranged as a partial day commitment or for a limited time working around other classes or the student's availability. Some theatres offer a hands-on training component in addition to working in the shop. As the individual demonstrates ability and learns the way of working in a particular organization, opportunities to work on larger projects usually are earned. Beyond learning professional technical skills, the individual is also exposed to the communication, organization, and leadership qualities needed to be successful.

To find an apprenticeship or internship, search the websites of regional or summer theatres. Online access is the same as with finding full-time employment. Start with a keyword search to narrow the region or kind of theatre company desired and find a listing of potential theatre companies. Many individual theatre webpages have links under a header such as: Opportunities, Employment, Jobs, Education, Training, or Internship. Application information is available, or contact information on how to inquire about potential openings might be listed. Contacting the theatre in person or by phone directly is a good way to explore available possibilities as well as to identify the correct contact person.

For internships in particular, if a theatre does not have an internship program in place, it is always possible to talk directly with the properties director about setting one up. Few theatres will turn away free labor, especially someone with an interest in the technical field who has some level of training and a passion for the work. Theatres with union contracts may be limited in offering contracts due to their particular agreement with the local stagehands contract.

Accepting an internship carries with it the same responsibility of accepting a paid position. The staff of the prop shop will expect the intern to be engaged, collaborative, and hardworking. In exchange, they offer the start of a successful career. An internship should not be viewed as a way to just see what goes on behind the scenes of a professional theatre but must be approached as an entry-level job with the same consequences of success dependent on assessment and review by supervising personnel.

TRAINING AND EDUCATION

Prop training can be as varied as the prop process itself. Many of the people working in prop shops across the United States were trained with a general theatre background and developed their prop skills on the job. Others came to the prop shop from a fine-arts, woodworking, architecture, or other related "craft" training track. Some may only have a passion for doing theatre and a knack for the kind of work done in a prop shop. Given its developmental track as an outgrowth of the scenery or costume shop, only a few universities offer props as a specific undergraduate training curriculum with a range of classes creating an arc of training developed for training a professional prop person. Those universities offer specialized classes in professional level properties production with specialty classes in soft goods/upholstery, casting/molding, woodworking/furniture restoration, fabric dyeing/painting, and properties crafts.

In a recent survey of over a hundred US universities and colleges, several dozen offered at least one class closely related to or specifically teaching stage properties. When considering a university curriculum, review past course catalogs (often available online) to see *how often* classes are taught and *who* is teaching them. Given the restrictions of state budgets in recent years, many colleges are finding the more highly specialized theatre production classes difficult to offer given smaller enrollments in these kinds of classes and the need for more individualized mentorship. Explore the arc of curriculum and what kind of classes and production work opportunities are available. The loss of a critical faculty or staff member can be devastating to a program, and past reputation of excellence does not guarantee the same level of training, opportunity, or educational offerings. It's best to visit the university to see the shops, talk with the professors and staff as well as enrolled students, attend a performance, visit a classroom to observe a class, and ask critical questions before making the choice of where to spend hard-earned money and years of educational commitment.

It may be difficult or financially problematic to move beyond a local university, but upon investigation, the theatre offerings are slim. It's still possible to get a foundational education to start a props career. If no specific props classes are listed, most universities have classes in stagecraft or costuming, teaching foundational skills adaptable to work in a prop shop. It may be possible, by reviewing the complete courses in the theatre department, to define a props curriculum from classes teaching millinery, sewing, carpentry, welding, metalworking, drafting, painting, design, décor, costume crafts, etc.

An aspiring prop person will also find classes offered in departments *outside* of theatre teaching skills and processes directly applicable to props. Classes in the art department might include sculpture, drawing, painting, jewelry, textile, puppetry, or computer graphics. Architecture departments offer interior design, drafting, and furniture design. Industrial Design explores wood, plastic, and metal processing classes with hands-on project work or a class in 3D printing and CNC programming. Within the university, classes in engineering, communications, marketing, and business can also apply for the entrepreneurial prop person. Through exploring the catalog of classes, a wide array of opportunities might open up to build a custom prop training curriculum. Convincing the theatre advisor to accept those classes as electives in a BFA track will depend on the flexibility of the curriculum, so it's best to keep advisors in the loop when planning classes. If a local theatre is nearby and the opportunity to do an internship might be available, college credit can often be earned by enrolling in an independent study class or a designated professional studies/internship and getting a double reward of experience as well as credits to degree.

Graduate level (**MFA**) professional theatre training programs often grant degrees in Production Technology or Technical Direction and may have a properties major, or properties classes may be included as part of the more general technical production curriculum. It is wise to thoroughly review the curriculum and frequency of class offerings as well as the credentials of the professors teaching the classes. A graduate level degree is not required for a properties job in regional theatre, but an advanced degree program will teach specialized theatre production skills and develop the administrative and leadership abilities of the graduate student, allowing for advancement to management level positions in the field. Those people anticipating a move to academia may want to seek out an MFA since it is almost always a requirement for teaching.

Given the expense of attending a graduate program, the prospective student should consider what would be the best investment of time and money. Having a scholarship or assistantship to pay for tuition, books, and expenses becomes almost mandatory unless self-funding is possible. Graduating with a heavy debt load from graduate school is an enormous burden considering the salaries of many theatre professionals. The hands-on training developed by working in the profession may have an equal value to graduate training and is comparable to the time commitment given while offering on-the-job access to experience and opportunity for a successful career.

Art is the essence of awareness.
—Louise Nevelson

Having the right set of skills and a passion for the craft of properties production is essential to finding, growing, and keeping a career in props. Many prop directors working at leading regional theatres came to the position by working up from assistant or artisan positions. Some started as interns and slowly moved up the chain of responsibility; others began as actors or designers but found their passion in the prop world. Regardless of the path, working in the prop shop brings new opportunities to solve the challenges of producing live theatre. Those with a commitment to creativity, collaborative art-making, and communication of those dreams, innovations, and expectations to all involved in the process will be rewarded with a joyous career in theatre properties.

Working as a Freelance Prop Maker

An interview with Deb Morgan, Freelance Props,
Kansas City, KS

What is a "freelance" prop maker?

A prop maker means I am responsible for the entire project and can either do all the work myself—shopping, upholstery, and crafts, or I can hire people to help me. A prop maker is

Deb Morgan
FREELANCE PROPS, KANSAS CITY, KS

someone who is hired to do a specific project such as making a puppet, upholstering a chair, or even shopping.

Do you work by the show—or on specific projects as part of the show?

In theatre, I most often work by the show, but I have also been hired to do a specific project. Some of those projects have included upholstering a chair, making some vintage airline stewardess bags, or babysitting a tech rehearsal.

I also work on different commercial projects, where I most often work for an art director. I may act as that person's assistant or be given specific props to find or build.

How do you find work/jobs?

I've been freelancing long enough the work usually finds me. Word of mouth is my friend. I sometimes get recommended for a job from a new client, so I do maintain a website which serves as a portfolio/resume. I will also contact theatres or people I've worked with before and let them know some dates I am available. If I have a big opening in my schedule, I check the performance dates of theatres around town and see if any shows would fit in my time frame. I will contact those theatres and let them know I am available if they need someone for props. That also goes for advertising and production companies; it's good to remind people you are around and available.

No matter where you live, the world of props is small. Don't hesitate to refer other artists for a job you may not be qualified to do. The other artists as well as the clients appreciate your desire to find the best person for the job. This will always come around and help you when they inevitably refer you for a job.

How do you determine what you should be paid?

I've set my fees/hourly rate on what the local market pays. I know what the hourly fee is for over hire in my area and price myself accordingly. My fee is determined by the amount of work to be done, the level of difficulty, and the theatre's ability to pay. For commercial work, the pay is usually based on a ten-hour day and depends what kind of work you will do. The more responsibility, the higher the pay. There is a definite hierarchy of jobs in the commercial world. Try to find other contractors to help you figure out your base day rate. If this is your first job in the commercial field, I've found employers receptive when asked what their average pay is for a similar job.

What expenses do you factor in—transportation, shipping, tools, shop use, hiring someone to help, etc.?

I try to factor all those expenses in and I have developed strategies with my tax accountant that work for me as well as my employers. I start with the tax benefits—my vehicle is a designated work vehicle and I write off all my work-related miles. For a show that requires a lot of driving and shopping, I may bump up my hourly wage to accommodate that. My employers are usually happy with that arrangement for it means a lot less paperwork if they don't have to calculate mileage. For me, the tax rate for mileage is higher than what most companies will pay.

I only factor in shipping when using Amazon Prime; I can write off a good portion of the yearly membership on my taxes. Most theatres have their own shipping accounts, so I try to use them whenever possible.

I consider my tools a convenience for me. The theatres I work for are not keen on paying a "shop fee" for me if they have their own shop or tools I could be using. I like my sewing machine and staple gun better than what most theatres provide. But I can factor in expendable items like thread, wood glue, hot glue, and staples. On commercial projects, if you use your own tools on a job site you can charge a "kit fee." If you are hired to build something for a commercial or photo shoot, you should calculate the use of materials and tools in your fee.

How do you track your business expenses and income for tax purposes?

I have a separate credit card I use just for business expenses. I also have a checking account separate from our home account, but it's simpler using the credit card statement every month. I have a big spreadsheet that I use to keep track of business expenses & income that my tax accountant helped me set up. The columns reflect what the itemized tax codes are. At the end of the year, I just send her my spreadsheet.

What has been one of your more interesting projects as a freelance artist?

I worked with an art director and we turned my van into a bird piñata complete with wings, beak, and a giant hat; carving a giant snowman that required an emergency dismantling of my sliding glass doors in order to get it out of my shop and to the shoot on time; and creating banquet tables full of fake food.

What is the most challenging part of the job?

Two things are challenging—trying not to stress over where the next job will come from and the schlepping of tools, materials, and props to and from a job site.

What is the advantage of freelance work over a seasonal contract with a regional theatre company?

The ownership of my time is the best advantage of being freelance. I can't always pick and choose my projects, but I can decide when and where I will work. With a shop of my own in my basement, I can work in front of the TV, listen to loud music, and work late at night if I choose. I can also decide to have lunch with friends knowing I have the freedom to work later in the evening if I need to.

The ability to pick up a quick job when they arise. "Hey, are you available for two days of shopping for me?" That's music to my ears.

If there is no work, you don't work. There is no busy work, though I tend to spend down time trying to clean up from the last project. I also like to sell props I haven't used lately or couldn't return on eBay, an easy way to make a few bucks.

What tips would you give to a person considering moving to freelance work?

Be prepared to spend money on tools and materials to set up your own workspace.

It's easier if you have a vehicle that can haul things—a minivan or SUV with seats that fold down is useful. You can always rent a truck for those big projects.

Don't burn any bridges with local artists or former employers—you never know when you might need their help or they will need yours.

Work out the terms of petty cash and how you will be reimbursed up front before you start a project. All companies should be able to give you seed money to start with. Make sure you can turn in receipts and get reimbursed during the project. If you use a credit card, be sure you can get reimbursed before your bill is due.

The beauty of freelance work is also its variety. Don't be afraid to branch out to production or advertising companies and even museums—they often need sculptures, painters, builders, people who can sew, and someone who can shop from a list. Send out resumes; often companies keep a list of artists they can call on when a project arises.

Have a nest egg of savings to fall back on when times are lean. Freelance work usually subsides around the holidays; don't let your first December and January with no work freak you out! Use the time to update your website, contact possible clients, and fix all your tools. If you find a skill you are lacking, take a class and make yourself more marketable. This is also a time to work on a project you have been dying to make; use it for a portfolio shot or to sell.

Think outside the box and be willing to do just about anything. You'll have great stories to tell and it will make you a more interesting person!

CHAPTER 12

The Prop Shop

During production work, the prop shop supports an enormous number of different activities. Mediums include wood, plastics, foam, and metal work similar to the scene shop; sewing, draping, dyeing, and distressing work similar to the costume shop; and painting, finishing, and crafting similar to work completed in the scenic paint shop. It is this overlap of skill sets and processes that generates the difficulty in creating a functional prop shop, and has historically forced the prop shop to work scattered about the other theatre shops with only a small space designated for props.

Given the fairly recent history of having props identified as its own separate craft, the common way of working was often to simply have a corner of the scene shop for prop construction and all other work was done in whatever clean nook or cranny could be found for craft work and soft goods. That worked in a limited way depending on the space available but often to the dissatisfaction of the props crew as well as the other theatre craftspeople trying to do their own work.

As the expense of producing massive scenic units increased and performance spaces evolved, bringing the thrust stage out and up close to the audience, the use of props to establish the scene increased the need to support the prop shop differently. Now that the identification of a separate staff to build props has become the industry standard, so has supporting a shop space dedicated to the production of props.

First and foremost, the prop shop must be a *safe* environment. This isn't just a wish; it's the law. With the enactment of the Occupational Safety and Health Act of 1970, Congress created the **Occupational Safety and Health Administration (OSHA)**. They are charged with setting and enforcing protective workplace safety and health standards. OSHA is part of the United States Department of Labor and their website (www.osha.gov) provides hours of reading on workplace regulations and standards. Since these are under constant review and modification with more information than can be adequately covered in a book, much less a chapter in this book, it would be wise to spend some time looking at the information provided there. Beyond safety standards for planning and maintaining a shop, look into subtopics on wages and work hours, the Fair Labor Standards Act, termination notices, computation of vacation, sick, or holiday pay, etc. In addition to extensive information for workplace safety and health standards, the website also has links to file a safety or health complaint, get whistleblower information, find an OSHA office, or report an injury/death. Free consultation services are offered to help employers identify workplace hazards, comply with standards, and set up safety and health programs. OSHA also offers a wide selection of courses and educational programs to train workers to recognize and prevent health hazards and to comply with safety standards in the workplace. Many of these courses are offered online, providing fantastic flexibility for anyone wishing to continue education in this vital subject area.

While OSHA is a national plan, individual states also have workplace safety and health standards. These must be "at least as effective" as OSHA standards; many are identical but may have some specific standards covering hazards not addressed by OSHA. The OSHA website has links to individual state safety and health standards and regulations.

Knowing and complying with these workplace regulations are the minimal level of managing a safe work environment. Prop artisans and managers spend countless hours doing an enormous variety of operations and work processes using a vast number of products. Designing and maintaining a safe environment allows the production process to flourish while maintaining the health and well-being of the artists practicing their craft.

In an ideal theatre world, the prop shop would be a calm, clean, spacious, and well thought-out work space. It would have good illumination including natural light; ventilation and dust collection far surpassing the minimums required by law; designated work spaces appropriate to the processes and products used; an organized tool and materials storage; easy access to a loading dock for materials and large prop deliveries; adjacent access to hand/furniture/dressing prop storage; a secure and separate space for an office; and would live contiguous to other production spaces and personnel.

Many theatres are undergoing the acquisition or renovation of real estate. Frequently, the production areas fall secondary to the public spaces and the level of planning and square footage allocation needed to function well is inadequate. It is critical that the voice of the artisans who spend hours upon hours in these spaces be heard and the needs and safety of these people considered in the planning of new production facilities and renovations of existing theatre areas. Production shop requirements often dwindle when budget and public interface determine priorities. It is important for management to provide safe, well thought-out, and pleasant work environments for the back-stage artists in the production shops, as well as for the audience, actors, administrators, or performance space. Not only is it the right thing to do, but these protocols are mandated by OSHA. Rather than risk high fines and penalties from hazardous environments, proper and sensitive planning allows for professional, creative, and *safe* work, leading to a win–win for all involved.

Maintaining the physical layout and keeping the functionality flexible to encompass the wide variety of projects asked of the prop shop regardless of the size of conveniences available is important. Shops should be analyzed periodically for safer ways of working, better utilization of space, appropriate storage of products and finished props, and easier communication between the staff. By advocating for a worker-friendly shop and setting up the space so tasks can be completed efficiently and safely, the prop shop can be a healthy and pleasant work environment.

SPACE, TOOLS, SUPPLIES, STORAGE

Given the various and, at times, conflicting projects needing to be accomplished on any given build, having adequate space designated by *function* is important in setting up a prop shop. The prop shop must function as a wood and metal construction shop, costume shop, crafts shop, paint shop, graphics shop, floral shop, and on and on through all the various skill sets. These areas do *not* function together and indeed may create havoc in the work processes if attempted in the same space at the same time. Sawdust and fabric and welding sparks are incompatible mediums and can even be dangerous when combined. Curing molds and castings can create irritating out-gases for artisans working on other projects. Completed props stored for check-in can be damaged or become dirty if not protected from the fabrication process. The need to house so many different kinds of processes and products demands the prop shop be a flexible workspace that allows the show needs to be accommodated. Setting up the shop to suit the required work is critical. These spaces may be actually physically separate rooms or they may be contained within one large shop divided into separate contained work areas. The properties director's job of managing these zones and directing the personnel is simplified if the areas are easily accessible or at least adjacent to each other. Defining work spaces allows projects to continue without creating overlap of space, tools, or product impact on other projects.

THE MULTIPLE SPACE SHOP

Larger regional theatres have a **multiple space shop** specialized into specific types of activity, while smaller organizations incorporate all work within one larger space, utilizing temporary set-ups to delineate zones as necessary for project management and flow. Having designated and specifically designed spaces for efficient and safe working on the widest variety of prop projects is the ideal. These separate workspaces are known colloquially within the business as a "dirty" room, "clean" room, and, additionally, often a "crafts" room.

The **dirty room** is primarily a wood and metal working space. In addition to the standard table saw, radial arm, band saw, etc. of a typical scene shop, the prop shop will have additional tools more specific to furniture construction like a power miter saw, wood lathe, vacuum form, shaper, planer, and jig saw, as well as hand tools allowing for the finer level of detail

Figure 12.1   Dirty Shop. Seattle Children's Theatre's main construction area with rolling work tables allowing custom setup work, overhead electrical pulldowns, natural light supplemented with general and task lighting, dust collection hard-piped to building system, and foot friendly flooring. Elizabeth Friedrich (Fried), properties shop manager.

and joinery seen in a prop shop. A wide variety of clamps also offers many solutions to the more unusual gluing and clamping challenges seen in prop construction and furniture work.

The activity in this shop is furniture construction, stripping, restoration, metal reinforcement, plastics and foam work and carving, and many other activities generating dust, smoke, dirt, or fumes. Dirty rooms often have a dust collection system to keep the sawdust generated by the woodworking process to a minimum. Sawdust has been documented as irritating to the lungs of many workers and can create a cumulative allergic reaction over time, as well as being a potential explosive hazard. A dust collection system on tools and a continuous dust filtration system pulling dust particles from the air make for a safer and healthier shop.

Access for loading in raw materials from an external loading dock or freight elevator as well as the delivery of props from the shop to the stage space is important. Adequate flat storage for plywood, lumber, metal, and plastics should be provided, as well as organized storage for fasteners and supplies such as staples, bolts, nails, screws, brads, hinges, glues, molding, sandpaper, etc. Fasteners in the prop area also include more furniture specialized items such as biscuits, table lags, and dowels. Hardware tends to be smaller and often more decorative in nature than the items found in the scene shop.

Wood stocked in the prop shop needs to be more select than what is usually found in the scene shop, allowing for strong joints and clear runs on furniture pieces. Poplar, ash, and birch are often used for prop furniture construction. Pine can be used for framing, but it is important to keep knots to a minimum. Hardwoods such as oak, walnut, or cherry are usually too expensive and too heavy for most prop work but may be used for trim or for turned pieces. Plywood with a faced surface such as oak-faced or birch-faced plywood offer the look of hardwood with the strength, durability, and ease of working associated with plywood.

Most regional theatre shops work off a pneumatic system for powering the various staple guns and nailers used in the prop shop. If the building is not supplied with an in-house system, an adequately sized compressor must be installed, including hard piping with appropriate outlets and pressure gauges. A sufficient number of electrical circuits and wall outlets allows flexible use of power hand tools such as drills, sabre saws, or routers. The safety hazard of cords running across the floor can be minimized by the installation of pneumatic and electrical cords pulled down from overhead reels and the installation of floor pockets near stationary tools.

Prop shop metal working areas often have a standard MIG welder for most mild steel welding, with an aluminum spool gun attachment to allow for construction of lighter weight or structural yet decorative elements utilizing aluminum. For larger jobs, an oxy-acetylene rig for

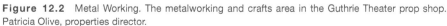

Figure 12.2 Metal Working. The metalworking and crafts area in the Guthrie Theater prop shop. Patricia Olive, properties director.

brazing metals and cutting is used. Smaller projects utilize handheld propane or gas torches for sweating copper and tiny butane torches for high-temp soldering requirements. Appropriate cutting and finishing tools such as chop saws, portable-band metal cutting band saws, grinders, wire wheels, buffers, pneumatic nibblers for delicate or small-scale grinding and metal shaping applications, benders for small scale steel stock, vices, etc. are needed. A metal table or cement slab for project work with a welding shield screen and appropriate ventilation makes it a safer process. Personal safety equipment such as welding gloves, fume respirators, face masks, etc. should be provided. Certainly, some prop shops will share welding facilities with the scene shop, but increasingly, prop shops are investing in designated equipment to meet more specialized metal construction requirements. Stock materials in the prop metal working area are again typically smaller in scale and more delicate than the corresponding structural components in the scenic department, although it is not uncommon for some vigorously used furniture to require steel structural reinforcement from the prop department on par with scenic construction techniques in steel.

The **clean room** is designated for fabric lay-out, draping, and upholstery-related tasks, paper goods and floral projects, graphics work, set-dressing modification, some crafts work, and other activities requiring a space free from airborne contaminants or dust.

Figure 12.3 Clean Room. Seattle Children's Theatre's clean room features large natural light windows, a rolling cutting table with enclosed storage beneath, pull-down electrical, fatigue floor mats, a small crafts area, tile floor for easy cleaning, and wall storage for materials and supplies. Elizabeth Friedrich (Fried), properties shop manager.

The graphics area requires a computer with a scanner and wide frame printer or color plotter for creation, alteration, and printing of photos, money, legal documents, newspapers, etc. supplemented by a drafting/light table for lay out work by hand. Computers today are evolving quickly, with corresponding digital software, memory, and computing power allowing a level of ephemera able to be created limited only by the skill and imagination of the artisan. Web access allows for image downloading and easy manipulation and printing for stage use. Document creation has been revolutionized and many prop items requiring hours of hand work in past years are now completed with the click of a computer mouse.

The upholstery and soft goods process utilizes much of the same equipment found in the costume shop, but requires tools capable of handling drapery and upholstery weight materials. In addition to heavy-duty sewing machines, most shops have a serger or marrow machine, an ironing table with industrial steam iron, patterning tables with surfaces allowing fabric to be pinned down, and hand tools such as scissors, measuring tapes, tack hammers, tufting needles, pattern weights, etc. When doing upholstery and sewing other types of theatrical or heavy-weight fabrics, a walking-foot sewing machine is often used. A walking-foot sewing machine has a special presser foot operating in two parts to help pull the fabric through the machine, allowing multiple layers of heavy weight fabric to be more easily sewn. This is especially useful when doing stage draperies. Having the machine inset into a large worktable assists in the handling of the material as it is walked through the machine.

The prop shop upholstery area ideally has a variety of webbing stretchers, pneumatic long-nose staple guns, tack pullers, and an electric foam saw for cutting foam rubber to size. Long nose staple guns allow upholstery fabric to be easily stapled deep in the folds and crevices of furniture. A foam saw is a long-bladed saber saw type of tool with a rolling base allowing upholstery foam to be cut with square edges and following patterned shapes. Upholstery and drapery supplies include cotton and polyester batting, muslin and cambric, foam rubber in various densities and thicknesses, spray adhesives, heavy-duty thread, tying twine, decorative gimp and fringes, drapery tape and webbing as well as various fasteners such as staples, webbing tacks, and decorative nail strips. Just as in the dirty shop, appropriate electrical and pneumatic outlets should be provided to minimize the use of extension cords.

Many upholstery and soft goods areas also have adjacent fabric cleaning and dyeing/distressing areas with an industrial washer and reversible dryer. Often this area is incorporated in a **crafts room**. The crafts room falls somewhere between the two other spaces supporting the wide variety of craft work done in the prop shop. It generally incorporates the *wet and hazardous* activities.

The crafts room often has a large steam vat for dye work (preferably stainless steel), dye mixing area with a stove or hot plate for heating water for dye solutions with a ventilation grill to pull dye fume away from the work area, a walk-in spray booth for exhaust of paint and curing materials, and a paint/plaster sink.

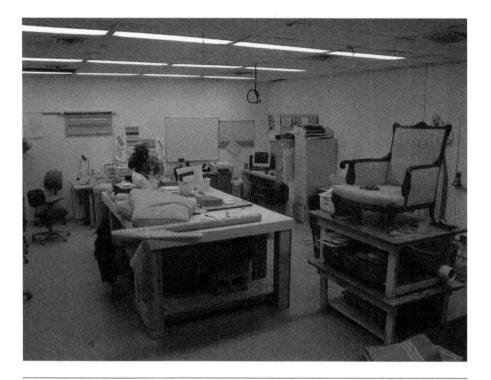

Figure 12.4 Upholstery Shop. The upholstery area in the clean shop. Note the large cutting table for large fabric manipulation, a tiled floor for easy clean-up of lost pins and upholstery waste, and work tables (stacked in photo) allowing for work at comfortable heights. Prop shop, UW-Milwaukee.

The spray booth and dye ventilation system allow contaminated air to be removed from the work area and exhausted via a filtering system to the outside. Any spray painting or work with finishes emitting an odor or fume should be done in this ventilated space. The prop shop utilizes spray paint and spray finishes more than any other area in the theatre due to the highly detailed nature of many of the items. Appropriate safety cabinets are necessary to store the flammable liquids (acetone, denatured alcohol, shellacs, etc.) and paints used in props work. Like the scenic paint studio, water-soluble latex or acrylic paint and glaze materials are standard for prop shop painting, supplemented by pure pigments for mixing into the glaze, dyes for FEV work, bronzing powders, and gold leaf. Supplies often include a wide variety of buckets and pails, brushes, wood combs, sponges, and specialty faux painting tools.

The crafts area usually has several tables for working on the wide variety of projects needed in props crafts work. Having at least one table with a stainless-steel top is handy when working with dyes and on casting and molding projects where keeping a clean surface is important as well as allowing easy cleanup. Besides the usual hand tools like pliers,

Figure 12.5 Crafts Room. Milwaukee Repertory Theater's crafts room has stainless steel work-tables, sinks, dye vat, a reversing industrial dryer, flammables cabinets for storage of paints/sealers/craft supplies and a small walk-in spray booth (on opposite wall, not in photo). Jim Guy, properties director.

screwdrivers, hammers, and small saws, specialty tools and supplies include corner and small hand clamps for custom picture framing and small construction or repair of hand props, small watercolor and acrylic paint brushes and paints for touch-up and re-paint of pulled hand props, an airbrush for detail work, floral wire, tape, and putty for creating silk floral arrangements, a variety of markers, sealers, and paper or parchments in different colors and weights for making ephemera. Molding and casting supplies might include mixing cups, stir sticks, a scale, Teflon pans, plaster, spray releases, a hot plate for melting materials, silicon spatulas, plastic tubs, and aluminum sheet pans. Standard supplies for this area include plaster, tape, glue, spray sealers, stamps, and seals.

The crafts room also might contain an area where furniture can be "stripped." This requires an area where entire furniture pieces can be covered with paint stripper and allowed to rest while the stripper works to dissolve the paint back to bare wood. Most pieces require vigorous washing following this process, so having a hose and large chemical floor drain to accommodate the dissolved paint and stripper is helpful.

THE SINGLE SPACE PROP SHOP

Some regional theatre and university prop shops are small multi-functional spaces requiring a juggling of processes and set-ups to allow for the widest variety of work to be accomplished. Managing the flow of materials and work processes within a single space to manage the dirty side of prop work from woodworking and foam carving to clean activities such as upholstery and floral work adds complexity to an already complicated job. In these one-room shops, the table saw lives with the sewing machine, the paint sink doubles as the area where props are washed and cleaned, and the shop graphics computer area is often the properties director's desk.

When possible, shops should have some method of defining and isolating work areas to allow for the safe and appropriate use of materials and work processes, but given the reality of most spaces, this is accomplished with limited success. Sawdust, paint spray, upholstery

Figure 12.6 Single Space Shop. A Contemporary Theatre's (ACT) prop shop is a single space shop with small areas for crafting/woodworking and sewing/upholstery tools to be stored. The shop has pneumatic and electrical pull-downs, a sealed cement floor, and a wall of storage for materials and supplies. A small hallway off this space gives access to the shared spray booth and a small room holds a washer/dryer and upholstery storage. Marne Cohen-Vance, properties master.

lint, wet glues and finishes, damp dyed fabric, noisy sawing, castings releasing gases, and the jumble of stock supplies all must thrive in the single space prop shop. Work may be compromised and the functionality of the prop shop limited simply by the need to constantly prioritize projects depending on how much space they require, how much of a mess (dust, fume, overspray, lint, trash, gas, etc.) will be created, drying time, etc. As projects flow through the shop, work spaces must be adaptable for a variety of projects, with the prop director and artisans determining what projects need priority in the build and what other projects complement the same use of tools, products, or process.

Just as in the multiple space prop shop, the one-room shop probably has a division of the space into working areas replicating the clean, dirty, and crafts rooms. Some overlap and dual usage occurs naturally as the build progresses through the shop, but many one room prop shops have artisans with multiple skills, allowing the shop to change as the project they are working on moves from start to finish. The same concerns for isolation to contain dust, contamination, fume, etc. should be addressed, and temporary barriers, mobile work tables, tools on rolling stands, and flexible/portable systems for ventilation and dust collection can go a long way to making the shop function quite well for properties production. Simple solutions such as storing supplies in plastic containers with secure lids, providing dust covers over prop storage shelves and dust sensitive equipment such as sewing machines or computers, or even rigging a physical barrier to temporarily divide the shop as needed gives the shop functionality.

Keeping an organized shop is critical in the one-room prop shop in order to keep a safe work area and manage tools and supplies. When specialty artisans work in designated multiple room prop shops, they are able to individualize their areas to their work style and manage the zone to suit their own process. Not so in a one-room shop, where the artisans often take projects from beginning to end and the spaces and tools are shared. Attention to cooperation, communication, safety, and the requirements of specific processes must be part of each artisan's work plan.

For example, prior to doing metal work, the shop should have a deep cleaning to remove wood dust and potential fire hazards. At the end of the metal working project, the area should be cleaned again to remove any scrap metal and oily materials able to stain fabric or other projects. Many crafts and soft-goods projects can successfully reside side by side utilizing similar tools and projects, but the spaces must be kept organized and materials and tools stored at the end of work call so each artisan can continue the following day without having to search for tools or clear an area to work on a project.

In the case where the prop space is really small, the prop artisans may share workspace with other areas having designated shops. For example, furniture construction or metal reinforcement of props may occur in the scene shop, allowing for similar material use and the mess of cutting, sanding, and grinding in a space set up to accommodate that activity. The prop staff may find clean space in the scenic paint studio to paint, stain, and seal furniture or props side by side with the artisans completing the scenery; this has the added benefit of allowing a collaboration on style and color palette in addition to having an environment safe from the dust and residue of construction work. The costume shop may allow the props artisan to complete a drapery project requiring a clean workspace with the use of a large cutting table and industrial sewing machine. Many smaller companies have a shared area for the costume and prop shop to do fabric washing and dye work. Expensive specialty equipment such as a wide frame color plotter may be shared by numerous areas, including marketing, design, and production, allowing the prop shop to produce posters and large graphics.

As with all shared resources, this requires the willing cooperation of the other departments and the allowance of their own activities to continue while accommodating the prop shop needs. Many theatres operate on increasingly limited budgets and when it is possible to share equipment or space, the overall benefit is increased; collaboration and smart use of resources allow the budget to be spent on show-specific purchases.

Figure 12.7   Seattle Prop Shop. The prop shop occupies the back portion of the larger scenic studio at Seattle Repertory. Sharing tools for many of the dirty room processes with the scene shop, a smaller crafting area is against the back wall while a clean room has been separated from the shop space by a storage wall and hanging plastic to the ceiling. Jolene Obertin, properties director.

RENOVATING OR PLANNING A PROP SHOP

If given the opportunity to be part of the planning team for a new building or even in the renovation of an old space, a variety of factors beyond size and division of space are important to consider. Like all areas where theatre artisans work, safety and personal comfort in the workplace should lead the decision-making process hand-in-hand with determining specific work areas. OSHA (Occupational Safety and Health Administration) has minimum guideline recommendations for the workplace and **ANSI (American National Standards Institute)** has publications on many aspects of workplace safety standards. This information is available through their websites or by writing directly to the organization. Please see Appendix for website links.

Setting up a shop involves more than dividing space by the kind of work done and the products used. It must consider the work flow through the shop. Any shop, large or small, uses materials and must access stock. Getting those raw goods into the shop, from sheet goods and lumber to furniture pieces, requires rolling access. Having a loading dock where lumber, metal, foam, and other materials can be unloaded onto a rolling cart allows for the delivery of materials to be safely and easily accomplished. Many theatres have a central loading dock for access to the entire building and utilize corridors with ramps and elevators to move goods between the floors and around the building. As the spaces are being planned, it is essential that adequate freight elevator support is provided when the prop shop is located on a floor different from the access point for raw materials. Utilization of a passenger elevator to move lumber and other cumbersome prop materials can create a problem for both the safe movement of the materials as well as for the public or other theatre personnel needing to use the elevator. Most personnel elevators are too small to move large furniture pieces and completely inadequate for moving lumber and large sheet goods.

Once at the prop shop, materials need to have a storage place where they can be placed until ready for use. Lumber should be stored flat to prevent warping but can take up too much space in most shops. Some theatres buy only on an as-needed basis and have only vertical storage available for sheet goods, metal, or lumber to be used on a specific build. Others work with the scene shop to access materials from a general stock and charge back against their particular budgets for goods used, allowing materials to be bought in quantities and available but not having to necessarily be stored in the prop shop. A balance of having materials on hand and available for work and yet not having too much quantity of materials taking up valuable working space is a constant consideration of priority and space. This is true of all work spaces, from the woodshop to the crafts room to the upholstery and soft goods area. Managing materials and knowing the inventory so materials can be purchased in appropriate quantity is one part of the artisan's work process.

Getting items from stock is an important part of the work flow through the shop. As the prop list determines what items might be pulled, those pieces are found in storage and brought to the shop for cleaning, alteration, or repair. Moving furniture pieces such as sofas, dining

Figure 12.8 Pull Cart. A wooden cart with castors and multiple shelves for prop pull is kept just inside the door of prop storage at Seattle Repertory Theatre. Its size allows it to be rolled down the aisles of prop storage as well as conveniently fit in the elevator for transporting props to the shop or out on stage. Jolene Obertin, properties director.

room tables, and other large heavy items requires wheeled dollies and furniture pads to allow them to be moved without damage to either the piece or the people doing the moving. Smaller items, such as clocks, glassware, picture frames, books, etc., are often moved in boxes loaded in a cart. All items should be secured in adequate padding to prevent accidental breakage. As the items are cleaned or repairs completed, a safe dust-free storage area should be provided in the prop shop. Some theatres have rolling prop run boxes for storing completed props allowing an easy transition at prop check-in time. Others simply designate particular shelves or a storage cabinet for completed props. The size of the show and the number of props may determine what kind of storage space is needed, with some shows requiring a great deal more and others far less. It is also perfectly acceptable to load completed props in storage boxes in anticipation of prop check-in.

The first step in planning for the **electrical needs** of the prop shop is to inventory the tools used in each area and know their electrical requirements. Welders, table saws, dye vats, clothes dryers and other large floor units may require 220V support. It is also important to consider circuit layout and how many tools may be in operation at any one time on a project.

For example, in doing casting and molding projects, it is common to have a hot plate running to boil water or melt a plastic, a hot melt glue gun plugged in to glue together a mold form, a hot air gun blowing to assist in drying or curing and a task lamp to help illuminate the work area. Having multiple circuits allows them all to be working at the same time without fear of tripping the fuse or circuit breaker.

Planning the layout of electrical outlets is partially determined by building codes and standards, but this is usually defining a *minimum* of outlets. In planning where outlets are installed, consider the work being done in the area. Installing outlets at the height of worktables rather than at floor level makes access for plugging easier and the use of an extension cord unnecessary for most applications. Installing drop down electrical boxes over open working space allows the cord to be retracted into a reel so the cord does not snake across the floor and create a hazard.

As in all things, shops evolve over time, and even in a given build the space may be altered to allow for a large project or one requiring special work processes to be successfully accomplished. Planning in flexibility and convenience for the future should be part of any proposal. Consider where a 220V dryer *might* be desired in the future if one is not available now and have electrical service anticipating the need included with the installation of all the other electrical runs; it's cheaper than adding it later. Add in electrical outlets where they might be needed in the future if staff are added or the shop reconfigured. Plan for what might be and not just what is needed for the present.

Planning safe and adequate lighting allows for an efficient and comfortable work environment. In the best of all worlds, the prop shop should be located where it can receive natural light. Natural light not only provides a more cheerful workplace and makes a connection to the outside world with the changing of light as the sun moves across the sky, but natural light is considered the best choice for matching colors and seeing the textures in fabrics . . . both valuable considerations in prop work. Given the design of theatres and the need to prioritize audience and lobby access, many prop shops unfortunately are situated in the basement of the theatre building or secured deep within the building away from any natural light source. Having natural lighting from skylights or exterior windows would be preferred, but when natural lighting is unavailable or insufficient, supplemental electrical lighting must be used.

In planning the **lighting** for the prop shop, several kinds of lighting should be considered. *General lighting* provides a uniform light level across the shop workspace. *Supplemental lighting* provides task-specific, intense light focused on a smaller area or worktable. *Emergency lighting* is used when power is disrupted to allow safe passage for occupants from the darkened room and is required by law, usually installed as part of the building plan.

Wall surfaces in the shops should be smooth to help eliminate the buildup of dust and toxins. Painting the walls of the prop shop area a light color allows the area to have a wash of illumination as light is reflected off all the surfaces. It also makes it easier to see when the walls need to be cleaned. In wet areas such as behind the paint sink or around the dye/washer area, having a solid water-proof covering allows for easy clean-up and prevents the development of mold or contamination from dye and paint processes.

Accidents resulting from a slip, trip or fall occur each year in theatre shops. Artisans complain about leg and back fatigue from working on hard **floor surfaces.** Providing appropriate walking and working surfaces can help to alleviate many of the hazards. Additionally, different processes require a different floor covering. What works in one part of the shop may be problematic in another. Having a cushioned tiled floor underfoot in the clean room makes for easy clean-up of loose thread, fabric trimmings, or paper and is also more forgiving on legs and feet for those artisans working in the space. The smooth surface allows an easy sweep at the end of the workday, is easily maintained by janitorial, and provides a light-reflecting surface. But a tiled floor when coated with a thin layer of sawdust makes for hazardous footing—problematic in a crafts or dirty room set up. In the dirty room, it is common to find a wood and/or concrete floor. Concrete floors can cause leg fatigue but are cost effective and useful when doing metal work since they are flame/heat resistant, but they should be sealed to prevent "dusting" and rubber mats provided near work areas where artisans may stand to prevent leg and back fatigue. A wooden floor provides the foot and leg comfort for the artisans and also provides a surface for nailing jigs in construction work. Wood floors will deteriorate over time and need replacing, especially in areas where foot traffic is high or if an area gets too rough or has raised areas/splintered surfaces. A shop may have a combination of surfaces to allow for the various processes to be accommodated or use a welding mat on a wood surfaced floor to protect against sparks.

Figure 12.9 Soft Goods Processing Area. Props artisan Moondancer Drake dyes some fabric in the UWM crafts room area. A top load washing machine and a large industrial reversing dryer is to her right. A ventilation slot hood pulls away any contaminants. A rubber drainage mat is on the floor to provide a non-slip surface as well as to cover the floor drain.

The crafts room should have a floor resistant to chemicals allowing easy water clean-up and is handy for many prop processes, including painting, general cleaning, specialty dye processes needing "drip" time, flame-proofing of fabrics or upholstered pieces, etc. Sealed concrete floors are common with containment curbs and fitted with a floor drain that allows excess water to be easily removed. In the fabric processing area, where the mess of dyeing and processing large yardages of fabric often creates excess water, a rubber floor grid may be installed to provide comfortable leg support as well as a non-slip surface as water empties away to a covered floor drain. Grids with sloped edges highlighted in caution yellow help prevent tripping.

An absolute must-have in any prop shop is an adequately sized dust collection and ventilation system. The crew will spend less time cleaning up, shop motors will last longer, and the air will be free of dust or spray settling on cleaned props—but most importantly, the environment will be far less hazardous to the health of everyone working in the shop. Sawdust can be hazardous to the health of theatre artisans. All woods have a variety of resins, alkaloids, and toxic organic and inorganic particles that, when inhaled as dust, can cause a wide variety of allergic reactions, skin problems, and respiratory ailments. Plywood, MDF, and particleboard,

Figure 12.10 ATL Shop. The prop carpentry shop at Actor's Theatre has large access doors from the scene shop and into the paint shop area and walk-in spray booth next door. Access curtains between areas allow for containment of dust and spray drift. A filtered ventilation system for dust control in the air supplements the dust collection system at tool sources. Mark Walston, properties director.

often used in theatre work, are especially problematic due to the glue resins necessary for their manufacture.

Dust collection at the tool source is important, keeping the air quality of the shop acceptable and pulling the sawdust away to a collection unit, preferably located in an exterior environment to control noise and ease of disposal without contaminating the workspace. Tools with a factory-installed collar have the size of port determined by the manufacturer as necessary for adequate exhaust. Each tool should be fitted with an open/shut port called a blast gate that allows each access point to be controlled and the system volume to be maximized. Some theatres have a whole building/shop dust collection plan configured by an air handling system expert. This is especially recommended when designing a new space to allow for appropriate duct sizing/runs and safe configuration/installation of the air handling units. Installation of the motors and collection units outside of the shop area can help create a buffer from the motor noise as well as make access for cleaning and maintenance easier. In other situations, adding in a stand-alone system similar to what one would find in a home workshop may be the best solution. In either case, knowing the volume of air to be moved or air volume in cubic feet per minute (CFM), divided by the number of branches in the system open and working at one time, allows an appropriate system to be installed. Most dust collection companies will have grids showing the performance ratings available on their systems, and most tool manufacturers will give a minimum CFM or FPM (velocity of air in feet per minute) required to evacuate the dust from the tool. Wood dust requires approximately 4000 FPM in the air system branches to adequately pull the dust to the main duct. Depending on how many tools are hooked up to the system and the length of the runs, one or several units may be required. When purchasing a system to install in a wood shop, a two-stage collector is recommended. A two-stage system has a first stage cyclone cone into which the air enters, which allows the coarse sawdust to settle out and removes the fine dust through a central outlet into the blower and on into the second stage after-filter. Allowing the coarse sawdust to settle out lessens the load on the blower, and filters are not filled as rapidly since they are receiving primarily only fine dust.

Proper installation and grounding of the collection system and especially the duct work is important to prevent static electricity from developing and to plan for appropriate negative pressure from the air ventilation. Like any other tool, consider cost, performance, safety, ease of use, ease of maintenance, and quality of construction in determining which unit to purchase. Complete and detailed information on selecting and installing a dust collection or air filtration system is available online, in many woodworking shop books, or from most tool companies selling wood dust collection systems.

Stopping the majority of airborne dust at the source is the first step, but each shop should also have an **air filtration system**. While most shops are part of an overall air system associated with the building, having additional units able to be activated when dust-producing work is occurring allows for the quick removal of small particulates from the air that a building

Figure 12.11   Downdraft Sanding Table. Downdraft tables are an easy way to keep the shop safe from excess dust when sanding or woodworking. The downdraft pulls the dust down into the large filter encased in the table keeping the air cleaner. UW-Milwaukee prop shop.

system would not dissipate quickly enough. Properly located and sized, these filtration units can circulate the air in a room multiple times per hour. Many filtration units contain permanent washable pre-filters capturing most particles three microns or larger. Smoke pre-filters are also available to capture even smaller particles. Electrostatic pre-filters enhance the performance of air cleaners and extend the life of the bag filter by working on the principle of static electricity to remove dust and mold from the air. Some units come with a remote control, allowing installation in practically any location.

The crafts area workhorse for ventilation should be a local exhaust ventilation system trapping toxic spray, mists, gases, fumes, smokes, and dusts, filtering them to an outside air source. Appropriate clean makeup air must be provided to allow the system to work properly. The common configuration for most shops is a **spray booth** with a hood to surround the work area, a large air filter grid holding the contaminants, and a fan to pull the air from the work space through the filter and out the exhaust ducting. Artisans working in the space must remember

Figure 12.12   Spray Booth. At Actor's Theatre production facility a walk-in spray booth is shared with the paint area and the prop shop (located through door to left). A rolling table allows for projects to be easily moved into the space, rotated for spray finishing, and removed. A suspended rod across the booth also allows for hanging objects to be painted/finished. Nearby flammable cabinets hold paints and solvents used in the booth, allowing for easy access and cleanup. Mark Walston, properties director.

to keep the workpiece between them and the filter screen. Airflow in the booth is directional, pulling from outside the booth to the filter. Artisans standing between the workpiece and the screen will be exposed to contamination. Local building codes often specify mandatory fire suppression requirements for all types of spray booths, and local authorities may perform periodic inspections of this equipment to check for maintenance, cleanliness, and safety compliance as they make the rounds on annual building inspections in all areas of the theatre facility.

Larger shops may have a walk-in variety spray booth where entire work pieces can be moved into the space and the back wall of the spray booth is covered with filters for the air to be exhausted. Smaller "bench" style vent booths are also available and work effectively in smaller shops where less space is available. Keeping a clean workspace inside the booth is important to prevent spills or contaminants from one project getting on another. An explosion-proof waste receptacle encourages the safe disposal of oily rags and debris but should be emptied daily. A separate plastic trash can should be provided and labeled appropriately for empty aerosol cans so they can be disposed of properly according to local hazardous waste policy. Many organizations have a **hazardous waste policy** for liquids requiring a chemically appropriate, usually plastic, removal container for any liquid not to be disposed down the drain. Disposal of nonhazardous materials can be accommodated through the normal and usual trash can disposal methods.

Having a **water source** in the prop shop is a necessity. The crafts area alone requires access to water for the washer, dye vat, and sink areas. Both hot and cold water must be available as well as good drainage. A deep stainless-steel sink in the crafts area is preferred to allow for easy cleaning and resistance to chemicals/dye. A separate paint/crafts sink with a plaster/paint trap prevents cross contamination of dye drift, plaster, paint, and other materials between the craft processes. The trap helps prevent drain clogs in a sink getting heavy use in the casting and molding/paint processes of a prop shop. A separate wash-up area free from contamination of dye or chemicals should be provided for the cleaning of food-safe hand props such as dishware, silverware, and glasses. This could be created on an as-needed basis with a dishpan and drip-dry area in a clean location of the shop.

An **emergency eye wash station** should be installed where artisans might be exposed to harmful chemicals or sawdust. These wash stations are designed to activate by a simple push lever to flush contaminants out of the eyes after exposure. Having access to a shower area in case of body contamination is important when doing processes which might accidentally splash or contaminate the body or clothing of the artisan to hazardous liquids. Planning a small shop bathroom with a shower provides for **drench decontamination** as well as a nice restroom amenity for the crew. Some shops may be adjacent to a backstage area where showers are provided to cast and crew, allowing access for a full body drench in an emergency situation. **First aid kits** should be available in a designated location in the prop shop for the treatment of minor scratches, burns,

Figure 12.13 Paint Sink. Paint sink and drench contamination shower head with emergency eye wash station in the prop shop at the Alley Theatre. Karin Rabe Vance, properties director.

headaches, nausea, etc. Often the first aid area is near a sink to allow easy access to water for washing hands before treatment and cleansing of small wounds. For minor first aid treatments, staff should be trained in basic first aid and can self-monitor appropriate care.

The prop shop, like all workplaces, can benefit from the implementation of and adherence to a written **health and safety program** to maintain a safe work environment, as well as to train employees in the safe handling of tools and materials. Most theatre workplace training programs also cover the use and disposal of hazardous materials, which can be common in the prop shop, as well as the proper use of **personal protective equipment** (**PPE**) often used in completing work in the prop shop. Theatre companies are required to document and investigate all workplace accidents, near-accidents, and work-related illnesses. By doing so, they can correct the circumstances leading to workplace accidents and illness. The production manager, assisted by the area heads in each shop, commonly manages many written health and safety programs. It is the properties director's responsibility to advocate for health and safety compliance in the prop shop and the artisan's responsibility to understand and follow the company's policies for protecting them.

At the start of each season, new employees and staff due for review or those being given new job assignments should be given appropriate training in accordance with the organization's written health and safety program. In the prop shop, when a new product, tool, or process presents a potential hazard, the prop staff should have appropriate training in handling, use, storage, disposal, etc. as deemed relevant. Many companies keep written documentation in the employee's personnel files acknowledging the safety and health areas the employee have received training in to ensure compliance with safe work practices. These forms often require a signature of the employee as well as the trainer verifying what training happened and the date. An Employee Safety handbook is commonly used to provide employees a resource for questions about emergency procedures or other health and safety concerns. If the company

Figure 12.14 Safety. A written safety handbook posted in the shop with protocols for training and workplace practices establishes the mindset of safety in the shop. Jolene Obertin, properties director, Seattle Repertory.

TOOL ORIENTATION FORM	NAME:		
	FULL TIME EMPLOYEE ↑	PART TIME EMPLOYEE ↑	
Prop Shop	CASUAL LABOR ↑	CONTRACTOR ↑	
Cannot use until trained on specified tool:			

TOOL	DATE	EMPLOYEE SIGNATURE	TRAINER SIGNATURE
Stationary Power Tools			
10" Delta tilting arbor table saw			
10" Radial Arm Saw, Craftsman			
Power Mitre saw, Delta (warehouse)			
Delta SawBuck (warehouse)			
Lathe			
Delta Radial Drill Press			
Bench Grinder, Dayton			
Belt/disc sander, Delta			
14' band Saw, Jet			
Wadkin C series Band Saw			
Delta 16" scroll saw			
MIG welders x 2, both Miller (shared with scene shop)			
Chop Saw – Milwaukee			
Dust Collector – Delta			
Handheld Power Tools			
Hand held Jig saws: Makita & porter Cable			
Circular Saw, Milwaukee			
Sawzall, Milwaukee			
Grinder – hand held, Milwaukee			
Porta band saw			
Porter Cable plunge router			
Dewalt Router			
Porter Cable cut out tool			
Dewalt Laminate trimmer			
Porter Cable biscuit joiner			
Fordham Flexible Shaft tool			
Dremel			
Random orbit sanders			
¼ sheet sander			
Porter Cable belt sander, mini hand held			
Pneumatic Tools			
Pneumatic die grinder, Campbell-Housfield			
Brad nailer, duofast			
Brad nailer, Senco			
Narrow Crown Stapler, Senco			
Upholstery Stapler, Duo Fast			
Sewing Machines/ Softgoods			
Bernina Sewing Machine			
Singer industrial Sewing machine			
Safety			
Spray Vent Booth, Binks			
Flammables storage			
Respirator			
Particulate dust masks			
Welding vapor masks			
Face Shields/eye protection			
Ear Protection			
Eye wash station			
First Aid supplies			
Hazardous waste disposal kit			
Lock out/ tag out center			
Fire extinguishers			
Circuit breaker box locations			
Emergency exit routes			
MSDS and tool manuals			
Warehouse safety protocols & 1st aid kit locations			

Figure 12.15 Tool Orientation Form. Example of a clean and easy-to-use form for documentation of shop tool orientation given at start of contract and as refresher reviews, assuring staff training is complete and all safety protocols are understood.

utilizes a written handbook, it should be available in the prop shop as well as be given to each staff member upon employment.

Each person working in the prop shop is responsible for their own personal safety. In the prop shop, this includes asking for assistance in completing projects requiring lifting or handling of awkward materials; cleaning up spills or contaminants immediately; wearing personal protective equipment such as gloves, safety glasses, respiratory protection, back support belts, etc. as necessary; using approved ladders or step stools when climbing; and seeking out assistance or training when encountering a new process or working with a new product. Safe working practices for tool usage should be followed in consideration of the tool handler as well as others working nearby. Think about the process being done and what hazard might be created that impacts the entire shop area as well as the workspace immediately present. Many prop shops provide PPE (personal protective equipment) for the staff including eye/face protection, hearing protection, gloves, respirators, and hard hats or back support braces when appropriate. For artisans working in processes or areas containing foot hazards, safety-toed footwear may be required; some companies contribute to the provision of a pair of safety shoes. Complete information on types of PPE and details on compliance is available at the ANSI or OSHA websites. Please see Appendix for website links.

Employees have the **right to know** the hazards associated with the products they are asked to work with and what safety procedures are required to protect them from exposure. They also have the right to question any instruction requiring them to disobey a safety rule that endangers themselves or others, or if asked to perform a task which they have *not* been trained to safely perform. The law protects employees from retaliation for demanding their safety rights. If a staff member feels a problem exists, they should work to resolve the problem. Verbal reporting of an immediate hazard to a supervisor or the properties director is best to insure the problem is resolved in a timely manner. Some shops utilize a safety suggestion form to report a continuing hazard or unsafe condition. Conditions requiring updating or maintenance to *prevent* a health or safety issue from developing can be reported using the form as well. The forms are generally submitted to production management or, in some companies, the safety committee, alerting the shop supervisor of the problem or to request janitorial/maintenance to fix the hazard. Review of safety suggestions also allows supervisors to advocate for possible changes in work practices or procedures, to suggest additional training needed, or to purchase protective devices or equipment. Any employee who knowingly commits an unsafe act or creates an unsafe condition, disregards the safety policies of the company, or is a repeated safety or health offender can be discharged.

The prop shop should maintain a binder with an **SDS (Safety Data Sheets)**, previously called MSDS (Material Safety Data Sheets), on the chemicals, products, and hazardous substances in the shop. The SDS provides handling and working information on a particular substance. These sheets are particularly helpful when working with a product that has not been handled in some time and the artisan wishes a refresher lesson in safe handling or processing

Figure 12.16 SDS and Tool Manuals. Binders holding SDS and tool manuals allow critical information to be readily accessible. Jolene Obertin, properties director, Seattle Repertory.

of the material. The SDS is available from the manufacturer or vendor and are often supplied with the product when purchased. Having access to the SDS on the various products used in the prop shop helps the artisans understand what precautions are needed and what kind of work processes are appropriate to use. Many websites are available to provide an SDS on a range of products as well as information on how to read and use an SDS.

All products should have appropriate labels listing chemical identity, appropriate use hazards, manufacturer name, and date of purchases. The date is especially important for those products having a limited shelf life. If pouring chemicals into a secondary container, label information should be transferred to the new container. Hazardous chemicals should not be poured into a cup or other container used for drinking or eating, to prevent accidental ingestion.

Local, state, and federal laws regulate disposal of hazardous materials. Failure to comply with those regulations can be very costly to the theatre as well as environmentally negligent. Properly labeled containers for hazardous waste disposal should be provided in the prop shop/s as necessary and final handling and waste removal completed in accordance with safe disposal regulations. This is usually coordinated with the janitorial and maintenance staff.

Fire extinguishers are the first line of defense in a fire. Fire extinguishers should be provided in the shop/s and clearly marked for easy location. Tools, equipment, or stored props should not interfere with access to the extinguisher in an emergency. Extinguishers should be inspected monthly to insure readiness and replaced immediately if damaged or discharged. Employees should be trained in safe firefighting procedures, including building evacuation, extinguisher usage, and fire safety protocols. Training and practice in using a fire extinguisher should be part of annual training or review for every employee. Containing a small fire with a fire extinguisher is preferable to letting a fire burn until the fire department arrives, but only if the fire is small and contained, and no imminent peril exists for the person/s fighting the fire.

When in doubt about controlling a fire, call for help, pull the fire alarm, close (but do not lock) the doors to the area, and evacuate the building to wait for the fire department.

At the end of each build, a handy method to insure workplace safety is to complete a **workplace inspection**. Having a written plan or checklist for tool maintenance insures all the tools are covered and properly maintained.

- Power tools examined for frayed or worn cords
- All tool guards checked for wear and secure attachment
- Fire extinguishers checked to be sure they are in their proper place and fully charged
- Floors swept and free of dust and debris
- All electrical cords coiled and racked
- All pneumatic cords coiled and racked
- Air compressor drained and clean
- Floor drains and mats are clear and clean
- Drains in sinks, dye-vat, and washing machine run freely
- All work surfaces wiped down and free of contaminants
- Spray booth is clean and clear of all materials/projects
- All materials appropriately stored
  - Plywood and lumber stacked or placed back in rack
  - Fabric rolled or folded/sorted into boxes
  - Upholstery materials boxed or rolled as needed
  - Paint/sealers/stain cans wiped clean and re-sealed—stored in fire cabinet as necessary
  - Crafts products sorted, re-sealed, and put in cabinet
  - Papers and flat goods sorted and filed
  - Hand props (not being used) returned to prop storage
  - Hardware sorted and put back into bins
- Leftover products/chemicals/trash disposed of properly
- All light sources are in working condition with functioning lamps/ballasts
- All filters have been cleaned or replaced
  - Clothes dryer
  - Spray booth
  - Air filtration system
- Dust collection bags/barrels have been emptied
- First aid kits inventoried and re-supplied as necessary
- Eye wash stations checked and cleaned.

Figure 12.17 Tool Storage. Having a lockable room within the shop to store tools and supplies keeps them safe and easy to inventory. A quick review of the storage slots at the end of work call shows any missing items. A small counter adjacent to the lock-up allows a dedicated space for tool maintenance/changing blades or attachments/and general inspection. Mark Walston, properties director, Actor's Theatre.

Performing maintenance service on equipment requires a correct **lockout/tag out** procedure. In a lockout situation, a lock is placed on the tool or machine that neutralizes all power to the system. Machine controls, switches, or disabled parts should be tagged with information relevant to why the machine should not be used, including name of person managing the maintenance, department, date and time of tagging, and reason for lockout.

Without a lockout/tag out procedure, an accident may occur when a machine is used that is faulty or needs maintenance. Following written procedure allows appropriate power sources to be identified, trained personnel to complete the maintenance needed to be authorized, and control of access to the locked-out machinery during the maintenance or upgrade procedures to be made possible. Most written procedures associated with a lockout/tag out process allow for inspections and documentation of each service prior to restarting any system and the removal of all locks and tags.

* * *

Running a safe shop starts with an investment in providing for a safe and healthy workplace. By demonstrating a commitment to the safety and well-being of all shop workers and providing the appropriate personal protective equipment, the prop shop can be a safe and productive work environment. Having a long and healthy career in the theatre begins with each individual's commitment to safe working practices carried out on a daily basis.

Appendix

SAFETY
Arts, Crafts and Theater Safety—Providing Safety and Hazard Information for the Arts
www.artscraftstheatersafety.org

ORGANIZATIONS
SPAM (Society of Properties Artisans/Managers)
OSHA (Occupational Safety and Health Administration) www.osha.gov
United States Department of Labor www.dol.gov
ANSI (American National Standards Institute) www.ansi.org
USITT (United States Institute for Theatre Technology) www.usitt.org
ESTA (Entertainment Services and Technology Association) www.esta.org

BUILDING PROPS/BEING A PROPS ARTISAN
The Prop Building Guidebook. (2nd edition)—ISBN 9781317292807
The Prop Effects Guidebook: Lights, Motion, Sound, and Magic—ISBN 9781138641136
To explore Toolkit series books on other specialties in theatre, see www.routledge.com

For those folks interested in exploring more about props, please view the original webpage at www.prophandbook.com to learn about how to set up a prop shop and see photos of prop shops from around the United States.

Index